# Black Cargoes

# Black

## A History of

DANIEL P. MANNIX

In Collaboration with

MALCOLM COWLEY

# Cargoes

# the Atlantic Slave Trade

# 1518-1865

THE VIKING PRESS · NEW YORK

VIKING COMPASS EDITION
Issued in 1965 by The Viking Press, Inc.
625 Madison Avenue, New York, N.Y. 10022

Sixth printing October 1968

Distributed in Canada by
The Macmillan Company of Canada Limited

Library of Congress catalog card number: 62-11674

Chapter 5, "The Middle Passage," appeared originally in
*American Heritage Magazine.*

Printed in U.S.A.

# Contents

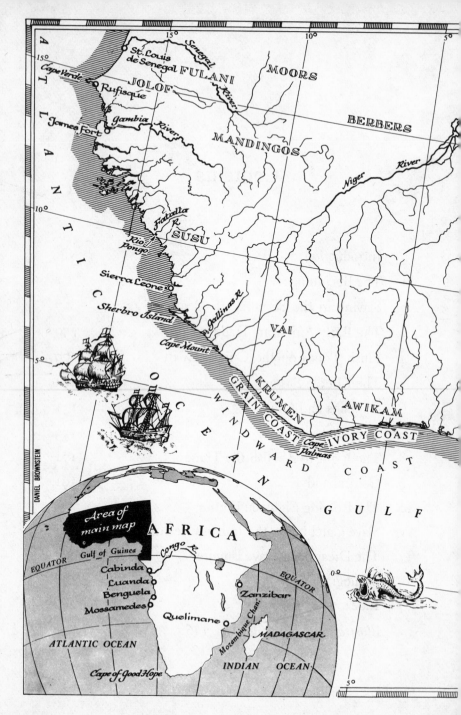

ATLANTIC

15°
Cape Verde
Rufisque
James fort

10°

5°

OCEAN

St. Louis
de Senegal    FULANI
JOLOF
Gambia  River

MANDINGOS

15°                    10°                    5°

MOORS

BERBERS

Senegal  River

Niger    River

Fatala R.
SUSU
Rio
Pongo
Sierra Leone
Sherbro Island
Gallinas R.
Cape Mount

VAI

KRUMEN

GRAIN COAST

WINDWARD  COAST

Cape
Palmas    IVORY COAST

COAST

GULF

DANIEL BROWNSTEIN

Area of
main map    AFRICA

Gulf of Guinea    Congo

EQUATOR
Cabinda
Luanda
Benguela
Mossamedes    Quelimane    Zanzibar    EQUATOR    0°

ATLANTIC OCEAN

Cape of Good Hope

MADAGASCAR
Mozambique Chan.

INDIAN    OCEAN

5°

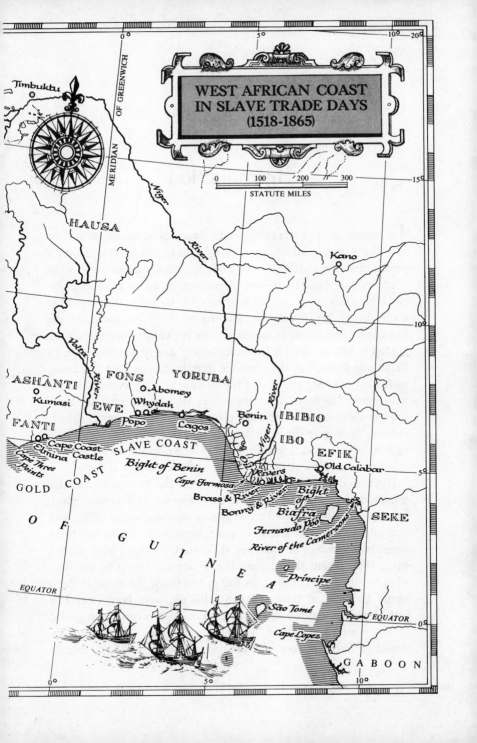

# Introduction

THE STORY OF THE ATLANTIC SLAVE TRADE IS ALSO THE STORY OF how the Negro colonists were brought to the New World over a period of nearly four centuries. They arrived almost as soon as the white colonists, and there were Negroes on the island of Hispaniola, or Haiti, as early as 1501. It was in 1518, however, that the slave trade proper began with the landing in the West Indies of the first black cargo direct from Africa. The last cargoes may have been landed as late as 1880, a few years before slavery was abolished in Brazil and Cuba, but the available records stop, as does this book, with the virtual suppression of the trade after 1865. Nobody knows how many Negroes had crossed the Atlantic before that time, though a conservative estimate places the total number at fifteen million. They were the victims of a forced migration that was more callous, more colorful, and immensely larger, in the end, than any other such movement of modern or ancient times.

It is true that a substantial proportion of the white colonists also consisted of forced migrants. Most of these were paupers or criminals or rebels condemned to be transported across the ocean and sold into bondage for a term of years, sometimes for life, but there were also thousands of kidnaped children. Often they were treated worse than Negro slaves, since the owner was trying to get back what he had paid for them in five or ten years, but most of them would be freed in time and their children were born free. The first Negroes imported to the English colonies were also regarded as indentured servants or "apprentices for life," whose children would be free, but soon the situation changed. After the middle of the seventeenth century, imported Negroes were chattels, condemned with their descendants to perpetual servitude, and for that reason they were preferred as articles of merchandise and units of labor power. That explains why they soon outnumbered the white indentured servants everywhere south of the Potomac. In the West Indies they outnumbered the whites of all categories, sometimes by more than ten to one. Because they did not reproduce themselves on West Indian sugar plantations, where many of the owners said that it was "cheaper to buy than breed," the entire slave population of some islands had to be renewed from Africa every twenty or thirty years. Comparative figures would be impossible to assemble, but it seems probable that, until the end of the eighteenth century, more Negro than white colonists had been carried to the two Americas.

This book tries to tell where the Negroes came from, how they were enslaved in Africa, how they were purchased by sea captains, how they were packed into the hold like other merchandise (though with greater losses in transit), and how the survivors were sold in West Indian and American markets. It tells how the trade got under way, how it rapidly expanded after 1650, with the development of the plantation system, how it was legally abolished by Great Britain and the United States in 1807, how it persisted and even grew, for a time, in spite of Her Majesty's Navy, and how it ended with the Civil War. The story has not been told on the same broad scale for the last sixty years.

During that time there have been many books that presented new facts about the trade or helped to explain its background. To mention only a few, there are various works by Melville J. Herskovits, notably *The Myth of the Negro Past*, which reveal how much Africa has contributed to the cultures of the two Americas, and there is Eric Williams' *Capitalism and Slavery*, which explains the effect of the trade on the industrial revolution. There is Elizabeth Donnan's four-volume collection, *Documents Illustrative of the History of the Slave Trade to America*, an invaluable source book containing the materials for a new history. In 1961 Basil Davidson published *Black Mother*, a fascinating work that demonstrates the effect of the trade on various African cultures, but without giving more than a few glances across the Atlantic. One might say, however, that there has been no attempt to offer a general picture of the Atlantic trade since John R. Spears' comparatively short and highly moralistic work, *The American Slave Trade*, copyright in 1900.

I do not find it a fault of the present book that it often presents history in terms of personality, or that it devotes not a little attention to the wildly colorful and often fatal adventures of sea captains, smugglers, African factors, and sailors before the mast. Adventure was part of the trade, which was a devourer of men, white and black. A high proportion of the Europeans engaged in slaving died on the Guinea Coast of malaria, dysentery, acute alcoholism, or gunshot wounds, and most of the survivors were physically ruined or morally degraded beyond redemption. There were a few, however, who managed to withstand both disease and the grosser forms of corruption, and these were among the extraordinary characters in maritime history. Sir John Hawkins, William Bosman, André Brue, Bartholomew Roberts the sober pirate, Captain (later the Reverend) John Newton, Captain Billy Boates, Captain Canot, King Gezo of Dahomey, Francisco Feliz da Souza, known as Cha-Cha, the prince of slavers, and the Georgia patriot and fire-eater, Charles A. L. Lamar: all these were men of exceptional courage, and all except Bosman and Brue, both company officials, obeyed no law but their own fierce will to survive and excel. They were not men of difficult consciences, except for John Newton in his later life. It was Newton who said, looking back on his Guinea voyages, that the trade "renders most of those who are engaged in it too indifferent to the sufferings of their fellow creatures," and that the necessity of treating the Negroes like cattle "gradually brings a numbness upon the heart."

That to me was the distinguishing feature of the trade: not its dangers, not the loss of life it involved, not even the cruelties it inflicted on millions, but rather the numbness of the traders and their loss of human sympathies. From beginning to end the trade was a denial of any standards except those of profit and loss. A black man was worth exactly what his flesh would bring in the market. If his flesh would bring nothing, he was tossed overboard as if he were a horse with a broken leg. But popular opinion is mistaken when it holds that Negroes were the sole victims of the trade. White sailors before the mast were also treated as mere items in the ledger. Because they had less value than the slaves, they were often given less food and more floggings, as we learn from the mass of testimony presented to Parliament in 1790–1791. There are figures to show that the rate of mortality among seamen on the Guinea voyage was higher, on the average, than the rate among slaves packed in the hold.

Also contrary to popular opinion, very few of the slaves—possibly one or two out of a hundred—were free Africans kidnaped by Europeans. The slaving captains had, as a rule, no moral prejudice against man-stealing, but they usually refrained from it on the ground that it was a dangerous business practice. A vessel suspected of man-stealing might be "cut off" by the natives, its crew massacred, and its cargo of slaves offered for sale to other vessels. The captains thought it safer to purchase their cargoes from native merchants, at a price per slave that was reached after hard bargaining.

The price was paid in consumer goods from Europe, and most importantly in muskets and gunpowder, which African nations had learned to regard as the requisites of survival. A nation with muskets and gunpowder could obtain a supply of slaves by attacking other nations; without them it was in danger of being attacked and enslaved. As the market for slaves expanded, each little tribe on the West African coast lived in a state of endemic warfare with its neighbors. Some of the vigorous nations of the interior— as witness the Susu of what was later French Guinea, the Vai of Sierra Leone, who had long refrained from selling slaves, the Ashanti of Ghana, and the rising kingdom of Dahomey—fought their way to the coast largely in order to maintain their supply of European weapons. In the Bight of Biafra, a monstrous sort of partnership was formed between the slaving captains and the coastal states. They cheated each other, they quarreled and sometimes opened fire, but they both profited from the business of exploiting the inland tribes, thus helping each other to spread fear and chaos deep into the continent.

In Africa the effects of the trade were uniformly disastrous. Elsewhere they were mixed, and we might as well admit that the trade produced some benefits, in the cruel and insanely wasteful fashion that history often chooses to produce them. England, France, and the Netherlands all profited from the trade; it encouraged the growth of their merchant shipping and furnished a market for the goods produced by their new industries. It also created more than its share of the primary capital that would later be invested in mines, railways, and cotton mills. But the best and almost the worst of its effects were felt in the Western Hemisphere, where the unwilling colonists from Africa contributed to the rapid settlement of two continents.

The problem for white colonists was finding a supply of manpower for the sort of work that is now performed by internal combustion engines. There was not enough of the manpower available in Europe, even after heavy drafts had been made on the rebellious Irish and the Scottish Highlanders. "I doe not see," a New England worthy wrote in 1645, "how wee can thrive untill we gett into a stock of slaves sufficient to doe all our busines, for our children's children will hardly see this great Continent filled with people." New England did manage to thrive without slave labor, but it was an exception. So too was Pennsylvania, where two-thirds of the white settlers from 1700 to 1800 were indentured servants. In almost all the English, Spanish, and Portuguese colonies south of the Potomac and north of the River Plate, it was the Negroes who chopped down the forests, planted the fields, ground the cane, and opened the mines. It was the Negroes, working in gangs under military discipline, who made possible the large-scale production of tobacco, sugar, rice, and later cotton, the four crops that did most to create the early wealth of the two Americas. The Negroes also proved to be a vigorous and enduring strain of immigrants, one that has contributed much—and will contribute more

—to the various American cultures, not least to that of the United States.

But along with these benefits, obtained at a vast cost in suffering, the slave trade left behind it a myth of Negro inferiority, an embittered racial conflict, and a sense of guilt that refuses to disappear. It is as if we were all responsible, now, for the sin of our forefathers, and as if the sin was so great that not even the Civil War could atone for it. That sense of guilt is nothing new; it began to appear in early times. After the middle of the seventeenth century, almost everyone who had not been corrupted by the trade felt that it was wrong in principle. Almost every European nation was by then engaged in it—except the Italians, the Austrians, the Poles, and the Russians, none of whom had colonies—and each nation excused itself by depicting the Africans as hopeless savages, while blaming every other nation for treating them badly. The Dutch asserted that French slavers were devious and cruel. The French said that the English were brutal and that the Portuguese were not only brutal but incompetent. The English laughed at the French for being excitable, and at the Portuguese for baptizing whole shiploads of slaves before taking them to Brazil.

In truth those wholesale baptisms must have been ludicrous affairs, yet they were not without meaning. They showed that the Portuguese at least regarded Africans as human beings with souls to be saved, and they help to explain why slavery in Brazil, though as cruel as slavery in the British West Indies, was in some respects a more liberal institution. The English were not in the least concerned with the souls of their black cargoes, and, unlike the Portuguese, they did not even send missionaries to Africa until the end of the eighteenth century; they sent only drygoods, gin, and firearms. In their practical way, and with their genius for large-scale undertakings, they probably inflicted more suffering on the Negroes than any other nation. On the other hand, they were also the nation that changed its heart, or found its heart, and did by far the most to abolish the trade.

In the end it is hard to assign the chief guilt to any national group. English, French, Dutch, Danes, Brandenburgers, Portuguese, Mandingos driving slaves from the Niger to the coast, the absolute kings of Dahomey, Yankee skippers, Congolese middlemen, and Egbo merchants in Old Calabar: the trade brutalized almost everyone who engaged in it. The guilt for it rests not wholly on the white race, or partly on the African kings and slave merchants, but beyond them on humanity itself, the same humanity that was responsible for Auschwitz and Matthausen and, in its blundering fashion, for Hiroshima and for the next catastrophe; I mean on the apparently inexhaustible capacity for greed and numbness of heart and the infliction of suffering that survives in the nature of man.

A word about the plan of this book. It is chronological by centuries rather than years, an arrangement made necessary by the fact that the narrative shifts back and forth across the Atlantic. Thus, there are two chapters on the seventeenth century, one dealing with the European slavers and the other with the early ventures of the American colonists. There are five chapters on the eighteenth century, since that was the flourishing period of the trade and was followed shortly by its formal abolition. The period of illegal slaving is covered in the last four chapters, which are based chiefly on the memoirs of smugglers and of the naval officers who tried to capture them. The struggles in Parliament and Congress over the suppression of the trade will have to be treated in a different sort of history.

This is Daniel Mannix's book, based on his researches in London and East Africa. My own contribution was chiefly editorial. There was a time, however, when I did a good deal of work on the slave trade in preparation for a book that was never written, and I was therefore able to contribute material and opinions from my new and old reading. I must accept most of the responsibility for the chapters on "The Middle Passage," "The Yankee Slavers," and "The Dream of a Slave Empire."

MALCOLM COWLEY

# 1

# The Beginnings

*[They came] from Angola and the Congo; from Dahomey, Lagos, Old Calabar and the Bonny River; from the Central Niger and Hausaland; from Portuguese Guinea and the Gaboon.*
—Sir Harry Johnston, *The Negro in the New World*

IN THE YEAR OF OUR LORD 1495, THE INDIANS ON THE ISLAND OF Hispaniola, or Haiti, rose against their Spanish oppressors. A great mob of them—the early historian Antonio de Herrera claims that it numbered a hundred thousand—marched on the little settlement of Isabella, where Christopher Columbus had arrived a few months before with three caravels after a prolonged voyage of discovery in the West Indies.

Columbus was a pious man, and Ferdinand and Isabella were conscientious monarchs who had instructed him to "honor much" the Indians and to "treat them well and lovingly," but they desperately needed gold. The Indians were unused to manual labor

1

of any sort, especially fourteen hours a day of panning gold from the mountain streams. They seem to have been a gentle people who had gone about naked, subsisting on wild fruits, fish, and whatever small animals they could snare. They were so innocent that at one time Columbus thought he must have reached the Garden of Eden and tried to identify every river he found with the Pison, Gihon, Hiddekel, or Euphrates, the four rivers of Paradise. But now the innocents had risen. If Spain was to have an empire, if Columbus was to continue his explorations, if the pagans were to be won to Christianity, their revolt had to be put down.

Columbus marched out against them, leading a force of two hundred infantry and twenty horsemen. With the Spaniards went twenty "bloodhounds": big, savage animals bred to pull down wild boars and bears in the forests of Central Europe. Ten leagues from Isabella the Spaniards met the Indian hosts. The Indians had no more idea of battle than children. Some of the men wildly hurled stones; others ran at the soldiers and struck at them feebly with sticks or tried to push their reed lances through the Spanish armor. A volley from the arquebuses and crossbows poured into the crowd. The naked Indians lay groveling in piles. Then the hounds were slipped, and the mounted men dashed in with their leveled lances. What followed was simply a massacre. The riders killed until their horses could no longer be coaxed into a trot. Later the survivors were hunted down with the hounds and put to work in the mines. Many of them died within a few days, totally unable to stand captivity.

Seemingly only one man was moved by the wholesale destruction of this once happy people: the man was Bartolomé de Las Casas, later bishop of Chiapa in Mexico and known as the Apostle to the Indies. Las Casas had come to Haiti as a colonist and had there been ordained to the priesthood. After watching thousands of Indians dying in corrals, and scores of men and women burned alive in the hope that their fate would induce the others to work, while those still left in the hills were pursued by *caballeros* as if they were foxes, Las Casas returned to Spain, determined to save the survivors. In 1517 he stood before the throne of Charles V, who had succeeded Ferdinand and Isabella, and implored him to spare the last of the Indians. Las Casas realized that there must be labor to work the plantations and the mines, but he had an excellent solution. Already a considerable number of Negro slaves had been brought to Haiti; they seemed happy and were hard workers. As an act of mercy toward the Indians, Las Casas begged his majesty to import other Negroes, twelve for each colonist.

Others made the same plea to Charles V, though not always with the same humanitarian motives. The king was moved to pity, and there was also the highly practical consideration that the Indians were worthless as slaves and the Negroes extremely useful. Charles granted one of his favorite courtiers a patent which entitled him to ship four thousand Negroes to the West Indian colonies. This was the beginning of the famous Asiento, an import license which carried with it the privilege of controlling the slave traffic to the Spanish dominions in the New World. For more than two centuries the Asiento was to be a prize in European wars. Thousands of Dutchmen, Frenchmen, and Englishmen would die so that each of their nations in turn could possess that valuable piece of paper. The Spanish courtier, however, had no idea of the value of the king's patent. For 25,000 ducats he sold it to a syndicate of Genoese merchants, who obtained most of their supplies from the slave markets in Lisbon, although one cargo was brought from the Guinea Coast as early as 1518. The Atlantic slave trade was under way.

The Genoese merchants bought their slaves in Lisbon because it was the Portuguese who carried them from Africa. The Portuguese had explored the Guinea coast and rounded the Cape of Good Hope, and their claim to exclusive rights in the whole African continent had been confirmed by two papal bulls issued in 1493. By that time they had already begun to build forts on the coast, as centers of national influence and also as depots in which slaves could be held for shipment. The first of the forts, Elmina on the

Gold Coast, was started in 1481. The local monarch, King Kwame Ansa, had made no objection to the white men's trading with his people, but when the Portuguese asked permission to build a fort, he had politely begged them to desist, in the first recorded speech of a Gold Coast ruler.

"I am not insensible," he said, "to the high honor which your great master, the Chief of Portugal, has this day conferred upon me . . . but never until this day did I observe such a difference in the appearance of his subjects. They have hitherto been only meanly attired . . . and were never happy until they could complete their lading and return. Now I remark a strange difference. A great number of richly dressed men are eager to build houses and continue among us. Men of such eminence, conducted by a commander who from his own account seems to have descended from God . . . can never bring themselves to endure the hardships of this climate. . . . It is far preferable that both our nations should continue on the same footing they have hitherto done, allowing your ships to come and go as usual."

But the king remained open to persuasion. In consideration of a yearly rent he permitted the Portuguese to lease a rocky peninsula, and they set to work immediately. Their "castle," as those early forts were called, took eighty years to finish. Unlike many of the others, Elmina was a true castle, with high towers and with walls thirty feet thick, protected on the landward side by two moats cut into solid rock. There were four hundred cannon, mounted to repulse attacks by land or sea. In the dungeons was room for a thousand slaves. John II of Portugal was so proud of the castle that, long before it was finished, he added "Lord of Guinea" to his other titles.

Beginning about the middle of the sixteenth century, Portuguese control of the African trade was challenged by other nations, notably by the French, the English, the Dutch, the Swedes (for a time), the Danes, and the Brandenburgers or Prussians, all of whom built forts of their own. The forts kept changing hands, either by purchase or else, more frequently, by force of arms. Thus Elmina was captured in 1637 by the Dutch, who retained it with some interruptions for more than two centuries. Cape Coast Castle, regarded as the second strongest fort on the Guinea coast, had a more violent history. It was started by the Swedes in 1652, captured by the Danes in 1657, captured by a local tribe in 1660, captured by the English in 1662, captured by the Dutch in 1663, and recaptured by the English in 1664. From that year it remained an English possession, notwithstanding a Dutch attack in 1665, a French attack in 1757, and various assaults by native tribes, until in 1957 it was peacefully transferred to the new government of Ghana.

In spite of wars between European states, the slave trade flourished from the beginning, and very soon it surpassed Charles V's original estimate of four thousand a year. Bishop de Las Casas proved to be right: Negroes could survive under conditions impossible for the Indians and would work hard under the overseer's lash. Antonio de Herrera wrote in 1601, "These negroes prospered so much in the colony that it was the opinion that unless a negro should happen to be hung he would never die, for as yet none have been known to perish from infirmity." Herrera also noted that the work of one Negro was more than equal to that of four Indians. As early as 1540 ten thousand Negroes a year were being imported to the West Indies. By the end of the century some nine hundred thousand slaves—by one estimate—had been shipped to the West Indies alone, not counting those sent to Mexico and South America. Bishop de Las Casas watched in agony the horror he had encouraged. He saw that the Indians, instead of being left in peace, had been virtually exterminated to make room for the newly arrived Negroes. Before his death in 1566, Las Casas became convinced that "it is as unjust to enslave Negroes as Indians and for the same reasons."

That the Negroes unquestionably made better slaves than the Indians—who either "died like fish in a bucket," as one indignant

Spanish planter complained, or else were intractable, like the mainland Indians whom the English colonists tried to enslave—is a fact
often quoted to prove that the Negroes are a naturally servile race.
The Indians, so the argument runs, were too "noble" to bend their
necks to the white man's yoke. But it was perfectly feasible to
enslave white men, and indeed much of the labor in the North
American colonies was performed by indentured servants—English,
Scottish, and Irish—who were slaves for a term of years. It does
not follow that they were culturally inferior to Haitian Indians.

The reason why members of most—not all—African tribes could
be enslaved might lie precisely in their having attained a relatively
advanced culture. "There is no case on record," says an English
anthropologist quoted by Arnold Toynbee, "of what we may perhaps call truly primitive societies, that is pure 'food-gatherers,'
being successfully brought within the orbit of a civilization, whereas
so-called primitive peoples who have passed through the agricultural revolution often so have been. Food-gatherers find the strain
of such forcible integration into an alien society too great, and die
out, like the West Indian islanders and most of the North American Indians; while African slaves are successfully—from the invaders' point of view—introduced to replace them." The anthropologist is wrong about the North American Indians; most of those
in Mexico had passed through the agricultural revolution and were
indeed reduced to serfdom by the Spanish invaders; while most of
those in the United States were primarily hunters rather than food-
gatherers like the Haitians. But hunting and fishing tribes are also
difficult to enslave, because of the value they place on personal
courage, and this seems to be true of Africa as well as America. The
Krumen, for example, were primarily fishermen and they refused to
be subjugated, although a few were sometimes procured as "captains" over the other slaves. On the east coast the Kikuyu, an
agrarian tribe, could be enslaved, but not their neighbors, the
Wacamba, who were a tribe of hunters. As for food-gathering
tribes, some of those in the Gaboon, for example, died off in
slavery almost as fast as the Haitian Indians.

Africans south of the Sahara are divided by ethnologists into five main groups, only two of which played an important part in the slave trade. The most convenient names for the groups are Bushmanoid, Pygmoid, Mongoloid, Caucasoid, and Negroid.

In the desert regions of southern Africa are the Bushmanoids, yellow-brown in color, with "peppercorn" hair (kinking so tightly that it leaves bare areas on the scalp). The true Bushmen are usually less than five feet tall, but the Hottentots, who are partly Bushmen by descent, stand nearly a head taller. Both peoples are frequently steatopygic, that is, possessed of huge buttocks which store up nourishment much as does a camel's hump. Although there is no record of Bushmanoid slaves' being landed in North America, it would appear that some of them were sent to Brazil. An English clergyman named Walsh, who visited the country in 1828–1829, reported in his *Notices of Brazil:* "People of Mosambique include generally all those of South Africa. They are distinguished by their diminutive stature and feeble limbs, but still more by their colour, inclining to brown and some even as light as mulattoes." He goes on to mention the "curious physical development" of a young girl, and this may be his clerical manner of describing her abnormally large buttocks.

In the Ituri forests of Central Africa are the Pygmoids, with an average height of four feet nine inches and an average weight of less than eighty-six pounds. They are brown-black in color and have high, bulging foreheads. There is the faint possibility that some of the slaves exported from Loango or the Gaboon were Pygmoids, but most slaving captains, if sober, would have rejected them.

On Madagascar are the Mongoloids, who reached the island from Asia many centuries ago, but who later mingled to some extent with a darker aboriginal people and with slaves imported from the mainland. The Malagasies, as natives of the island are called, resemble the Southeast Asians in stature and pigment; they speak a language classified with the Malayo-Polynesian group. There were shipments of slaves from Madagascar to the American colonies, but not enough, it would seem, to leave anything more than a small Mongoloid strain in the Negro population.

In a long strip extending from Senegal, at the westernmost extremity of the African continent, to Ethiopia and northern Kenya on the east are the Caucasoid—formerly called the Hamitic—peoples. They have deep black to light brown skins, curly but not woolly hair, and thin lips and noses, and they tend to be tall, long-legged, and slender. As a result of unceasing wars among Sudanese kingdoms, they contributed their share of the slaves exported by the French from Senegal and by the English from the Gambia River, but this Senegambian trade declined after the first quarter of the eighteenth century.

Finally, on the west coast from the Gambia to southern Angola and stretching across the continent to Kenya and Mozambique, are the Negroids. The inhabitants of this vast area are often divided into two groups, the "true Negroes" in the northwest and the Bantu in the south and east, but this distinction appears to be more linguistic than truly racial. Both groups—although with more variation from tribe to tribe among the Bantu—have dark skins, woolly hair, thick lips, and broad noses, and are usually described as being of "average" height, that is, the height of average Europeans. Since the great centers of the Atlantic trade were on the west coast from Senegal to Angola, the vast majority of slaves shipped to the New World were Negroids.

It would appear, moreover, that a smaller but still absolute majority consisted of the so-called "true Negroes." This was especially true of the slaves brought to North America and the West Indies. The Portuguese, whose markets were in Brazil, recruited more of their labor from the Bantu tribes of the Congo, Angola, and Mozambique, all south of the equator. Usually their priests would baptize a whole shipload of Angolans before the vessel set sail. The English, like the French and the Dutch, obtained more of their slaves from the "true Negro" population of Upper Guinea. They also traded to Angola, but the bulk of their cargoes came from the great slaving ports of Elmina, Cape Coast Castle, Whydah, Lagos, Bonny, and Old Calabar, east or west of the Niger delta. The Niger and its many mouths, later known as the Oil Rivers, were highways for native slave traders, who carried much of their merchandise to market in canoes that were as long as fishing schooners.

Melville J. Herskovits, the famous student of West African cultures, believes that most of the New World slaves belonged to the coastal tribes, but this was a rule with many exceptions. In 1795 Mungo Park, the Scottish explorer, traveled for months with a coffle—that is, a string of bound slaves—most of whom had been purchased in the market of Segu, on the upper Niger, more than six hundred miles from the mouth of the Gambia. In the present century Herskovits himself, while traveling in northern Nigeria, talked with old Arabs in Kano who remembered taking coffles of slaves to the coast in the 1880s. Kano is five hundred miles from the coast, but the route followed by the Arab traders was three times as long. Cases have been reported of slaves captured in Mozambique and sold at the mouth of the Congo. Such incidents, however, cannot be regarded as typical. Most of the New World slaves came from tribes living within two hundred miles of the coast for the simple reason that they could be sold without a perilous long journey through the jungle. A disproportionate share of them belonged to the Twi-speaking, Yoruba-speaking, or Ewe-speaking peoples living in what are now Ghana, Dahomey, and Nigeria. In his researches into African culture patterns transported to the New World, Herskovits found that many of the surviving patterns could be traced back to Dahomey, the kingdom that controlled the populous farmlands west of the Niger delta.

Before Europeans appeared on the coast, the Negroes of West Africa had created a number of brilliant empires, one succeeding another. The first to be recorded in history was Ghana, which, before the year 1000, ruled over most of the territory from the Sahara on the north and the Niger on the east to the Atlantic ocean. The king of Ghana could put two hundred thousand soldiers into the field. He maintained a system of highways with rest houses for travelers at regular intervals. His subjects had fine buildings, a code of laws, and an advanced knowledge of agriculture and medicine. The name "Guinea," formerly applied to the whole west coast of Africa, is often said to be a modified form of "Ghana," although there is argument over this derivation. The first African country to achieve its independence after having been a colonial possession was the new republic of Ghana, named after this ancient empire.

The earlier Ghana was weakened by drought in its northern territories, which were gradually taken over by the desert, and its capital city was sacked by the Moors in 1076. After a lapse of years the Ghanese empire was replaced by the Mandingo empire of Mali (or Melle), which has also given its name to one of the new African republics. It was in the days of Mali that the great city of Timbuktu became famous over the world for its wealth and its Mohammedan university with a faculty more advanced in knowledge than most European scholars of the fourteenth century. But Mali declined in turn, and during the fifteenth century it was replaced by the Songhai empire, which was still expanding when the Portuguese founded their first trading stations on the Guinea coast. The Songhai empire was overthrown by a Moorish army that crossed the Sahara and captured Timbuktu in 1591. The proud city was reduced by pillage and misgovernment to a huddle of mud houses around its once famous mosques.

The Portuguese learned little about the Songhai empire, which was in the interior. Of the coastal states with which they had dealings, the largest territorially was the kingdom of Kongo, at one time almost the size of California. After the king and his successors became Christians, their dominions shrank rapidly in size and wealth. A smaller but richer and more civilized kingdom than Kongo was Benin, in what is now Nigeria. The capital city, also called Benin, was six miles in circumference and was surrounded by a wall ten feet high. Shade trees lined the broad streets, and the houses were made of red clay polished to such a high degree that the first explorers thought they were made of red marble. One explorer reported that the palace of the king, called the Oba, "is as big as all Haarlem and it has square galleries, the pillars of which are covered with bronzes representing heroic deeds." Some of those bronze plaques, saved from the British destruction of the city in 1897, are still in existence, the treasured possessions of a few museums.

The first white man to reach Benin was a Portuguese, Ruy de Sequeira, in 1472. Before Sequeira was ushered into the king's presence, he and his party were taken to a caravanserai and carefully washed. He then prostrated himself before the Oba, whose arms, covered with golden ornaments, were each supported by a courtier. Sequeira received permission to trade for ivory, gold dust, and slaves. Later the Oba sent an ambassador to the king of Portugal and expressed some interest in Christianity; he even took a Portuguese, or half-Portuguese, wife from the island of São Thomé to add to his harem of a thousand women, and he ordered one of his sons to become a Christian. The Oba himself could not be converted without losing his throne. He was a largely ceremonial monarch, regarded as a representative of God on earth, and Benin was actually ruled by a theocracy of priests; it was the holy city of the Bini nation. Its sanctity, or powerful juju, was maintained by the yearly sacrifice of hundreds of slaves and captives. Its subject peoples, who provided most of the victims, revolted one after the other, and great Benin declined into a squalid town. It has been rebuilt, however, and it is still ruled over by an Oba. In 1960 the ruling monarch complained because all of his fifty-two grandsons wanted to go to Eton or Harrow.

The period when Europeans first arrived on the Guinea coast was marked, in general, by the decline of great African kingdoms, by Moorish incursions from the north, by raids from the south by savage tribes like the Fang, who were then cannibals with filed teeth, and by almost continual warfare among the smaller states. That warfare was encouraged by the slavers, who provided both sides with muskets, powder, and lead on condition that they return from the war with slaves for sale at low prices. Nevertheless a vast majority of the west-coast nations were far from being "naked savages" living in primitive squalor. Several towns near the west coast were more populous, at the time, than any but the largest European cities. There were kingdoms and commonwealths comparable in size with many European nations, and even the smaller tribes had definite and often complex cultures. The West Africans had invented their own forms of architecture and their own methods of weaving. Many of them possessed flocks of donkeys and great herds of cattle, sheep, and goats. They were skilled workers in wood, brass, and iron, which last they had learned to smelt long before the white men came. Many of their communities had highly involved religions, well-organized economic systems, efficient agricultural practices, and admirable codes of law. We have only in recent years begun to appreciate West Africa's contribution to sculpture, folk literature, and music.

There were, however, notable gaps in the African cultures, and it was the gaps that impressed Europeans. The Negro peoples had never devised a written language that became widely known (although the Vai of Sierra Leone, a branch of the great Mandingo family, reduced their own speech to writing toward the end of the eighteenth century). They had never invented either the wheel or the plow, and in most technological matters even the more advanced African peoples were little removed from the early iron age. Thus, African craftsmen were able to fashion muskets after European models, but only a few of the northernmost Negro states had learned to make their own gunpowder, that hallmark of an advanced culture.

But the great advantage of the slavers lay in what President Nkrumah of Ghana has called "the Balkanization of Africa." One tribe could not understand another. There were 264 Sudanic languages (those spoken by the "true Negroes"), 182 Bantu languages, and 47 Hamitic languages. A single people, such as the Wolof of Senegal, might be divided into two or three hostile kingdoms; the Yoruba of Nigeria had ten separate states. Neither these little kingdoms nor the warring tribes around them would join together against a common enemy, and hence it was easy for the slavers to set one group against another. It was as though an invading force had arrived in Europe during the Dark Ages and had exploited the continent by pitting each feudal lord against his neighbors. The Africans remained independent, however, during the whole of the slaving era. What saved them from being conquered for nearly four hundred years after the white men appeared was partly their courage and skill in using European weapons, and partly the fact that slavers of various nations were as hostile to one another as were the African tribes.

But it was chiefly mosquitoes and malaria, dengue and yellow fever, that protected the vast continent from conquest and even exploration. One portion after another of the African coast—first Senegambia, then Sierra Leone, then the Bight of Benin—was called "the white man's grave." The Portuguese, who tried at first to penetrate into the interior, became discouraged by their losses. To the slavers who followed them Africa was chiefly a coastline; or rather it was three parallel lines, one of boiling white surf, one of brown sand, and finally a green line of jungle beyond which few of them ventured and from which fewer still came back.

Of course certain facts, or supposed facts, were known about the interior. There was a huge river, the Niger, called the Nile of the West, which rose in the Mountains of the Moon and reached the sea no one knew where, although it was believed that the Senegal and the Gambia were two of its mouths. In Abyssinia lived Prester John, the Christian monarch of a powerful nation surrounded by pagan tribes. The king's banquets were lighted by trained elephants holding torches in their trunks, and his trappers caught unicorns with the aid of young virgins. Farther south was the kingdom of Monomotapa, a gold-encrusted land that was even richer than Eldorado. In Madagascar was a giant bird called the roc, which was capable of carrying off elephants (possibly the legend was based on the aepyornis, a gigantic ostrich that did not become extinct until the eighteenth century). In Central Africa was a nation of pygmies only six inches high who fought pitched battles against the cranes. Another tribe consisted of people with such huge lower lips that they used them as sunshades. There were cannibals everywhere, including the Niam-Niam—the name of a real tribe, incidentally—who were reputed to have tails, which they used to knock down their victims. Africa, in short, was a continent where any sort of beast or monster could flourish, but where white men died like fish on the sand.

For European geographers of the eighteenth century, West Africa or its coastline had three divisions: Senegambia, Upper Guinea, and Lower Guinea. For slaving captains, who sometimes used different names, the coast was further subdivided by its physical features, such as harbors or the lack of them and prevailing winds, and by the type of slaves coming from each locality.

*Senegambia*, a term used chiefly by geographers, was the westernmost projection of the continent. Essentially it was the land between two navigable rivers, the Senegal (controlled by the French) and the Gambia (controlled by the English). The principal African peoples were the Fula, Wolof, and Serer in the north, the Felup south of the Gambia—described by Mungo Park as "a wild and unsociable race"—and the Mandingos in wide sections of the interior. The Fula or Fulani were a people of herdsmen with long hair, fine features, and comparatively light complexions; their neighbors called them "the whites." They were devout Mohammedans, and the young men of good families could read and write Arabic. The Wolof were very black and very tall, with big chests and slender legs; they made good soldiers. The Mandingos were farmers—sometimes big planters with hundreds of slaves—and merchants who circulated everywhere, trading in gold dust, slaves, salt, iron, and ivory.

None of the Senegambian peoples (except the Felup) was regarded as being suitable for hard work in the cane, rice, or cotton fields. John Barbot, a seventeenth-century slaver, describes them as being "genteel and courteous . . . but leud and lazy to excess." "For this reason," he adds, "they are not reckoned so proper for working in the American plantations as are those of the Gold Coast of Ardra and Angola, but the cleanliest and fittest for house servants being very handy and intelligent." In addition to their use as house servants, the Mandingos were also widely used as plantation coopers and blacksmiths.

From the Gambia south and east to the Bight of Biafra were two thousand miles of coastline shaped like a dog's leg and known as *Upper Guinea*. Another name for most of it in the early days was the Windward Coast, because of the onshore winds. For English slavers as late as 1700 the dividing point was Cape Coast Castle, the English stronghold on the north shore of the Gulf of Guinea. Anything west and north of Cape Coast Castle was "windward"; anything east and south of it was "leeward." After 1750, however, the term "Windward Coast" was restricted to a smaller area that centered on Cape Palmas.

Directly south of the Gambia was a region known in early slave-trading days as the *Rivers of the South*; it included the territories that later become Portuguese Guinea and French Guinea, and sometimes the term was extended to cover Sierra Leone. Among the rivers were the Rio Grande, the Rio Nuñez, the Rio Pongo, the Great and Little Scarcies, and the Great Bum, most of them with swift upper courses and broad estuaries choked with marshy islands. It was so easy to hide among the islands that the Rivers of the South became the haunt of illegal slavers after 1807. In the days when the trade was legal, it was largely conducted by sending boats up the rivers to native towns, but there were also three famous slave depots on the coast: the islands of Los or Delos, the Sierra Leone River, and Sherbro Island, each with an excellent harbor. The slaves exported came from many small tribes; most often mentioned in the records are the Baga and Susu of French Guinea and the Chamba of Sierra Leone, all of whom brought fairly high prices in the New World markets.

Next came the *Grain Coast*, north and west of Cape Palmas, which corresponded to modern Liberia. It produced a great deal of rice, often sold to slaving vessels, but the product for which it

was named was malaguetta pepper, or "grains of paradise." This
African pepper was thought to prevent dysentery and was used to
season the food of the slaves on their voyage to America. There
were no good harbors on the Grain Coast, and ships standing inshore were in danger of being wrecked on sunken rocks. Trade here
(and on the Ivory Coast as well) largely took the form of "smoke
trading." Standing offshore, a European vessel would fire a gun to
attract attention. The natives, if they had rice or pepper or slaves
to sell, would send up smoke signals, then launch a canoe through
the surf. They were always apprehensive, and with good reason,
of being kidnaped. Among the coastal tribes the most famous was
that of the Krumen, fishers and boatmen who were rarely sold to
the slavers unless they were criminals. They were big, very dark
men with enormously powerful muscles from their constant paddling. Later many Krumen enlisted in the Royal Navy, and more
than one English captain went on record as saying that he considered them superior to white sailors.

The *Ivory Coast*, east of Cape Palmas, sometimes bore the other
name of Tooth Coast, since the tusks that once formed its principal
export were also known as "elephants' teeth." Here again there
were no good harbors, and the trading was usually from canoes.
Many of these were manned by Krumen, who were spreading eastward along the coast. The true natives of the region distrusted
Europeans and would not permit them to set up trading stations or
penetrate inland. The Europeans retaliated by describing the inhabitants as "the most savage, thievish, and revengeful upon the
African coast." When sold in American markets, they were usually grouped with the natives of the Grain Coast and Sierra Leone
as "Windward Coast Negroes."

The *Gold Coast*, extending as far as the Volta River, corresponded to what is now the Republic of Ghana. It was named for
the gold that was mined in the hills and panned from many of the
streams. Until the streets of Accra were paved within recent years,
gold nuggets were occasionally picked up on main thoroughfares
after a heavy rain. There were no harbors on the Gold Coast, but

there were dozens of European forts and "factories"—depots for goods and slaves—often in sight of each other. Some of the famous forts were Axim (Dutch), Elmina (Dutch), Cape Coast Castle, Anamabo (English), Cormantine (the first English fort, built in 1631, but captured and held by the Dutch in 1665), and Accra (where Dutch, English, and Danish forts stood within gunshot range). From the forts and factories slaves were ferried to the waiting ships by Krumen, through what was always described as the "terrible surf."

Slaves from the Gold Coast were highly regarded by the English and usually sold at a higher price than those from other regions. In the West Indies they were called Coromantees (a name spelled in various fashions) after the port of Cormantine, from which many of them had been exported. It was not an African tribal name, and the Coromantees may have belonged to several different tribes; but it seems likely that most of them were either Fanti, from the largest of the coastal nations, or else Ashanti from a hundred miles in the interior. No other group of slaves aroused so much controversy. Captain William Snelgrave says, writing in 1734, "I know that many of the Coromantine Negroes despise punishment and even death itself, it having often happened that on their being any ways hardly dealt with twenty or more have hang'd themselves at a time." They were often the leaders of slave mutinies. Edward Long, who wrote a *History of Jamaica* (1774), calls them "haughty, ferocious, and stubborn." He mentions a slave uprising in which "thirty-three Coromantes, most of whom had been newly imported, murdered and wounded no less than nineteen Whites in the space of an hour." The Jamaica House of Assembly, in describing a series of slave revolts during the middle of the eighteenth century, reported that "all these disturbances . . . have been planned and conducted by the Coromantin Negroes who are distinguished from their brethren by their aversion to husbandry and the martial ferocity of their dispositions." In 1765 a committee suggested a tax of ten pounds on each Coromantee to discourage their importation, as their "turbulent savage and martial temper was well known."

On the other hand, everyone admired their courage. Bryan Edwards, writing in 1792, tells of Ibo children who screamed with pain while being branded by their owners, whereas the "Koromantyr" boys took the pain without wincing and ridiculed the Ibo. Christopher Codrington, governor of the Leeward Islands, became lyrical when describing the Coromantees in his official report of 1701. They are, he said, "not only the best and most faithful of our slaves but really are all born heroes. There is a difference between them and all other Negroes beyond what 'tis possible for your Lordships to conceive. There was never a raskal or coward of that nation. . . . My father, who had studied the genius and temper of all kinds of Negroes for forty-five years with a very nice observation would say no man deserved a Corramante that would not treat him like a friend rather than a slave." If many of the Gold Coast captives were Ashanti, members of the proudest and most warlike nation in all the lands that bordered on the Gulf of Guinea, treating them as friends rather than slaves must have been a wise policy.

East of the Volta River was the *Slave Coast*, which included all the regions that faced the Bight of Benin. Here, where the trade was briskest, the native kings would not permit any European nation to build a fort and install a garrison. Instead they encouraged all nations to compete on equal terms. Any nation that wished to maintain a stock of trade goods was permitted to store them in a mud-walled factory, so long as the factory was situated at least three miles from the shore. Most of the slaves exported belonged to the Yoruba-speaking or Ewe-speaking peoples, the latter including the warlike Dahomans. In many cases they owed their captivity to the wars between the expanding Dahoman empire and its neighbors. Both the Yoruba and the Dahomans were disciplined, industrious nations used to cultivating the soil, and the price of both in the British West Indies was only less than that of the Gold Coast slaves. In French Haiti, where the Coromantees were feared as troublemakers, the price of Dahomans was highest. The Spanish, for their part, preferred Yoruba.

East of Cape Formosa, which is the tip of the Niger delta, lay "the terrible Bight of Biafra." The lands that border on it, swampy and malarial, were sometimes known as "the Bight" for short, and sometimes generically as Calabar. Here the chief ports, all lying on rivers and sheltered from equatorial storms, were New Calabar, Bonny, and Old Calabar. Slaves from these ports were usually sold as Ibo, although many of them belonged to other nations, notably the Ibibio and the Efik. They were popular in some of the New World markets because they had the reputation of being gentle and tractable, but elsewhere they were distrusted as being subject to fits of despondency. When Henry Laurens, later president of the Continental Congress, was the leading commission merchant of Charleston, South Carolina, he wrote in 1757 that he could not sell a newly arrived shipment of slaves unless no others came in. Planters would hesitate to buy them because they were "Aboes" and known to commit suicide. Even today there is a current expression in Haiti: *Ibos pend' cor' a yo,* "The Ibo hang themselves."

*Lower Guinea* included more than fifteen hundred miles of seacoast from Calabar to the southern desert. This vast area was divided into the Cameroons, Gaboon, and Loango, all north of the Congo, and Angola south of the river. From Gaboon southward the seaports were more or less controlled by the Portuguese. The natives of Lower Guinea, all Bantu-speaking, were less advanced or industrious than those of Upper Guinea and brought a somewhat lower price in the New World markets. A seventeenth-century slaving captain said of the Gaboon, "From thence a good Negro was scarcely ever brought. They are purchased so cheaply on the coast as to tempt many captains to freight with them; but they generally die either on the passage or soon after their arrival in the islands. The debility of their constitutions is astonishing"; and in this respect they seem to have resembled the Haitian Indians. By the last quarter of the eighteenth century, another type of slaves was being exported from this area, for geographers began to describe them as "a bold and hardy race."

"Angola" was a broad term, and it was sometimes applied to all the Portuguese missions and trading stations, including those to the north of the Congo. South of the river the largest and busiest port was Luanda, but some slaves were exported from Benguela and from Mossamedes, which lies not far from the edge of the southern desert. An early American school geography, compiled by William Channing Woodbridge, says of Benguela that it is "a region south of Angola, inhabited by a rude and barbarous race. The air is very unwholesome. Strangers are advised not to land; and those who survive attempts to reside there, resemble men coming from the tomb." Of Angola, Woodbridge says, "It is resorted to only for slaves of an inferior order, of which 40,000 are annually sold, chiefly to the French." An anonymous Englishman explained in 1763 that Angola was an extremely fertile part of Africa, where the natives have everything they need for the mere trouble of picking it from trees. "On that account," he said, "the men never work, but lead an indolent life, and are in general of a lazy disposition and tender constitution . . . so that when these people are carried to our sugar islands, they are obliged to be nursed, to be taken care of, and brought to work by degrees." But in spite of these complaints about the laziness and debility of the Angolans, they could be cheaply purchased from the Portuguese, and English planters learned to like them better as time went on.

By the year 1798 no less than 69 of the Liverpool slavers—out of a total fleet of 150—went to Angola, and 34 went to Bonny, on the Bight of Biafra, whereas only 11 bought Gold Coast Negroes and not a single vessel cleared for the once busy factories on the Gambia. The trade had moved south, where human merchandise was cheaper.

But that was toward the end of the legal slave trade, and almost all the ancestors of present-day American Negroes had already reached this country. Most of them belonged to the relatively advanced and highly industrious peoples of Upper Guinea. Much as these peoples differed among themselves, their national characteristics disappeared after two or three generations in the colonies, and the American Negro evolved into a new type, almost—some anthropologists say—a new race. But ancestral traits of physique or temperament may reappear in unexpected fashions, and one is tempted to recognize the Fula in a particularly fine head, the Wolof in an immensely tall and slender-legged basketball player, and the Ashanti in a boxer. Some evidence might even be assembled to show that the Mandingos, a race of traders in Africa and one that was prized in America as house servants, have furnished more than their quota of the new Negro bourgeoisie.

The early slavers were as mixed a lot as the slaves. There were respectable merchant captains taking on a little extra cargo, derelicts who had no other means of making a living, sadists finding an opportunity to gratify their passion for cruelty, picturesque "gentlemen adventurers," money-mad speculators, serious young clerks sent out by their firms (and dying of fever before they got home with their savings), seamen treated almost as harshly as the slaves, criminals planning to be pirates, diligent surgeons, and pious Christians.

Possibly the most colorful of the early slavers was Captain John Hawkins, who later played an important part in the defeat of the Spanish Armada. Hawkins, born in 1532, was bred to the sea as an Arab is born to the desert. His father was a merchant captain who had been to Guinea and who, during the long winter evenings, would tell the boy what he had seen: the endless beaches lined with waving palms, the great surf that threw spray as high as a galleon's crosstrees, the murky rivers full of crocodiles as big as a ship's longboat, and the naked blackamoors who traded gold dust and elephants' teeth for tawdries and trinkets. The blackamoors themselves would fetch a good price in Hispaniola or the Spanish Main. Alas, the slave trade was controlled by Portugal, backed by the power of imperial Spain. What a pity that this path to riches was blocked by foreign Papists!

Young Hawkins' first voyage to Guinea was in 1562. He commanded a little squadron of "private" ships (not sailing under government orders), whose combined crews numbered fewer than a hundred men. "Partly by the sword and partly by other means," as he put it, Hawkins acquired three hundred Negroes. He exchanged them in Hispaniola for a cargo of hides, sugar, ginger, and "some quantitie of pearles." With amazing effrontery Hawkins sent some of his cargo to be sold in Spain, but the authorities seized it because of his illegal raid on Guinea. In spite of this loss, he still showed a handsome profit on the voyage.

When Queen Elizabeth heard of Hawkins' slaving venture, she said "It was detestable and would call down vengeance from heaven upon the undertakers." Hawkins went to see the queen and showed Her Majesty his profit sheet. Not only did she forgive him but she became a shareholder in his second slaving voyage. That was in 1564, and Hawkins then had four vessels. Before setting out he issued his famous sailing orders, which became a tradition in the British Navy: "Serve God daily, love one another, preserve your victuals, beware of fire and keep good company."

Since the Portuguese regarded Hawkins as a pirate, he could not get his cargoes from their forts along the coast and was forced to make his own arrangements. Off Sierra Leone he stopped at Sambula Island, where the original inhabitants, the Sapie, had been enslaved by the Sambose from the mainland. Hawkins enslaved both tribes. His fleet spent several days at the island, "going ashore every day to take the inhabitants with burning and spoiling their towns." Continuing southward along the African coast, Hawkins met with his first serious reverse. The English heard of a little community named Bymba, where "there was not only a great quantity of gold but also not above 40 men and 100 women and children." Trusting to their armor for protection, the English landed and attacked the town. While the English were looting it and capturing the women and children, the men of Bymba counterattacked. Hawkins lost seven of his sailors, who were drowned or killed by arrows as they tried to launch the boats, or cut off by the furious natives and hacked to pieces. He gained only ten Negro slaves.

The little fleet continued southward, seeing "canoes that had three score men in a peece," attacking and being attacked by various native communities. Having at last filled their holds with slaves, the vessels set sail for the Spanish Main. Hawkins tried to sell his cargo in Venezuela, but the governor refused to accept it. Hawkins thereupon landed a hundred sailors armed with "bows, arrows, harquebusses and pikes," and the governor changed his mind. The business having been brought to a successful conclusion, Hawkins returned to England a comparatively wealthy man.

Hawkins made one additional slaving voyage in 1567. He had with him as captain of the *Judith* a young man named Francis Drake. Although Drake had taken part in a previous slave-raiding expedition, this was his first command. The expedition had its troubles and at one point was driven off by poisoned arrows, but at last Hawkins managed to enter into an alliance with three kings who had a feud with another tribe. The procurement of slaves had changed for Hawkins—as it had already changed for the Portuguese—from simple man-stealing by the whites to a partnership with some Africans at the expense of other Africans. John Hartop, who was with the expedition, wrote, "The three kings drove seven thousand Negroes into the sea at low tide, at the point of land, where they were all drowned in the ooze except for five hundred which we took and carried thence for traffique to the West Indies." In spite of this success, the expedition ended in failure. Hawkins took his ships to Vera Cruz, but was trapped in the harbor by a large Spanish fleet, which disapproved of his smuggling. The captured sailors were executed as heretics. Only two English vessels escaped, the flagship and the *Judith*, Captain Drake.

Another early slaver, much more typical than Hawkins, was Andrew Battel, a young English sailor who found himself involved in the trade much against his will. In 1599 Battel joined the complement of the *May Morning*, a pinnace of fifty tons, one of the "rovers" designed to prey on Spanish treasure galleons. The boy must have set out in hopes of returning soon to England, his pockets full of golden ducats, and of astounding his friends with his adventures in the fabulous Indies. His future was to be more fantastic than the wildest of his boyish dreams.

The *May Morning* set out for Brazil and first tried to raid the ports of Cape Lopo and São Tomé, but was beaten off. She continued along the coast until supplies ran short; then the captain sent some sailors ashore to get water and fresh fruit. In the shore party was Andrew Battel. The party was attacked by Indians, and the ship's captain, deciding that it was no use losing more men, sailed off leaving Battel and the others to their fate. It was a better fate than the captain's, since the *May Morning* was never heard of again.

The Indians sold their captives to the Portuguese governor of Rio de Janeiro, for at that time there was no color line in the slave trade, and whites were as acceptable as Negroes or Indians. The governor, impressed by young Battel, sent him on a Portuguese ship to the Congo to purchase Negroes, promising him his freedom if he did well. Battel, however, tried to escape on a Dutch ship trading along the African coast. He was recaptured and thrown into prison, where he found himself in the company of some Moorish and Egyptian slaves, in addition to a few Portuguese criminals. Battel joined a mass prison break, but the fugitives were attacked by natives and then retaken by a Portuguese patrol. Probably Battel would have died in prison if there had not been an uprising in the interior of the colony. The local governor needed every man he could find and offered the prisoners a pardon if they would help in putting down the revolt. Battel went out with a force of four hundred men, who spent the next two years destroying crops, burning villages, and driving coffles of slaves back to the stockades or barracoons on the coast.

Battel then joined the crew of a slaver. The vessel sailed slowly down the coast of Angola, stopping at every likely point to see if the local community had slaves for sale. At one point the men had a stroke of luck. A tribe called the Gaga was at war with another tribe and offered the white men all the prisoners captured if they would join in the campaign. The slavers joyfully accepted. As a result, Battel says, "We loaded our ships with the slaves we purchased which did not cost us more than a rial each, which in the city would be worth 12 mille-reys." But now came an unexpected complication. The Gaga were so delighted with the white men's help that they refused to let them go. The Portuguese captain solved the problem by leaving Battel with the Gaga as a "pawn." The custom of leaving "pawns" or hostages as assurance of good faith was well known along the coast. This time the promise to the Gaga was that the vessel would return in two months, but Battel was a foreigner, a heretic, and a slave, and the captain never bothered to redeem the pawn. Battel was at the mercy of the Gaga, who decided to kill and eat him. He persuaded them, however, that he would be of more use as a mercenary soldier. With his knowledge of native warfare, he soon distinguished himself and received his share of the loot acquired on the raids.

On the whole Battel preferred the Gaga to the Portuguese. They were cannibals, it is true, but to a man living in the era of the auto-da-fé, of keel-hauling and flogging on shipboard, and of piratical raids on foreign commerce, the dietary habits of the Gaga were at most times no more than a local eccentricity. There was a period of famine, however, when the Gaga had completely devastated the surrounding country and found themselves with nothing left to eat. Battel came to the conclusion that his new friends were looking at him a little hungrily. During the night he slipped away into the jungle and set out for the coast. There he was fortunate enough to be picked up by a passing vessel and so reached England again.

Battel's story illustrates some important points connected with the early slave trade. It was something else than mere aggression by heartless adventurers against peaceful tribesmen. Except for the slavers' weapons and ships, there was little to choose between them and many of the predatory coastal tribes. Race was not as yet a central question. Battel was enslaved by both Portuguese and Negroes, while being quite ready himself to enslave either whites or blacks. He writes of his masters impartially, seeing good and evil in the customs of both. At this time slavers seldom bothered to make excuses for their profession; it was an institution accepted by all nations. Religion was often used to justify the trade, but the racial excuse was seldom offered in the sixteenth century. As for brutality and suffering, they were universal. Anthony Knivet, another Elizabethan "rover," tells of being marooned together with eighteen other sick men because their captain did not think it worth while to nurse them. Knivet, like Battel, was captured by Indians and sold as a slave to the Portuguese.

# 2

# Slaving in the Seventeenth Century

Beware and take care of the Bight of Benin,
Few come out, though many go in.
                    —Seventeenth-century slavers' saying

**D**URING THE PERIOD OF MORE THAN A HUNDRED YEARS WHEN THE
Portuguese controlled the slave trade, they invented or adapted
many terms that became a permanent part of the slavers' jargon.
Some of the commonest terms were *palaver* (for any sort of talks,
negotiations, or disputes), *caboceer* (a headman or official, from the
Portuguese *cabociero*), *pickaninny* (from *pequenino*, very little),
*fetish* (from *feitiço*, charm or sorcery), *barracoon* (possibly from
the Spanish), *customs* (meaning native rites involving human
sacrifice), *panyaring* (kidnaping), *dash* (a gift or bribe), and
*bozal* (an adjective applied to slaves fresh from Africa: bozal
Negroes). By the end of the sixteenth century, however, the Portuguese no longer had the armed power to support their words.
    Portugal was united with Spain in 1580; for the next sixty years

it was governed as a separate kingdom by the Spanish kings. It retained its colonial possessions, but the Spanish Navy was unable to protect them, and other nations demanded a share of their trade. During the long wars between Spain and Holland, the coast of Guinea was harried by Dutch raiders. In 1630 a Dutch fleet captured Pernambuco, then the chief port of Brazil, and the Dutch extended their control over the northern half of the colony. In 1640 the Portuguese regained their independence, but the fighting continued. It was not until 1662 that it was ended by a Dutch-Portuguese treaty, with the Dutch surrendering their claims to Brazil in return for control of the Guinea trade.

Other nations had taken advantage of the fighting to establish themselves in Senegambia and Upper Guinea. In 1626 the French built the fort of St. Louis on a sandy peninsula between the Senegal River and the ocean. The English first built a fort at Cormantine, on the Gold Coast (1631), but later they captured the originally Swedish fort of Cape Coast Castle, not far distant, and made it their principal trading center. Another English center was James Fort, near the mouth of the Gambia, which—except for the Senegal —was the only West African river navigable for a considerable distance by seagoing vessels.

English interest in the slave trade had been intensified by the acquisition of colonies in the West Indies, beginning with Barbados. These "sugar islands," as they came to be called, needed slaves, so English merchants tried to break the foreign monopoly. In 1663 an English company was chartered under the Duke of York, brother of Charles II, to supply a minimum of three thousand slaves yearly to the new colonies. It had the romantic title of "The Company of Royal Adventurers of England Trading to Africa," and, as a tribute to the duke, its slaves were branded with the letters DY. To advertise the company, in which he had invested money, King Charles had a new coin issued; it was made of gold from West Africa and was called a guinea. The coin was intended to have the same value as the pound sterling, but the reddish "guinea gold" was so pure and in such demand that at one time (1694) it was worth thirty shillings in silver. Finally the value of the guinea was fixed at twenty-one shillings.

The Company of Royal Adventurers started by establishing a chain of new forts and factories along the Guinea Coast, but, as a prelude to the Second Dutch War, in 1664–1665 the famous Dutch admiral de Ruyter swept down the coast and captured all the English establishments except Cape Coast Castle. The captured forts remained in Dutch hands by terms of the treaty of peace (1667), and the Royal Adventurers, including Charles, lost almost their whole investment of more than 120,000 pounds.

For a time the slave trade was chiefly in Dutch hands, but the English did not abandon the struggle. They started building a new chain of forts, and in 1672 they founded the Royal African Company to maintain the forts in return for a monopoly of the trade. The company proved to be a mine of guinea gold for its investors (once more including King Charles); in one of the early years they received a stock dividend of 300 per cent. Outdistancing foreign competitors, the Royal African Company gradually came to exercise control of the trade everywhere from the French ports in Senegal to Loango and Angola, which remained Portuguese. Its chief difficulty, as time went on, was with English "interlopers"— independent traders who refused to recognize its monopoly. Obligated as the company was to garrison the forts, "dash" the native kings, and pay dividends to its stockholders, it suffered more and more from competition with the interlopers, who traded where and when they could and had almost no overhead.

Interloping was made a capital offense, but still the company's slaves had to be sold at higher prices than the planters thought they could afford to pay. In 1689 the Barbados planters issued a pamphlet entitled *Groans from the Plantations.* "Heretofore," they said, Negroes "stood us about seven pounds a Head . . . and now we buy . . . [at] twenty pounds. And we are forced to scramble for them in so shameful a manner that one of the great

Burdens of our lives is the going to buy Negroes." In a "scramble" the whole cargo of slaves was sold at a uniform price for each "piece of India," and the purchasers, all admitted to the slave yard at the same moment, scrambled to put ropes or handkerchiefs around the best of them. The slaves could not complain, but the planters did.

Their groans became so loud that in 1698 the trade was thrown open to all English merchants who would pay a 10-per-cent tax on their cargoes for the benefit of the company. The tax, however, did not yield enough to reimburse the company for the cost of maintaining its forts. Although the trade flourished as never before, the Royal African Company by now was steadily losing money. Many prominent men tried to preserve the company, fearing that if its forts were lost the trade would go with them. James Oglethorpe, the great philanthropist who founded Georgia as a refuge for English debtors, was one of its directors during the 1730s. But nothing could save it, in the end, and the Royal African Company was dissolved between 1750 and 1752. After that time the forts were maintained by a committee of English merchants with the help of government subsidies.

Some of the Africans were by no means passive victims or mere observers of these conflicts. Indeed, the trade would have languished without their wholehearted cooperation. Supplying slaves for the European powers was both the profession and the recreation of many native kings. It would be a great error to suppose that the rulers of Dahomey and Ashanti, for example, or the Damel of Cayor, in Senegal, were any more high-principled or tender-minded than Charles II, John Hawkins, or Queen Elizabeth I.

The African monarchs continued to control the coastal areas and in most cases owned even the land on which European forts were built. On the Gold Coast almost every local chief possessed a "note" or "book," that is, a legal contract issued by the European power controlling the fort in his area; the contract acknowledged his title to the land and fixed a yearly rent. Chiefs fought for possession of these "notes" exactly as European powers fought for the Asiento. Except in Portuguese Angola, the Africans remained independent of the foreigners encamped on their shores. When the Dutch, in 1637, tried to subjugate the local tribes around Elmina, they suffered a costly defeat. The chiefs were sometimes taken to Europe, where they were lavishly entertained and met the European rulers. The king of Whydah acted as an arbiter in disputes between the European nations trading in his little dominion, and his decisions were accepted without question. The king of Dahomey seldom shook hands with a white man, and then only as "a very uncommon mark of royal condescension." A French trader complained in 1680, "The great wealth of the Fantineans [Fanti] makes them so proud and haughty that an European trading there must stand bare to them." A Dutch slaver reported that in Anamabo (1690), "The English factors dare not in the least contradict [the local kings] but are rather obliged to bear with them and are sometimes so invested that they are close confined to the castle without daring to stir abroad. Nay, if the Blacks dislike the English chief factor, they send him away in a canoe to Cape Corso [Cape Coast Castle] or oblige him to pay a heavy fine." Salutes had to be fired in honor of the local king by every ship that put into port, and an English captain who omitted this courtesy on the Gambia was arrested by the king and heavily fined.

Even with their forts, men of war, and cannon, the Europeans hesitated to retaliate against such treatment. The forts would be worthless—perhaps they could not even be held—if the local chiefs were hostile, and both sides knew it. William Mariner, "a person well experienced in the affairs of Africa having for many years frequented these coasts," tells how the English, in 1662, had made an attempt to capture Cape Coast Castle, had been repulsed, but had returned the following year with native help and had taken the fort—"By which it appears that the Natives are the best Bulwark to defend any hold the English have upon these Coasts and for want of the Natives good will, Cormanteen Castle was taken by the Dutch in the year 1664 and they have it in possession to this day." In 1665 the Danish castle at Accra was captured by the natives, and the governor had to flee to the English for help.

Still more important, the native kings saw to it that slaves were provided to European ships. By the year 1600 the hit-or-miss raids of John Hawkins and Andrew Battel were things of the past. Except for a comparatively few natives kidnaped by the more unscrupulous captains, slaves were sold by Negro merchants and caboceers under supervision of the coastal kings, most of whom were slave-traders themselves. Thus the trade acquired an air of complete legality. During the seventeenth century the social, political, and economic life of West Africa became reorganized to produce one result, a steady flow of slaves for the ships anchored along the coast.

To suggest the immensity of this traffic, here are a few figures. In the years from 1575 to 1591, 52,000 slaves were sent from Angola alone to Brazil and the Spanish Indies, with the shipments rising to an average of more than 5000 a year by the end of this period. They continued to rise, and, by 1617, 28,000 slaves were being shipped annually from Angola and the Congo. From 1680 to 1700, 300,000 slaves were shipped in English vessels alone. From 1680 to 1688 the Royal African Company had 249 slavers in operation, and these embarked 60,783 slaves, only 46,396 of whom survived the voyage. As against some 900,000 slaves shipped from all parts of Guinea to the New World in the sixteenth century, the total figure for the seventeenth century is thought to be 2,750,000, or an average of 27,500 a year.

Supplying, shipping, and disposing of this vast number of human chattels became a gigantic international operation and one that favored the growth of new industries in England especially, but also in France and the Netherlands. There was no such industrial growth in Africa, but only a vast disruption of native culture. The Europeans did not introduce manufacturing plants, agricultural methods, business communities, political systems, or Christian ideals, as they were trying to do in the New World. What they introduced were muskets, gunpowder, dry goods, and rum, all as means to advancing the slave trade, which was so enormously profitable that nothing else could compete with it. In 1853 an experienced British official on the Gold Coast was writing regretfully, "It may be safely affirmed that from our first settlement on the coast until the abolition of the slave trade in 1807, we did not confer one lasting benefit upon the people."

The slaving captains did not want to stay longer on the coast than was absolutely necessary. Their profits depended on loading their ships as rapidly as possible and then racing for the West Indies under a full press of sail before their close-packed cargoes perished. Also their crews sickened and died when exposed to the "noxious vapors" rising from coastal marshes. It was necessary, therefore, to create a group of middlemen who would live permanently on the coast, buy slaves from the local merchants or kings when the coffles were driven down to the ports, prepare the slaves for the long voyage, and keep on hand a stock of healthy Negroes ready to be loaded into the hold of any slaver anchoring in the road. These middlemen were usually employees of the big trading companies, and hence they were called "factors," a factor being someone who represented a large firm. Their establishments, if not fortified, were known as "factories."

In general the factors were a degraded lot, many of whom had been in trouble at home. William Bosman, a Dutch factor on the coast—and an exception to the generality—remarked that "no one came here who could live in Holland." Factors were poorly paid, even by the standards of the time. Writing at the end of the seventeenth century, Bosman reported that the Dutch Director-General received 315 pounds a year, but his assistant only 37 pounds, 16 shillings. The factors fought a losing battle against heat, disease, and most of all boredom. They took refuge in drink and native women. Bosman says, "They are as zealous Votaries to Venus as Bacchus and so waste the small portion of Strength left them." John (or Jean) Barbot, a French factor of this period, says of his colleagues, "They are generally men of no education or principles, void of foresight, careless, prodigal, addicted to strong liquors, as palm-wine, brandy and punch which they will drink to excess and then lie down on the bare ground in the open air . . . without any other covering but a single shirt, nay, some, and perhaps no small number are over-fond of the black women whose natural hot and leud temper soon wastes their bodies and consumes that little substance they have." Bosman adds, " 'Tis incredible how many are consumed by this damnable Liquor (pardon the expression) which is not only confined to the soldiers but some of the principal People are so bigotted to it."

Thomas Phillips, who wrote an account of his voyage to Guinea from 1693 to 1694, as captain of the *Hannibal*, tells a story, here condensed, about the degradation and death of one English factor.

The 20th in the morning [he says] Capt. Shurley and I went ashore to our castle at Succandy [Sekundi, on the Gold Coast] where we found the factor, Mr. Johnson, in his bed raving mad, cursing and swearing most wretchedly at us, not in the least knowing Capt. Shurley, tho' he had a long former acquaintance with him. I pity'd from my soul this poor man, who had plunged himself into this condition thro' resentment of an affront put upon him by one Vanbukeline, the merchant of the Mine Castle [Elmina] which, as we were informed by his second, was as follows:

One Taguba, a noted Negro woman in Cape Corce town, being got with child by some of the soldiers of our castle there, was brought to bed of a Malatto girl who growing to be about 11 years old, Mr. Johnson had a great fancy for her and purposed to take her for his wife (as they take wives in Guiney) and about that time he being removed to Succandy to make sure of the girl took her there to live with him until she was of age fit for matrimonial functions, using much tenderness and kindness to her and taking great pleasure and satisfaction in her company for two or three years.

When she was grown man's meat and a pretty girl, Vanbukeline by bribes and presents corrupted her mother Taguba and prevailed with her to go to Succandy and under pretence of making a visit to her daughter, to steal her away and bring her to him, he

having ordered a swift canoe to lie ready under the Dutch fort at
Succandy for that end. The mother accordingly came and having
been kindly treated by Mr. Johnson, who suspected nothing, went
with her daughter to take a walk and being come near the canoo
that lay perdue, the canoo men took hold of her and put her per
force into it, her mother following, and carried them both away
to the Mine Castle, and delivered the young one to Vanbukeline
who soon cracked that nut which Mr. Johnson had been so long
preparing for his own tooth.

When I dined with the Dutch general at the Mine, I saw her
there, being brought in to dance before us, very fine, bearing the
title of Madam Vanbukeline. This, and some other old differences
between that Dutchman and he did so disturb and vex him, that
it threw him into distempers and quite turned his brain. We
were entertained by the young second as well as he could and
about three in the evening we went aboard.

I have been informed since my being there that the adjacent
negroes, instigated by Vanbukeline and the Dutch general, had in
the night surprised and seiz'd the fort, cut Johnson to pieces,
and plundered all the goods and merchandise.

Not all the factors succumbed to dissipation. A few, especially
those in responsible positions, were brilliant men who devoted
their time to studying the African people, the soil, the flora, and
the fauna. One such man was John (or Jean) Barbot, who, writing
in English, describes himself as "agent-general of the Royal Company of Africa and Islands of America, at Paris." Barbot made at
least two voyages to Guinea between 1678 and 1682. At that time
France had forts at St. Louis and Goree and a number of stockaded
strong-points. Barbot traveled up and down the coast for his company, making elaborate notes of everything he saw and even draw-
ing diagrams of the scales of unusual fishes. He recorded the
quality of the malaguetta pepper and how it was grown, the operation of the gold mines, and methods of cattle raising, and observed
how the natives raised millet, wove their cloth, made pottery,
fished, and operated forges.

Toward the people themselves Barbot was on the whole sympathetic and understanding. He admired their system of govern-

ment and tax collection, while noting that the tax collectors were
"not popular." He reports that the kings were elected and could
be deposed. He distinguishes between the true native religion and
the "fetish" worship of images, which was, he says, a superstition
practiced chiefly by the lower classes. He suggests that Europe
might do well to copy certain African techniques: for example,
the police force of Guirrala, south of the Gambia, kept off slave-
kidnapers by maintaining patrols of trained attack dogs wearing
armor made of animal hides. He was especially interested in the
Negro law courts and noted approvingly that there were no law-
yers, each man pleading his own case. (This was not a universal
rule, since the Dahomans, to name one nation, had professional
pleaders to conduct their suits at law.)

Barbot did not know whether to be angered or amused by the
natives' ingenuity in outwitting the white traders. In the gold-dust
trade, a matter of prime importance to the factors, "the dexterity
of the Blacks in sophisticating their gold," Barbot says, was "scarce
imaginable." The natives alloyed their nuggets with copper or sold
brass filings for gold dust. A gullible French captain exchanged his
whole cargo for brass filings and sailed off with "twenty marks of
dross." Barbot acknowledges, however, that the factors also cheated,
blowing in the scales when weighing the dust, using false weights,
and even letting their fingernails grow especially long so they could
collect a few additional grains of dust while weighing it.

But principally Barbot was interested in the slave trade. He
speaks approvingly of Fida (Whydah, that is, or Ouidah) because
"The Blacks of Fida are so expeditious at the trade of slaves that
they can deliver a thousand every month." Wars between the
native states were, he thinks, the great source of slaves. "I remember that in 1681 an English interloper got three hundred good
slaves almost for nothing as the Commando brought them from
the field of battle having taken a great number of prisoners. At
other times slaves are so scarce that in 1682 I could get but eight
from one end of the Coast to the other . . . by the reason that
the tribes were at peace. At another time, I had two hundred slaves

at Accra only in a fortnight or three weeks time and the upper coast men, understanding that I had those slaves aboard, came down to redeem them giving me two for one of such as I understood were their near relations who had been stolen away by inland Blacks, brought to Accra, and sold to us."

Barbot sums up the situation by saying, "If the Negroes be generally crafty and treacherous, it may well be said, the Europeans have not dealt with them as becomes Christians, for it is too well known that many of the European nations trading among the people have very unjustly and inhumanly without any provocation stolen away from time to time abundance of the people . . . when they came aboard their ships and in a harmless and confiding manner carried great numbers away to the plantations and there sold them with the other slaves they had purchased for their goods."

Another outstanding factor was the William Bosman mentioned previously, who went out to the coast as clerk for a Dutch company but exhibited superior business ability and understanding of the natives, so that he soon rose to chief agent. In a series of long letters to a friend in Holland, he described everything he saw, birds, beasts, and fishes as well as people, and related his adventures with such a dry wit that it is often difficult to know whether to take him seriously. At first Bosman hated Africa. He went to Elmina, Cape Coast Castle, and Accra, but found that "The Negroes are all without exception Crafty, Villanous and Fraudulent. . . . A man of integrity is as rare among them as a white falcon . . . herein they agree very well with what authors have told us of the Muscovites." They were also dangerous and had killed the factor at Acoda by breaking all his bones. It was no use trying to learn their language, as a new one could be heard every ten miles along the coast and "there is indeed a vast difference in their Languages." True, the natives had a few good qualities. There were no beggars. The young men and women showed great respect for their elders. The music was interesting. But in general Bosman hated the country, the climate, and above all the people.

He went to Popo on the Slave Coast, where the king claimed

that he could produce several hundred slaves within three days. Bosman did not believe him and kept on to Whydah. He later found that the king had been as good as his word and had captured two hundred slaves in a raid, but, as Bosman had gone, sold them to a Portuguese trader. Meanwhile Bosman reached Whydah and fell in love with it at first sight. It was a lovely, level country, "not one hillock to interrupt the view," happily wrote the Dutchman used to the level expanses of Holland. Also, the Whydahns were such expert slavers that they could slave four ships in five to six weeks' time. The king was a prosperous monarch, as he collected four hundred pounds for every ship slaved, and there was an average of fifty ships a year.

Bosman settled down happily in Whydah. He got along well with the king, who gave him a seven-room suite in the royal palace, including a court with a covered gallery. Here Bosman spent most of his time except when he was forced to take trips for the company up and down the coast. The government seemed to him benevolent. There were only two capital crimes, murder and adultery with the king's wives. Since in Europe a man could be hanged for stealing a sheep, this seemed to Bosman like foolhardy magnanimity. The natives had such huge families that it was an act of kindness to take some off their hands for slaves. An official told Bosman apologetically that he had only seventy children by his various wives, although most of his friends had at least two hundred. One particular family, counting grandparents, parents, and children, numbered nearly two thousand.

The king could not do enough for Bosman. When the king gave one of his daughters in marriage to an English trader, Bosman jokingly asked His Majesty why he had not been given first choice. The king seriously replied that he did not know that Bosman was interested in the girl, but that he could easily get her back from the Englishman. "The mischief is," wrote the gay Dutchman, "marrying a king's daughter in this country is not very advantageous. Otherwise I had not failed long since to be happy that way."

Perhaps the most capable of all the company officials in Africa at the end of the seventeenth century was Sieur André Brue, who was sent to the Coast in 1697 by a newly formed French slaving concern. In 1695 the French had captured James Fort near the mouth of the Gambia, but the English retook it in the year of Brue's arrival. His double task was to establish a working agreement with the English, so that both nations could trade in peace, while at the same time maintaining cordial relations with the irascible king of Cayor, styled the "Damel," who controlled the coastal region south of the Senegal. In general he found that the English were easier to get along with than was the native king.

The Damel was a powerful monarch, for the Coast, with an army consisting of two thousand infantry and two hundred knights in chain mail, as well as a camel corps for desert raiding. Brue says, "This is the negro manner of making War. It is a great chance if they come to a pitched Battle. Their campaigns are usually mutual Inventions to plunder and carry off Slaves which they sell to the Traders on the coast." The Damel was also in the habit of seizing his own subjects and selling them. On one occasion when Brue wanted a slaver loaded in a hurry, the Damel obliged by sending his army to capture three hundred local villagers. Brue offered him a fine suit of armor and a bed for another lot, but the Damel was afraid of a revolution if he pressed his luck too far.

The Damel was a shrewd politician as well as a ruthless tyrant. He became an expert at playing off the various European powers against one another. When the English sent ambassadors to the king's court to ask permission to trade for slaves, the Damel gravely listened to their arguments and accepted their valuable gifts. Although he knew that his treaty with the French gave them a monopoly of the trade, he assured the Englishmen that, if they accompanied him, he would set out with his army on a gigantic slave raid. The English traders eagerly agreed, and for the next few months the Damel marched them around Senegal, stopping occasionally to demand more gifts, until the exhausted and impoverished traders staggered back to the coast.

Although Brue considered this trick uproariously funny, he was to have trouble with the king himself. When an English ship came into the mouth of the river to trade, Brue resolved to have the fort open fire on her. The Damel protested, "Let her land her trade goods first . . . then fire on her," but Brue refused to condone such double-dealing. As a result there was a rupture between him and the king. When war broke out between France and England in 1701, the Damel decided that his opportunity had come. He invited Brue to a palaver and then seized the Frenchman and held him for ransom. The sum demanded was so large that Brue had to wait until it could be sent up from Goree. Brue was released, but he resolved to get his revenge. Under his orders French frigates were sent to blockade the Senegal coast, stopping all trade and destroying the native fishing canoes. As the economy of Cayor depended on its trade and its fishing fleet, the Damel was forced to yield. He sent Brue a message offering to meet him in neutral territory to discuss terms. Brue agreed. What he intended to do at the meeting, as he later acknowledged, was to pay back the Damel for his former treachery by seizing him and selling him as a slave in the West Indies. Before the meeting could take place, however, Brue was recalled to Paris (1702).

The governor who followed him was unable to handle the situation, and Brue returned to the coast twelve years later. In spite of his troubles with the Damel and the English, he laid the foundations for the French occupation of Senegal, which continued, with a few interruptions, until 1958.

African natives became merchantable slaves in any one of five ways. They were criminals sold by the native chiefs as punishment; or they were individuals sold by themselves or their families in times of famine; or they were persons kidnaped either by European slavers or, more often, by native gangs; or they had been slaves in Africa and were sold by their masters; or else they were prisoners of war.

Punishing dangerous malefactors by selling them as slaves had been an established practice in many African communities, but after European vessels began to frequent the Guinea coast, many kings formed the habit of punishing any and every offense by enslaving the accused. According to Brue, the Damel of Cayor issued an edict that any woman taken in adultery was to be sold as a slave. "This severe punishment," he says, "keeps the Wives pretty honest or at least makes intriguing very troublesome." Other kings would go to a village, marry half a dozen of the most attractive girls, and leave them there. Sooner or later the girls were almost certain to be unfaithful to his majesty with some able-bodied young man, and the outraged monarch could then sell the adulterers to a slaver.

Subversive plots against the local government became surprisingly common in seacoast towns off which the slavers dropped anchor. The king almost always discovered a number of dangerous conspirators, and they naturally had to be sold. To eliminate all possible danger, the king also sold the conspirators' wives, their children, and their brothers. Often the crime was something less romantic than adultery or subversion. If an Englishman of the time went into debt, he was hustled off to debtors' prison. If an African went into debt—as frequently happened with members of commercial nations like the Hausa and the Mandingo, when they made unsuccessful ventures with borrowed funds—their household servants were sold to the slave merchants. Then, if the debt was a large one, the failed merchant was also sold, together with his wives and children.

In the Gulf of Guinea—though not in Senegambia, where most of the rulers were Mohammedans—witch doctors proved helpful in identifying criminals. After "dashing" the king with a keg of rum and a few muskets, the slavers would dash the witch doctor. This personage would then announce that black magic—or some other un-Fantian, un-Whydahn, or un-Calabarian activity—was rampant in the town, and he would proceed to "smell out" the culprits. The population was assembled in the square, and the witch doctor danced around them, loudly sniffing. At intervals he would rush into the crowd and drag out an able-bodied person, who was sold to the slavers.

Famine was a lucrative period for the trade, as most of the tribes had no means of storing food for long periods. Bosman notes that "one barren year occasions an incredible famine . . . and sometimes free-men have sold themselves for victuals. An English ship . . . got his whole shipfull of slaves without parting with any other merchandize than victuals." Barbot recalls: "In times of darth and famine, abundance of these people will sell themselves for a maintenance and to prevent starving. When I first arrived at Goree in December 1681 I could have bought a great number at very easy rates if I could have found provisions to subsist them." Fathers might sell their children to keep them from starving.

"Panyaring," or kidnaping persons into slavery, was such a widespread practice that panyaring anecdotes are common in accounts of the trade, although merchants and even priests officially denied that the practice existed. As early as 1610 a Portuguese priest, Father Sandoval, became troubled by stories of panyaring and wrote to Brother Luis Brandaon in St. Paul de Loando, the great port of Angola, asking if the rumors were true. Brother Brandaon answered, "Your Reverence should have no scruples on this score . . . no negro will ever say he has been captured legally. Therefore your Reverence should not ask them whether they have been legally captured or not. . . . There are always a few who have been captured illegally . . . but these are few in number and to seek among ten or twelve thousand who leave this port every year for a few . . . is an impossibility."

If Brother Brandaon was correct at the time, which one doubts, panyaring had greatly increased by the end of the century; or perhaps it had always been a commoner practice in Senegambia and Upper Guinea. Barbot says it was almost impossible to induce natives to come aboard a vessel, "so great is their mistrust of Europeans since some have basely carried away or kidnaped several of them." Panyaring by the natives themselves was wide-spread. Barbot also says:

> Those sold by the Blacks are for the most part prisoners of war
> . . . others stolen away by their own countrymen and some
> there are who will sell their own children, kindred and neighbors.
> This has been often seen and to compass it, they desire the per-
> son they intend to sell to help them in carrying something to the
> factory by way of trade and when there, the person so deluded
> not understanding the language is sold and delivered up as a slave
> notwithstanding all his resistance and exclaiming against the
> treachery.
>
> I was told of one who designed to sell his own son after
> that manner, but he understanding French dissembled for a
> while and then contrived so cunningly as to persuade the French
> that the old man was his slave and not his father by which means
> he delivered him up to captivity. . . . However, it happened that
> the fellow was met by some of the principal Blacks of the coun-
> try as he was returning home from the factory with the goods he
> had received for the sale of his father all of which they took away
> and ordered him sold for a slave. . . . Abundance of little Blacks
> of both sexes are also stolen away by their neighbors . . . in the
> Cougans or corn-fields when their parents keep them there all
> day to scare away the devouring small birds.

Many of the Negroes transported to America had been slaves in Africa, born to captivity. Slavery in Africa was an ancient and widespread institution, but it was especially prevalent in the Sudan. Mungo Park, after his journey to the Niger, estimated that three-quarters of the inhabitants of the many kingdoms through which he passed were slaves. It has been claimed that African slavery was a very different institution from slavery in the New World, as the owners were not driven by the desire to make large profits from their chattels. Gustavus Vassa, the only slave shipped from Africa who acquired a sufficient mastery of English to write an account of his life, says in recounting his boyhood memories, "Those prisoners [of war] not sold or redeemed we kept as slaves but how different was their condition from that of the slaves in the West

Indies. With us they do no more work than other members of the community, even their masters' food, clothing and lodging were nearly the same as theirs (except that they were not permitted to eat with those who were free born) and there was scarcely any other difference between them than a superior degree of importance which the head of a family professes in our state." Mary Kingsley, the English missionary-anthropologist, defines African slavery as "a state of servitude guarded by rights."

John Barbot gives a very different picture. "These slaves," he says, "are severely and barbarously treated by their masters who subsist them poorly and beat them inhumanely as may be seen by the scabs and wounds on the bodies of many of them when sold to us. They scarcely allow them the least rag to cover their nakedness which they also take off from them when sold to Europeans. . . . This barbarous usage of these unfortunate wretches makes it appear that the fate of such as are bought and transported from the Coast to America . . . is less deplorable than that of those who end their days in their native country . . . not to mention the inestimable advantage they may reap of becoming Christians and saving their souls."

Barbot, of course, was trying to justify the transatlantic trade, by which he earned his living. But he was also overlooking the distinction, familiar to Africans, between household slaves and those captured in war or purchased in the market. Household slaves were regarded as natives of the kingdom and were usually treated with some degree of kindness. They were allowed to earn money, with which they were sometimes able to purchase their freedom, and in the Calabar region there were known examples of slaves who rose to be kings. Those who remained slaves ran the danger of being sacrificed when a king died, to be his servants in the other world, but otherwise they led a fairly secure life. Unless the master went into debt, they could not be sold except for crimes of their own, and then only after a public trial. "But these restrictions on the power of the master," says Mungo Park, "extend not to the case of prisoners taken in war, nor to that of slaves purchased with money. All these unfortunate beings are considered as strangers and foreigners, who have no right to the protection of the law, and may be treated with severity, or sold to a stranger, according to the pleasure of their owners." In other words, these "strangers and foreigners" were treated as heartlessly by African slave merchants as they were by Europeans.

Mungo Park believes that the vast majority of Negroes exported from the Gambia had been slaves from birth. He also says that it was African warfare, not African slavery, that provided the slave ships with the bulk of their cargoes. This apparent paradox he explains by saying that in Africa both slaves and freemen went to war, but that the freemen were better armed and more likely to escape after a lost battle. Moreover, a freeman could be ransomed by his relatives in exchange for two slaves, whereas a slave-born captive had no hope of being rescued. After his two years in the interior, Park sailed from the Gambia on a small American vessel with a cargo of a hundred and thirty slaves, with whom he talked in their own language. He found that about twenty-five of them were free-born Africans, and that the others had been slaves from birth. All the free-born and most of the slave-born had been captured in warfare.

After a sufficient number of slaves had been assembled and taken down to the coast, they were sold either to merchants and factors or else directly to the captains of slaving vessels. Purchasing Negroes was generally a long-drawn-out process, requiring bargaining skill, a judicious use of "dash," and some medical knowledge. The process is described by James Barbot, who made a slaving voyage to Guinea in 1699. James was the brother of the more famous John Barbot, and the two men had a nephew, also named James, who made a slaving voyage to the Congo in 1700; apparently the whole Barbot family was in the trade. Brother James was supercargo and part owner of the *Albion-Frigate*. He wrote that it took him from June 25 till July 2 to reach an agreement with the king of Bonny regarding the price of slaves and the value of trade goods. The king's brother, Pepprell, was "a sharp blade" and handled the negotiations. It was not until the king had been dashed a hat, a firelock, and nine bunches of beads, and his caboceers two firelocks, eight hats, and "nine narrow Guinea stuffs" (bolts of cloth), that the deal could be closed. Even so, it was necessary to get everyone connected with the court royally drunk.

Thomas Phillips, captain of the *Hannibal*, gives an account of how the slaves were examined for purchase:

The king's slaves . . . were the first offer'd to sale, which the cappasheirs would be very urgent with us to buy, and would in a manner force us to it ere they would shew us any other . . . and we must not refuse them, tho' as I observed they were generally the worst slaves in the trunk, and we paid more for them than any others, which we could not remedy, it being one of his majesty's prerogatives. Then the cappasheirs each brought out his slaves according to his degree and quality, the greatest first, etc., and our surgeon examined them well in all kinds, to see that they were sound wind and limb, making them jump, stretch out their arms swiftly, looking in their mouths to judge of their age; for the cappasheirs are so cunning that they shave them all close before we see them, so that let them be never so old we can see no grey hairs on their heads or beards; and then having liquor'd them well and sleeked with palm oil, 'tis no easy matter to know an old one from a middle-aged one, but by the teeth's decay. But our greatest care of all is to buy none that are pox'd, lest they should infest the rest aboard; for tho' we separate the men and women aboard by partitions and bulk-heads, to prevent quarrels and wranglings among them, yet do what we can they will come together and that distemper which they call the yaws, is very common here and discovers itself by almost the same symptoms as the *Lues Venerea* or clap does with us; therefore our surgeon is forc'd to examine the privities of both men and women with the nicest scrutiny, which is a great slavery, but what can't be omitted.

After examination, the selected slaves were branded. John Barbot says that each of them was "marked on the breast with a red-hot iron imprinting the mark of the French, English or Dutch companies so each nation may distinguish their own and to prevent their being chang'd by the natives for worse as they are apt enough to do. In this particular, care is taken that the women, as tenderest, be not burnt too hard."

Payment for the slaves was in trade goods. For English slavers these consisted largely of woolens and linens from Manchester and Yorkshire, calicoes from India, silks from China, and knives, cutlasses, muskets, powder, iron bars, and brass basins from Birmingham and Sheffield, besides old bedsheets (much in demand), fancy hats, glass beads, and various distilled liquors, which were, by a trade custom, generously mixed with water. Already an industrial nation, the English could supply most of the trade articles from their own resources and thus make a double profit. The French and the Dutch also produced articles for export, but the Portuguese were at a disadvantage; they had to buy most of their trade goods in Holland. Each section of the African coast had its particular and peculiar form of currency. In Senegambia and Upper Guinea as far as the Slave Coast, the value of a slave was reckoned in bars of iron. In Lower Guinea it was reckoned in "pieces"—of cloth, that is; so many yards of cloth, or so many gallons of rum, or so many strings of beads made a "piece," and so many "pieces" could be exchanged for a Negro. The Slave Coast preferred sea shells, called "cowries," which were strung together, forty to a string or "toque." A hundred toques made a "grand cabess," at one time equal in value to a pound sterling.

After the slaves were branded, they were marched toward the beach. Many of them, coming from the interior, had never seen or even heard of the sea. They were terrified by the distant sound of the surf and thought it was the roaring of some great beast. Then they saw the Atlantic, the great mountains of white-crested breakers, and beyond them the waiting ship. This was the critical moment when even the hippopotamus-hide whips of the Negro traders and the white man's cat-o'-nine-tails sometimes proved useless. The slaves flung themselves on the beach, clutching handfuls of sand in a desperate effort to remain in Africa. Some tried to strangle themselves with their chains; but the slavers, white and black, were prepared for every form of rebellion. Special "captains of the sand" had been posted along the beach. The slaves were beaten, pushed, dragged, and even carried to the big canoes, often manned by the famous Krumen, which were waiting to ferry them through the surf.

By the end of the seventeenth century the Krumen, who started as a fishing people on the Grain Coast, had largely abandoned their traditional way of life and had made a profession of carrying slaves through the breakers. Each canoe had a captain who acted as coxswain, giving his paddlers the beat while steering his craft with a long paddle. As some of the canoes were seventy feet long, required twenty paddlers, and carried eighty slaves at a time, steering them required unusual skill. If a canoe turned broadside to the surf for even an instant, its slaves and its crew as well were likely to be drowned or eaten by the sharks.

Captain Phillips says, "The negroes are so wilful and loth to leave their own country, that they have often leap'd out of the canoos, boat and ship, into the sea, and kept under water till they were drowned, to avoid being taken up and saved by our boats, which pursued them; they having a more dreadful apprehension of Barbadoes than we can have of hell, tho' in reality they live much better there than in their own country; but home is home, etc. We have likewise seen divers of them eaten by the sharks, of which a prodigious number kept about the ships in this place, and I have been told will follow her hence to Barbadoes, for the dead negroes that are thrown overboard in the passage."

John Barbot adds, "Many of those slaves we transport from Guinea to America are prepossessed with the opinion that they are carried like sheep to the slaughter and that the Europeans are fond of their flesh; which notion so far prevails with some as to make them fall into a deep melancholy and to refuse all sustenance, tho' never so much compelled and even beaten to oblige them to take some nourishment; notwithstanding all which they will starve to death." Better to starve in sight of the African coast than to be carried across the river of salt water and sold not to the white men—so many of them were convinced—but to a race of gigantic cannibals called *Koomi*, whose country was named in Mandingo *Jong sang doo*, "the land where the slaves are sold."

# 3

# The Early American Trade

*About the last of August came in a Dutch man-of-Warre that sold us 20 negars.*
  —John Rolfe reporting the landing of the first Negro slaves in the English colonies, 1619

TWO INNOCUOUS CROPS, SUGAR AND COTTON, HAD A PROFOUND EFFECT on the slave trade and so have been responsible for the death and suffering of millions of human beings. Cotton did not become crucial in the trade until the invention of the cotton gin in 1793, but sugar began to be cultivated on a large scale about the middle of the seventeenth century. It made the slave trade a seeming necessity for the New World, and especially for the West Indies.

It was in 1605 that the English laid claim to Barbados, their first possession in the Caribbean area; later it would be called "the mother of the West Indian sugar islands." The first English settlers, who began to arrive twenty years later, cultivated their own small holdings and raised a diversity of crops: tobacco, cotton, indigo, ginger. Later they were joined by royalist refugees from the Civil War in England, who brought with them indentured servants, mostly Scottish and Irish prisoners of war. By that time, however, the cultivation of sugar cane, first introduced in 1641, had begun to revolutionize the economy not only of Barbados but of England as well. England had formerly depended for sweetening almost entirely on honey and on what little sugar she could purchase from Spain, the sugar being so precious that it was sold by the ounce. But with the acquisition of West Indian colonies and an unlimited supply of cheap labor, sugar could be produced by the ton and molasses by the hogshead. When the molasses was fermented and distilled, it became a potent beverage called rum, and the demand for rum was universal.

Sugar has never been a little man's crop; to yield a profit, even in the seventeenth century, it had to be cultivated on a broad scale, with gangs of slaves. Barbados was rapidly transformed. In 1643 the little island—hardly bigger than Martha's Vineyard, but with rich soil, every inch of which could be tilled—was divided into nearly ten thousand separate landholdings. The population included eighteen thousand white men "capable of bearing arms" and only five thousand Negroes of both sexes. By 1666 most of the small holdings had been absorbed into eight hundred sugar plantations. Half the white men had emigrated to other islands, but there were then forty thousand slaves. In 1684 there were forty-six thousand slaves and only twenty thousand whites of all ages.

Even before the intensive cultivation of sugar began to exhaust the soil of Barbados, the plantation system spread to other islands, beginning with those of the Leeward chain: Antigua, St. Kitts, Nevis, Montserrat. In 1655 the English took Jamaica from the Spanish and, after some financial reverses in the early years, transformed the island into a collection of big plantations. The years of financial hardship were those when the local government tried to limit the importation of slaves, in order to avoid the danger of uprisings. As late as 1673 there were only 9504 slaves on the island, as compared with 7768 whites. But it proved impossible to continue this cautious policy, in view of the quick fortunes to be made in the cane fields. From 1698 to 1707, 42,572 slaves were shipped to Jamaica and 34,583 to Barbados, and not long afterward the slaves in Jamaica outnumbered the whites in a proportion of ten to one. Then, as even the rich Jamaican soil began to be exhausted in its turn, Haiti became the greatest of the sugar islands and did not yield its place to Cuba until the end of the century.

It was widely admitted that slaves in the West Indies were treated more harshly than those in the English colonies on the mainland. One reason was that sugar—much more than such mainland slave crops as tobacco, rice, and cotton—was grown and prepared for market by factory methods. There was little room for human regard between master and slaves; often the West Indian master was an absentee landlord or a joint stock company. The slaves, says Ulrich Bonnell Phillips, were regarded as work units, not as men, women, and children. "Kindliness and comfort, cruelty and hardship, were rated at balance-sheet value; births and deaths were reckoned in profit and loss, and the expense of rearing children was balanced against the cost of new Africans." Usually the cost of new Africans was lower, even though it included a "seasoning" process that lasted three or four years: the process consisted largely in getting used to new hardships and a new group of tropical diseases. Phillips thinks that 20 to 30 per cent of the bozal Negroes failed to survive.

Defenders of slavery often argued that, as slaves were worth money, the planter's interest lay in keeping them well and happy; he could not afford to be brutal. The fact seems to be that brutality was often profitable. Henry Coor, who visited Jamaica in 1774, was told by an overseer, "I have made my employers 20, 30 and 40 more hogsheads per year than my predecessors and tho I have killed 30 or 40 negroes per year more, yet the produce has been more than adequate to the loss." Many planters frankly said that it was "cheaper to buy than breed." Men outnumbered women by two to one on most plantations, and "children were rare." One reason they were rare was the high infant mortality, which was estimated at 40 to 50 per cent. One year there were 2656 Negro births on the island of St. Vincent, and 4205 Negro deaths.

Slaves were kept in a state of terror. After a tour of the islands in 1688, Sir Hans Sloane reported that they were punished for major crimes by "nailing them down on the ground with crooked sticks on every Limb and then applying the Fire by degrees from the Feet and Hands, burning them gradually up to the Head, whereby their pains are extravagant; for Crimes of a lesser nature Gelding or chopping off half of the Foot with an Ax. Their Punishments are suffered by them with great Constancy. For running away they put Iron Rings of great weight on their ankles or Pottochs about their Necks which are Iron rings with two long Necks rivetted to them or a Spur in the mouth. They are whip'd till they are Raw; some put on their Skins Pepper and Salt to make them smart, at other times their Masters will drop melted Wax on their Skins and use several very exquisite Torments." Sir Hans was not tender-hearted, for he adds: "These punishments are sometimes merited by the Blacks who are a very perverse Generation of People and though they appear harsh, yet are scarce equal to some of their Crimes and inferior to what Punishments other European Nations inflict on their Slaves in the East-Indies."

There was a far more potent reason for the punishments than simple cruelty or hope of gain. With the slave population far outnumbering the white, it had to be overawed by the white man's power. Almost from the earliest days, there were slave revolts in the islands; perhaps the first large one was a Hispaniola revolt of 1522. When the British took over Jamaica in 1655, many of the Spaniards' slaves escaped to the hills, where they became known as "Maroons." They constantly encouraged other slaves to escape, and they became so powerful that in 1730 troops had to be sent from England to put them down in a campaign that lasted for years and ended with a treaty of peace. There were insurrections in Surinam all through the middle years of the eighteenth century, and the escaped slaves—called "bush Negroes" or "Djukas"—have retained their independence until this day. There were Maroons in Haiti as early as 1620 and later slave uprisings there in 1679, 1691, and 1704, all of which culminated in the successful revolt at the end of the eighteenth century. The horrors of such revolts were not a popular topic of conversation, but they were always in the back of a planter's mind. Rather than win his slaves' loyalty by kindness, he preferred to earn a large profit as soon as possible and then return to France or England to live in luxurious safety.

Nobody knows who was the first Negro slave to reach the mainland of the New World, but he must have arrived there at an early date. Balboa had thirty Negroes with him when he discovered the Pacific. Cortez brought three hundred slaves to the conquest of Mexico. By 1530 there were so many Negro slaves in Mexico that they plotted an uprising. When Pizarro was murdered by his own men in Peru, his body was carried to the cathedral by his Negroes. There were also Negroes with Alvarado when he went to Quito, Ecuador, in 1534. The first Negro slaves were brought to Brazil in 1538. By the seventeenth century 44,000 were being imported annually. The first reliable census, in 1798, showed 1,582,000 slaves and 406,000 free Negroes in a total population of 3,250,000.

Probably the first Negro slaves to arrive on the United States mainland were imported by Lucas Vásquez de Ayllón in 1526. He attempted to found a colony at what may have later been the site of Jamestown, Virginia. He brought with him five hundred colonists, one hundred slaves, and eighty-nine horses. Three months after founding the colony, Vásquez de Ayllón died of fever, the slaves revolted, and the survivors returned to Haiti.

There were Negro slaves in other North American Spanish settlements. From its founding in 1565 to the end of the Civil War in 1865, a period of exactly three centuries, there were slaves in Saint Augustine, Florida. But as far as the English colonies to the north were concerned, the slave trade did not begin until 1619, when a Dutch man-of-war, probably a privateer sailing under letters of marque from the prince of Orange, put into the newly established colony of Jamestown with twenty Negroes, whom she may have "highjacked" from a Spanish merchantman in the Caribbean. She probably met the *Treasurer*, the first privateer to sail from the colonies, for the *Treasurer*'s log shows that somewhere in the West Indies she was hailed by a Dutchman who told her that slaves were wanted in Virginia.

That nameless Dutch vessel which arrived a year before the *Mayflower* was hardly less important in American history. She carried not only twenty Negroes but, for the future, everything those Negroes and their successors would contribute to American wealth and culture, including Carolina rice, Louisiana cane, and the Cotton Kingdom. She carried, or announced, the maritime trade of New England and the training of the first sailors in the United States Navy; then the plantation system, the Abolition Society, the Missouri Compromise, and the Civil War; then Reconstruction, the Solid South, Jim Crow, and the struggle for integration. She carried the spirituals, jazz, the researches of such Negro scientists as George Washington Carver, the contributions to American culture of younger Negro musicians, statesmen, scholars, and writers; and she also carried, for this age of international struggles, the first link between the United States and Africa.

But for all she promised, the Dutch vessel "that sold us 20 negars" did not immediately begin the wholesale importation of slaves to the English colonies. Not until the latter part of the century were Negroes imported by the thousands. There were several reasons for this long delay. The plantation system had not yet developed. There were no great fields of sugar cane that required a huge force of unskilled labor to harvest. The English still had no slaving fleet and no forts in Africa. But what was probably the most important reason for the slow growth of the slave trade in the English colonies was the abundant use of indentured servants: men and women bound to their masters for a period of years, sometimes for life. Possibly as many as half of the early white immigrants were indentured servants.

In general it was cheaper and easier for the English colonists to use indentured servants than to purchase Negro slaves. The servants spoke the same language, they required no "seasoning" period, and they cost little more to maintain than Negro slaves. Since the bond of indenture was usually for five or ten years, the master did not need to worry about his servant's health, could work him harder, and did not have to provide for his old age. In the West Indies, where bozal Negroes were cheap, these considerations were not of prime importance, but the Virginia colonists had to repurchase their Negro slaves from the West Indies in the early days, and hence a Negro represented a considerable investment.

Because of the high cost of importing Negro slaves, several attempts were made to breed them. One of the earliest of these attempts was definitely a failure, as Josselyn tells in an account of his two voyages to New England in 1664. A Mr. Maverick had a Negro woman who had been a queen in her own country and for that reason looked down on the other slaves. However, "Mr. Maverick was desirous to have a breed of Negroes and therefore seeing she would not yield by persuasions to company with a Negro young man he had in his house; he commanded him will'd she nill'd she to go to bed to her which was no sooner done but she kickt him out again."

Exporting white indentured servants became a big business in many English communities and closely resembled the African slave trade. Drunkards were carried on shipboard, children were lured away with promises of candy, and officials were bribed to turn over convicted criminals to the procurers. These procurers, called "spirits" because their victims were spirited away, became as common and as efficient as the "panyarers" of the African coast. J. Wesley Bready, the historian, writes that "kidnapping . . . reached the proportions of a considerable business and was winked at, if not encouraged in high places." In 1617 an affidavit was sworn out against William Thiene, who in one year had spirited away 840 people. In 1668 there were three ships at anchor in the Thames, full of kidnaped children. "Though the parents see their children in the ships, without money they will not let them have them," reported a contemporary writer. It was only natural that Bristol, one of the main ports for procuring indentured servants, should later become a center of the African trade.

Some of the white servants were convicted criminals who were openly labeled as slaves and bound to their masters for life. In 1652, 270 Scotsmen who had been captured in the battle of Dunbar were sold in Boston. After Monmouth's Rebellion in 1685, hundreds of the rebels were sold into slavery in America and the West Indies, the king giving his favorite courtiers gifts of one or two hundred rebels to dispose of as they would. J. C. Jeaffreson, a young English country squire of the period, tells in his journal of selling three hundred of the rebels for £4125, less £1500 for transportation to the colonies. The king received a commission of forty shillings a head for the slaves, and the warden of the prison who was holding the captives also demanded a share.

In some cases the slaves were children suffering for the sins of their parents. In 1659 the children of Quakers, then a persecuted sect, were ordered sold. A court order has been preserved that authorized such a sale: "Whereas, Daniel Southwick and Provided Southwick, son and daughter of Lawrence Southwick, absent themselves from public ordinances . . . resolves that the treasurers of the several counties are and shall be fully empowered to sell said persons to any of the English natives at Virginia or Barbadoes." It should be noted, however, that no captain from the port of Boston would transport the children.

The conditions on vessels carrying these "servants" were sometimes even worse than on the slavers, since the Negroes were more valuable merchandise. A governor's wife coming to the North American colonies in 1639 wrote, "While crossing the Atlantic we have been pestered with people so full of infection that after a while we saw little but throwing dead bodies overboard." Another ship lost 130 out of 150 of the white slaves. A Dutch ship lost 100 out of 150. The usual procedure was to batten both men and women below hatches and leave them there until the ship dropped anchor. Then, under armed guard, the hatches were opened and the living allowed to go ashore to their new masters. The dead were thrown into the bay.

The use of indentured servants continued well into the eighteenth century. Between 1750 and 1755 more than two thousand bodies were tossed into New York harbor alone. In 1768 Henry Laurens, a Charleston slave dealer, protested, "Yet I never saw an instance of cruelty [to the Negro slaves] in ten or twelve years' experience equal to the cruelty exercised upon those poor Irish." As late as 1775 a seventeen-year-old girl named Elizabeth Brickleband was decoyed into an office and then put on the brig *Nancy* for sale abroad. The office-keeper and his wife were caught, and it was proved that they had kidnaped a hundred other young girls by a similar technique. A ship's captain went to the Clerkenwell House of Correction, got the girls drunk, and with the connivance of the warden carried them off. It was the abundance of cheap white labor that prevented Negro slavery from becoming an important institution anywhere in Europe (except, for a time, in southern Portugal, emptied of its Moorish peasants).

During the early period there was no racial issue involved in slavery, although it aroused some religious questions. Generally it was considered that enslaving heathens was more ethical than enslaving Christians. Negro slaves were simply listed as "servants" in the census of 1623–1624. The first Negroes were generally required to serve for a stipulated term, but were then freed and given some land, as was done with the white indentured servants. Negro and white servants not infrequently ran away together, and no distinction was made between the fugitives, as the following advertisements show:

Run away in April . . . a Mulatto slave Named Richard Molson of Middle Statue, about forty years old and has had the Small Pox. He is in company with a White Woman Named Mary who is supposed now goes for his wife. . . . Whoever shall apprehend the said Fugitives . . . shall be well rewarded. (*American Weekly Mercury* of Philadelphia, August 11, 1720.)

RUN AWAY, the 2nd. of last month from the subscriber . . . a mulattoe servant named Isaac Cromwell. . . . Run away at the same time, an English servant woman named Anne Greene. . . . Whoever takes up the said servants . . . shall have Five Pounds. (*Pennsylvania Gazette*, June 1, 1749.)

White indentured servants were offered for sale together with Negroes, as witness this advertisement from the *Boston News Letter*, May 3, 1714: "Several Irish Maid Servants time most of them for Five Years and one Irish man Servant who is a good Barber and Wiggmaker, also Four or Five Likely Negro Boys."

Although there were many advantages in using white indentured laborers, there were serious problems in dealing with them. They were so nearly on the same cultural level as their masters that it was hard to keep them in a state of subservience. When they ran away they could not be identified by color. Lastly they were Christians, and this presented a moral difficulty. It was generally felt that slavery required some justification, and so the Biblical verse was used: "Both thy bondmen and thy bondmaids, which thou shalt have, shall be of the heathen that are round about you; of them shall ye buy bondmen and bondmaids" (Leviticus XXV, 44). But this commandment could hardly be applied to fellow Christians, especially if they were Scottish Protestants.

And what about the Negroes who had been converted to Christianity? By the middle of the seventeenth century it had become imperative to find some new reason for holding them in bondage. And in what sort of bondage should it be? Since the first Negroes to reach Virginia had been regarded as servants indentured for life, their children were born free and were also reared in the true faith. But those children were valuable possessions of the planters, who in many cases refused to let them go. Some excuse had to be found for transforming indentured servitude into chattel slavery. At this point there occurred an inevitable, under the circumstances,

but ultimately disastrous change in apologetics. The religious justification of slavery—that the Negroes were heathens whose souls
might be saved—gave way to a racial justification that condemned
all Negroes to bondage. This new excuse could also be supported
by texts from the Bible. Negroes were children of Ham, or Canaan,
on whom Father Noah had laid his famous curse: "And he said,
Cursed be Canaan; a servant of servants shall he be unto his
brethren" (Genesis IX, 25). Some of the slave-owners went far
beyond the Bible, arguing that it might be wrong to enslave
Christians, but that the Negro was not a human being and therefore could not become a Christian. One pious lady said, when
asked if her Negro maid was to be baptized, "You might as well
baptize my black bitch." Bishop Berkeley put the same idea into
philosophical language. Negroes, he said, were "creatures of another species who had no right to be included or admitted to the
sacraments."

Virginia was the first colony to meet the issue officially. In 1661
the assembly ruled that Negro slaves were to be "perpetual servants." In 1663 the Maryland assembly passed a measure providing
that all Negroes in the colony should be regarded as slaves, and
another forbidding racial intermarriages. Part of the law read,
"Divers free-born English-women, forgetful of their free condition
. . . did intermarry with slaves. Such women are to be slaves of
their husbands' masters." In 1667 Virginia ruled that baptism did
not confer freedom. Maryland passed a similar law in 1671, New
York in 1706, and other states followed. The servile position of the
Negro race as a whole became definitely established.

Many attempts were made to obtain slave labor from another
source that seemed to be convenient. Both the English and the
Dutch colonists tried to enslave the Indians, as the Spanish had
done in the West Indies. Wall Street in New York City gets its
name from the wall which the Dutch erected to keep their Indian
slaves in and their slaves' relations out. In 1645 the Massachusetts
settlers hoped that the Indians would solve their labor problems.
Emanuel Downing wrote his brother-in-law, John Winthrop, in

expectation of a war against the Narragansetts, "If upon a Juste warre the Lord should deliver them into our hands, wee might easily haue men, woemen & children enough to exchange for Moores, which wilbe more gaynefull pilladge for us than wee conceive, for I doe not see how wee can thrive untill wee gett into a stock of slaves sufficient to doe all our busines, for our children's children will hardly see this great Continent filled with people, soe that our servants will still desire freedom to plant for them selues, & not stay but for verie great wages. And I suppose you will verie well see how wee shall maynteyne 20 Moores cheaper than one Englishe servant."

After King Philip's War in 1675, many of the captured Indians, including King Philip's wife and child, were sold in the West Indies and Virginia. But the Indians never made satisfactory slaves; either they proved intractable or they simply died. By 1712 the Massachusetts legislature forbade the importation of Indian slaves, adding that they were "of a malicious, surly and revengeful spirit; rude and insolent in their behavior, and very ungovernable."

The answer, then, was to import Negroes. George Moore wrote in his *Notes on the History of Slavery in Massachusetts*, "At the very birth of foreign commerce from New England ports, the African slave trade became a regular business."

The first definitely authenticated American-built vessel to carry slaves was the *Desire*, built in Marblehead and sailing out of Salem. Like almost all the early slavers, she was small: 120 tons burthen and 79 feet long. In 1638 the *Desire* carried a cargo composed, among other items, of seventeen Pequot Indians, whom she sold in the West Indies. On her return voyage to Boston she carried "cotton, tobacco, salt and negroes," these last being such an unimportant item that their number is not given. The first American slaver definitely known to have reached Africa was the *Rainbow*, in 1645. We know about the *Rainbow* because of an interesting trial that resulted from her voyage.

The *Rainbow* reached the "coast of Guinea" and found some

English slavers waiting for a cargo. As no slaves were being offered for sale at the time, the slavers "landed a murderer [the highly descriptive name of a type of small cannon], attacked a Negro village, killed many of the inhabitants and made a few prisoners." Captain Smith of the *Rainbow* got two of the slaves for his share. When Captain Smith returned to Boston, he became involved in a lawsuit with the owners of the vessel over a division of the profits, and the story of how he obtained the two slaves was revealed. It turned out that the raid had occurred on a Sunday. Smith was tried for "murder, man-stealing and Sabbath-breaking," but was acquitted because the action had taken place outside the jurisdiction of the Massachusetts court. However, the two slaves were confiscated and returned to their home at the expense of the Massachusetts legislature.

Aside from being the first account of an American slaver in Africa, the story is interesting because it shows there had been a change since the days of Hawkins' raiding and that capturing slaves by force was now considered unethical. The trade was legitimate only if the slaves were obtained legally—purchased from a native king or some other recognized dealer, not taken by force. How the original owner obtained the slaves was not the trader's concern, but he himself had to observe certain standards.

In the first half of the seventeenth century, New Amsterdam rather than New England was the principal North American slaving center. In 1621 all the Dutch private slaving concerns were incorporated into the Dutch West India Company. By then Holland had firmly established herself on the Guinea Coast and the West India Company had the full support of the government. From 1619 to 1623, the company carried 15,430 slaves to Brazil alone. In 1625 the first slaves were landed in New Amsterdam, and in 1652 the Dutch shipowners in the New World were authorized to trade directly with Africa.

On November 19, 1654, two citizens of New Amsterdam, Jan de Sweerts and Dirck Pieterson, obtained permission to sail their ship, the *White Horse*, to Africa for a cargo of slaves. They returned the next year and the slaves sold for an average of £125 each. The slaves were in such poor condition that some dropped dead before their new owners could get them home. Four years later, the *Oak Tree* set out. Like nearly all of the early slavers, she was a small craft—120 feet long, 25½ feet wide, and with gun-wales a scant 11 feet above the water—but she could carry 350 to 400 slaves at a time. How successful she was, we do not know.

There are ample records of the *St. John* (1659), as we have the accounts kept by the supercargo. The *St. John* went to Bonny, where she shipped 219 slaves. She went on to the Cameroons, where she picked up another 171. But then she encountered a run of hard luck. Dysentery broke out and many of her crew died, including the master. There was no one to treat the sick, for the surgeon had died. The water casks fell to pieces and could not be repaired, as the ship's cooper was also dead. Luckily the *St. John* met another of the company's ships, the *Peace*, and transferred half of the slaves to her. The *St. John* then took on five thousand coconuts and five thousand oranges to make up for the lack of water, and set sail for Curaçao.

A careful list was kept of deaths during the passage: "July 10. Men—2. Women—1. Boys—1. Aug. 14. Man—1 (did spring over-board)." On November 1, when almost within sight of her goal, the *St. John* struck a reef. "We escaped in the boat to the island of Curacoa leaving in the ship 85 slaves [she had started with 390] as there was no hope of saving the slaves when we were compelled to leave the vessel in the heavy surf." The company sent another ship, which rescued the slaves, but on her return the rescuer and her cargo were captured by an English privateer.

The *King Solomon*, sailing the same year, was more successful. She arrived in Curaçao with 331 slaves. The vice-director of the company at Curaçao wrote to the New Amsterdam office that he wished there had been a thousand of them, so great was the de-mand. Peter Stuyvesant received five of these slaves, "branded with the letter 'M.'" The last Dutch slaver to reach New Amster-dam before the English captured the city was the *Gideon*. She brought in a cargo of between three hundred and four hundred slaves only two weeks before the English blockaded the port. Stuyvesant claimed that having to feed those extra mouths was one reason why the city could not stand a siege.

It was not until after the Royal African Company was chartered in 1672 that the North American slave trade began to flourish. Earlier in the century there had been comparatively few Negroes even in the southern colonies. In 1625 there were twenty-three of them in Virginia; by 1650 there were still only three hundred. In 1663 the newly named proprietors of the Carolinas offered twenty acres of land to settlers for every slave imported. Cheap labor was the first necessity for opening a new country. Georgia, founded in 1733, was the last of the colonies and the only one, North or South, in which slavery was forbidden by law. But the planters' favorite toast was "Here's to the one thing needful," and the law was repealed in 1750.

There were slaves in all the New England and middle colonies, but only a few in each. William Penn, the founder of Pennsylvania, was himself a slaveholder, unlike his brother Quakers. Slaves were introduced into Delaware as early as 1636. In Massachusetts there were slaves almost from the founding of the colony. Cotton Mather had slaves, although he cautioned himself, "I will remember that they are in some sense my children," and condemned those who regarded them as "domestic animals." Rhode Island, later the center of the African trade, had the largest percentage of slaves among the New England colonies, but even so they were less than 5 per cent of the white population. New York, as a result of the early Dutch trade, had the highest proportion of Negroes in the middle colonies: 2170 of them at the end of the seventeenth century, as against 15,897 whites.

Since the Royal African Company was launched under protection of the Crown and contributed to the fortunes of the royal family, the government itself encouraged the colonies to buy slaves. By 1700 they were being imported, mostly into the Southern colonies, at the rate of a thousand a year. Many of them were being carried direct from Africa, though it would seem that more of them still came from the West Indies.

With the growth of the slave trade, the plantation system began to spread through the South. Particularly in South Carolina its growth was encouraged by the arrival of colonists from Barbados. South Carolina and later Georgia were the "rice colonies"; Virginia and Maryland were the "tobacco colonies." Tobacco was, for a time, such a remunerative crop that it was being grown even in town marketplaces. Cotton was not yet profitable on a large scale, and sugar cane, after a few experiments, was left to the French in Louisiana. By 1700 the average Southern plantation covered seven hundred acres, and many of the Virginia and South Carolina plantations were much larger.

Most of the North, however, was not adapted by soil or climate to the plantation system. It might have succeeded in a few areas, and notably in the broad limestone valleys of southeastern Pennsylvania, but there most of the settlers were Quakers or Mennonites who did not believe in owning slaves. Elsewhere the controlling factor was economic. The small fields, the long winters, the need for supplementing agriculture with commerce and home industry, all made slave labor impractical. Men worked alone or by twos and threes instead of in gangs under overseers. Slaves were a household luxury of the rich, or a few of the rich, and the Royal African Company met with little success in its efforts to sell them to other colonists.

Governor Bradstreet of Massachusetts wrote in 1680 to the Privy Council: "There hath been no company of Blacks or Slaves brought into the Country since the beginning of this plantation for the space of Fifty Years, onlly one small Vessell about two yeares since after twenty months' voyage to Madagascar brought hither betwixt Forty or Fifty Negroes, mostly Women and Children, sold here for Ten, Fifteen, and Twenty pounds apeice. . . . Now and then, two or three Negros are brought hither from Barbados and other of his Majesties' plantations and sold here for about Twenty pounds apeice. So that there may bee within our Government about one hundred or one hundred and twenty and it may be as many Scots brought hither and sold for Servants in the time of the warr with Scotland." Governor Dudley of New Hampshire wrote (1708): "There are in New Hampshire negro servants to the number of seventy. And about twenty of them in nine years past have been brought in." Governor Leete of Connecticut was equally unenthusiastic: ". . . and for Blacks, there comes sometimes three or four in a year from Barbadoes."

But the slave trade itself was a different matter, and vessels from all the Northern colonies were eager to engage in it. Often it is difficult to say whether some of the vessels that took part in the trade were slavers, pirates, or privateers. Wars between European powers were endemic, and almost any ambitious captain could find some nation willing to issue him letters of marque to prey on the commerce of its rivals. The situation became so confused that historians are still uncertain whether the notorious Captain Kidd, who sailed out of New York in 1696 and was later hanged for his activities on the east coast of Africa, was a pirate or a legal privateer. At all events, capturing merchantmen on the high seas was a lucrative profession. There came into being a special class of merchants, called "Red Sea Men" (as much of the raiding went on in that area), who subsidized the raiders and received their goods but seldom advertised the nature of their investments.

One such vessel was the *Fortune*, operating out of New York in the latter part of the century. She specialized in seizing slavers coming through the Mozambique Channel between Madagascar and the mainland. This, incidentally, was also Captain Kidd's great hunting ground. The *Fortune*, it would seem, displayed no petty prejudice about the nationality of her prizes. Some of them were American vessels, and there were violent protests from New York merchants involved in the slave trade. The accusation was made that ex-Governor Fletcher of New York had been bribed to ignore the *Fortune*'s activities. Fletcher explained, "The case (as I recollect it) was thus. There were several English and Dutch merchants of New York who had hired the ship *Fortune* to fetch Negroes from Madagascar as was every year usuall with them." The merchants were forced to accept his explanation.

There are contemporary records of several other American vessels engaged in the trade. One of them was the *Arms of Amsterdam*, out of what was still New Amsterdam, which fell prey to a Portuguese privateer in 1663. The *Sunflower*, out of Boston, carried forty-seven slaves to Rhode Island in 1696. Since the Royal African Company had a monopoly of the west-coast trade, American vessels sailing to Africa either had to obtain their cargoes illegally or else get them on the east coast, to which the company's jurisdiction did not extend. That explains the comparatively large number of voyages made by American slavers to Madagascar and up the Mozambique Channel. By 1698, however, it became obvious that the company could not supply the enormous number of slaves needed, and the trade, as we have seen, was thrown open to all.

The War of the Spanish Succession radically reduced the influence of France and Spain, establishing England as the dominant power in Europe. In the treaty that ended the war, England obtained effective control of the Guinea Coast from the Gambia to the Congo. That same Treaty of Utrecht (1713) gave her the famous Asiento, with the privilege of supplying 4800 slaves each year to the Spanish possessions. Of course English slavers could carry as many more Negroes as they wished to almost any part of the world.

The boom that followed has seldom been equaled in history. Du Bois estimates that the annual exportation of slaves from Africa after 1713 was between 40,000 and 100,000 a year. J. D. Fage puts the average number at 70,000 a year. Most of them were sold in the West Indies, with Jamaica the principal market, but more every year were reaching the North American mainland. In 1738 the Carolinas alone imported 2800 slaves. Thirty years later there were twice as many Negroes as whites in Charleston. Even the Northern colonies increased their quotas. In 1700 there were only 1000

Negroes in all New England; but by 1715 there were 2000 in Boston alone.

Profits from the trade would finance the rum distilleries that furnished the most popular export of New England. In the American South great plantation houses were rising, and a manner of life came into being that had formerly been unknown in the New World. The South was not yet the Cotton Kingdom, but already more slaves were being bought to raise more tobacco and rice, to buy more slaves, to raise more tobacco and rice. In 1714 the total slave population of the British colonies in North America was only 59,000. By 1754 it had risen to 298,000. Part of this growth was due to the excess of births over deaths, for the North American planters lived on their own land and took better care of their human stock, but much of it was owed to new cargoes from the West Indies and Africa. The census of 1790 showed a slave population of 697,897, almost all of it south of the Mason and Dixon Line. It was the eighteenth-century trade that established the "peculiar institution" of slavery as the economic foundation of one-half the United States.

# 4

# Flush Times on the
# Guinea Coast

*Heaven is high and Europe far away.*
—The Guinea factors' motto

LONDON WAS THE HEADQUARTERS OF THE ROYAL AFRICAN COMPANY
and hence, until the end of the seventeenth century, it was the
principal English slaving port. After the trade was thrown open to
independent vessels, or "ten percenters," in 1698, Bristol out-
distanced London, but meanwhile a new rival had appeared in the
North. Liverpool had been slow to enter the Guinea trade. In
1700 her principal export had been coarse linens, called "osna-
burgs" and "checks," from the textile industry that was rising in
Manchester. By 1730 these Manchester goods had acquired a monopoly of the West Indian market. Many of the Liverpool cargoes
were smuggled into the Spanish islands, where the merchants also

demanded slaves, so Liverpool entered the trade in a modest fashion; she had fifteen slave ships in 1730, when Bristol had more than a hundred.

Then, in the middle of the century, came a series of events that transformed the Guinea trade. England fought a war with Spain called the War of Jenkins' Ear, which was later merged with the War of the Austrian Succession. Captain Robert Jenkins' ear, sliced off by a Spanish *guarda costa* and preserved in a bottle, which the captain showed to Parliament, was only an excuse for fighting; the real issue was the Spanish slave markets in the West Indies. By the treaty of peace, signed in 1748, England preserved the market for slaves, but other provisions of the treaty dealt a blow to the smuggling of textiles. Two years later England surrendered the famous Asiento in return for a cash reimbursement. Without the Asiento, smuggling became still more difficult, and the Liverpool merchants had to find a new source of revenue. But the Royal African Company started its process of dissolution that same year, so that there were splendid openings in the Guinea trade, and Liverpool rushed into them. Her slaving fleet was doubled in a year. By 1764 Liverpool had seventy-four vessels sailing to Africa, and Bristol had only thirty-two.

As a slaving port Liverpool had advantages over her English rivals. She was geographically much closer to the source of goods for the Guinea trade; that is, to the looms, foundries, and workshops that produced cheap linens and woolens, iron bars, copper pans, glass beads, cutlery, gunpowder, and muskets. Most of these supplies came from Manchester, Birmingham, or the West Riding of Yorkshire and could easily be carted to docks on the River Mersey. Liverpool was also comparatively new to the trade, with the result that she was able to build larger and faster ships, especially designed for transporting black cargoes. But her greatest advantage was the notorious parsimony of Lancashire merchants. They drove harder bargains, paid lower wages to their crews, and offered fewer privileges to their captains and factors than London or Bristol merchants. Where the London captain received extra pay while in port and was able to dine ashore with a bottle of madeira, the Liverpool captain dined somberly on shipboard, washing down his salt beef with a flagon of small beer. The result of these economies was that Liverpool slavers undersold their competitors in the West Indian markets, often charging four or five pounds less for an able-bodied slave.

The London and Bristol slaving fleets dwindled; the Liverpool fleet continued to grow. In 1771 London had only fifty-eight ships engaged in the trade, and Liverpool had one hundred and seven. As for the total extent of the eighteenth-century trade as carried on by all nations, figures are impossible to assemble. J. D. Fage's estimate of 7,000,000 carried to the New World during the century seems high; it does not allow for the interruptions caused by European wars. But an average of 70,000 slaves a year during all the years when the trade was unimpeded would be a modest figure. The English were supplying more than half of these, or an average of 40,000 a year. The trade came to a partial stop during the American Revolution, when for seven years the seas were infested with cruising frigates and privateers of all nations, and especially with fighting and plundering Yankees, but it was grandly resumed in 1783. During the eleven years from 1783 to 1793, Liverpool ships sold a total of 303,737 slaves in the West Indies (not counting those who died on shipboard). According to "an Eye Witness, Liverpool, 1797," the following propositions were generally accepted:

"First. That one-fourth of the ships belonging to the port of Liverpool are employed in the African trade.

"Second. That it has five-eighths of the African trade of Great Britain.

"Third. That it has three-sevenths of the African trade of all Europe."

During the last years of the legal slave trade, from 1794 to 1807, Liverpool enjoyed something close to a monopoly. In 1800, for example—a nearly average year—she sent one hundred and twenty vessels to the African coast, with accommodations for 31,844 slaves (and possibly a few more thousands packed between decks, in violation of the new law against overcrowding). In that same year London sent out only ten ships, and Bristol only three, all smaller than the Liverpool average. Counting by slaves, not ships, Liverpool had by then engrossed more than ninety per cent of the black cargoes. She had no European rivals trading north of the equator, since French and Dutch commerce had been driven from the ocean by English frigates and privateers. Her only new rivals were Yankee slavers hailing from Newport and Bristol, Rhode Island.

Income from the trade was an important element in the economic growth of Lancashire, Yorkshire, and the Midlands. It must be remembered that the eighteenth-century pound, with a gold value close to that of eight post-depression dollars, had an immensely greater purchasing power. Dr. Johnson told Boswell that "a man can manage to exist on six pounds a year and live comfortably on thirty pounds." Swift's Stella lived almost luxuriously on an annual income of a hundred pounds. As compared with these figures, the adjusted gross income of the Liverpool merchants from the 303,737 slaves they sold in the West Indies in eleven years was £12,294,116, or an average of £1,117,647 a year. During the same period Liverpool slavers made 878 voyages to the Guinea Coast, each lasting an average of nine or ten months and yielding an average cash return of £14,002 per voyage.

Exact profits are hard to determine, because Liverpool merchants had their own systems of accounting; they might or might not include the charter cost or depreciation of their vessels in reckoning their outlay of capital. But another computation, this time for the one year 1786, shows that the average cost per voyage, including depreciation, was £11,313, and the average net profit was £3431, or almost exactly thirty per cent. The Liverpool profit for that year, for eighty-seven vessels, was £298,462. This, incidentally, was the profit from slaves alone. It does not include extra revenue from palm oil, beeswax, and ivory carried with the slaves on many voyages, nor does it include the cargoes of sugar and ginger carried from the West Indies to Liverpool. The Guinea trade was "three-cornered." It consisted in carrying Manchester goods to Africa, where they were exchanged for slaves; then carrying slaves to the West Indies, where they were exchanged for cash or three-year notes-of-hand bearing six-per-cent interest; then buying sugar, cocoa, coffee, indigo, and ginger to carry home—and sell to buy Manchester goods and repeat the process. A ship seldom had to make part of its run in ballast and was expected to show a profit for every leg of the voyage—though of course the profit was highest on the run from Guinea to the West Indies, which was known as the Middle Passage. It should be added that Liverpool slavers were heavily armed and that many of them succeeded in capturing French or Spanish vessels with rich cargoes.

The whole city, except for its squalid lanes and rookeries, was excited by the prospect of sudden fortunes. "Almost every man . . . is a merchant," said the author of *A General and Descriptive History of Liverpool*, "and he who cannot send a bale will send a bandbox. . . . It is well known that many of the small vessels that import about an hundred slaves, are fitted out by attornies, drapers, ropers, grocers, tallow chandlers, barbers, taylors, etc., some have one-eighth, some a fifteenth [sixteenth], and some a thirty-second." A thirty-second part of a small slaving venture yielded very little return, as the author took pains to demonstrate. The big profits were made by about ten houses, each with a very few partners; these were the houses that sold a thousand or more slaves every year, and they accounted for almost two-thirds of the traffic. It was their enterprise that led to the construction of longer and lower ships, the predecessors of the famous clippers.

A new system of docks had to be constructed to hold the ships, and this was the beginning of the docking system that made Liverpool the greatest port in the world. Nor was shipping the last of the undertakings. The slave trade led to an accumulation of capital in ruthless hands, and much of the capital was reinvested in textile mills, foundries, coal mines, quarries, canals, and railways. The economic effects of the trade have been described in Eric Williams' interesting book, *Capitalism and Slavery* (University of North Carolina Press, 1944). He makes it clear that the trade quickened the tempo of the whole Industrial Revolution. James Watt's first steam engine was subsidized by wealthy merchants who had made their money in the West India trade. The slate industry in Wales was created by slaving money, and the Great Western Railway was built with funds from the same source. An early economist described the trade as "the first principle and foundation of all the rest, mainspring of the machine which sets every wheel in motion."

Liverpool made no secret of the source of its sudden wealth. The town hall was covered with stone reproductions of elephants' teeth and "blackamoors." Shop windows were full of handcuffs, leg irons, collars, and slave chains for outgoing vessels. Goldsmiths advertised "Silver Locks and Collars for Blacks and Dogs," and before 1772, when slavery was ruled to be illegal in Great Britain, ladies of fashion appeared in public each with a monkey dressed in an embroidered jacket and a little black slave boy wearing a turban and baggy silk pantaloons. "Young bloods of the town deemed it fine amusement to circulate handbills in which Negro girls are offered for sale," reported one shocked observer. The famous actor George Frederick Cooke appeared drunk on the stage of the Theater Royal in Liverpool and was booed by the audience. Reeling to the footlights, he shouted, "I have not come here to be insulted by a set of wretches, every brick in whose infernal town is cemented with an African's blood."

During the eighteenth century, before and after Liverpool merchants acquired control of the trade, there were many changes on the Guinea coast. The "castles" or forts were becoming less important. They were no longer so much needed as protection against natives, since most of the coastal tribes were eager to exchange captives from other tribes for European products. Nevertheless, they were felt to be useful as safe depots for trade goods and as a sign of English, Dutch, French, or Danish presence and prestige. After the dissolution of the Royal African Company in 1750–1752, the English forts were maintained, as has been said, by a committee of merchants with the help of government subsidies. There were still forty forts in operation at the end of the century, including thirty on the Gold Coast, and there were innumerable barracoons along the coast and up the rivers, presided over by petty factors.

The factors too had declined in relative importance, now that the natives had learned to do their own trading. Some of the biggest slave merchants were native kings, who gathered in their captives on a grand scale. Some were caboceers or headmen, some were Portuguese half-castes professing to be Christians but maintaining several wives, some were honest native merchants, and some were gangsters maintaining bands of professional kidnapers. A few of the coastal monarchs boasted that their towns could supply a thousand slaves a month. "You shall be slaved in a week," they sometimes promised an English captain when persuading him to anchor and pay the royal customs. But they seldom kept this promise, and "slaving" a ship was a process that usually lasted for two or three months, sometimes for more than a year. Therefore the petty factors, with a supply of slaves waiting in their barracoons, were still considered useful.

Most Europeans forced to serve a tour of duty in Africa led miserable lives. In particular the military garrisons of the forts were subjected to ruthless discipline in an effort to keep them from completely degenerating under the combined effects of the climate, insufficient food, cheap liquor, and native women. In 1782 a private soldier who had run away from Cape Coast Castle was blown from the muzzle of a cannon. The governor did not bother to record his name, but he did mention that the cannon was worth twenty pounds. At Goree in the same year a sergeant died as the result of being given eight hundred lashes for some minor offense. But such repressive measures could be employed only in the garrisoned forts, and the factor in a lonesome barracoon was a law to himself.

As the factors operated solely by consent of the native kings, they needed no such protection as the castles afforded. Each factory was surrounded by a stockade of sharp-pointed logs, sometimes with the additional protection of a moat filled with thorns. There might be watchtowers at the four corners and a couple of rusty old cannon commanding the entrance. The factor usually lived alone, unless he had native mistresses, but he would be protected by a small guard of Negro mercenaries armed with old muskets. The heart of the factory was the barracoon or slave pen. The barracoon was a stockade within the stockade and resembled a corral for cattle. A long shed ran down the center to protect the slaves from sun and rain. Down the middle of the shed was stretched a long chain fastened to a stake at either end, the men slaves being secured at intervals along the chain. The women and children were allowed to run loose. At one corner of the barracoon was usually a tower where an armed guard kept watch over the slaves.

There were scores of these factories scattered along the coast from Senegal southward to the mouth of the Niger. Some were very elaborate communities. Most were ramshackle affairs holding ten to twenty slaves and presided over by some down-and-out white man condemned to spend his life on the fever-ridden coast. Typical of the small factors was Nicholas Owen, who operated a small barracoon in Sierra Leone from 1746 to 1759. Owen was an Irishman whose father had impoverished himself as the result of a long lawsuit, leaving his family "to the world destatute," as Owen says in his journal. Owen joined a merchant ship and was captured by West African natives when he and some of his fellow seamen went ashore in the ship's longboat to fill water casks. Owen was sold as a slave to a neighboring tribe, among whom he lived for several years; then he was ransomed by a Mr. Hall, a merchant visiting the coast, with the understanding that Owen would operate a slave factory for his rescuer. Many of the smaller factories were maintained like this one, for the benefit of private merchants.

According to his journal, Owen spent most of his time trying to keep the land crabs from destroying his little garden of watermelons, guinea peas, and pumpkins, which were the only things he could eat without falling victim to dysentery. He despised the natives ("These people are very lazey, seld'm provideing any thing but just what necery for the pressent") and quarreled constantly with the chiefs over the amount of their "dash" ("one complaining I gave him no dram, another says as much for tabaco and a third is hungary"). He was terrified of the witch doctors who performed some simple sleight-of-hand tricks for him ("these must be aledged to the power of some evil spirit sent by that great enemy of mankind to draw these ignorant wretches to him self") and fearful of the terrible creatures that lived in the jungle ("one monster has body, arms and head like a man in all things but is covered over with strong hair and exceeds 2 common men in size"), but above all he suffered from homesickness: "O how I long for the produce of Europe, such as milk, sallit and a hundred other things that's good for a sick man which I can't get here. I have had a voilant favour the 5 or 6 days. In my sickness I had the misfortune to have a prime slave run away in the middle of the day and my man brought a small slave that's not marchantable. I have been sick so that I never had power even to walk in my house."

Owen never recovered from his "voilant favour." He died in Africa, leaving behind the journal, in which he minutely described everything he saw, from the color of a chameleon to the chiefs' royal robes.

A far more important factor than poor Nicholas Owen, who seems to have been worse off than his slaves, was Francis Moore, sent out by the Royal African Company in 1730 to James Fort at the mouth of the Gambia, an important area which then exported two thousand slaves a year. Moore's duties were to travel up and down the Gambia, checking on the thirteen factors stationed at key points along the river, while also expediting and organizing the shipment of slaves. He was expected to maintain friendly relations with the chiefs of the nineteen tribes along the river, especially with the king of Barsally, a powerful and temperamental monarch.

Moore describes how the king obtained the slaves.

Whenever the King of Barsally wants Goods or Brandy, he sends
a Messenger to our Governor at James Fort, to desire he would
send a Sloop there with a Cargo; this News being not at all un-
welcome, the Governor sends accordingly. Against the arrival of
said Sloop, the king [plunders] some of his enemy Towns, seizing
the People and selling them for such Commodities as he is in
want of, which commonly is Brandy, or Rum, Gunpowder, Ball,
Guns, Pistols and Cutlasses. . . . In case he is not at War with
any neighboring King, he falls on one of his own Towns, which
are numerous, and uses them in the very same Manner. . . . It
is [owing to] that insatiable Thirst of his after Brandy that his
Subjects' Freedom and Families are in so precarious a Situation. . . . He often goes out with some of his Troops by a
Town in the Day-time and returns in the Night and sets Fire
to three parts of it, placing Guards at the Fourth to seize the
People that run out of the Fire, then ties their Arms behind them
and . . . sells them.

"Since this Slave-Trade has been us'd," Moore observes, "all
Punishments are chang'd into Slavery." A man was brought to him
in Tomany "to be sold for having stolen a Tobacco-pipe." Another
native saw a "Tyger"—a leopard, that is—eating a deer that he
had killed and hung up near his house. Firing at the leopard, he
accidentally killed a man; and the king "not only condemn'd him,
but also his Mother, three Brothers and three Sisters, to be sold."
From the king of Barsally and his court, Moore was forced to suffer
all sorts of indignities. Once the king's brother took a mouthful of
water and spat it into Moore's face. The king looted the company's
stores, invaded one factor's house, threw the factor out, and then
went to sleep on his bed. In spite of everything, Moore considered
him "a good natured man when sober."

Moore had his troubles not only with the king but also with the
factors and factories he supervised. One factory was destroyed by
the heavy rains. Another was burned to the ground by its factor,
who had gone mad. Moore gives an imposing list of the casualties
among white men. Mr. Robert Forbes died "after a short Illness
contracted by hard Drinking." Mr. Railton, the company's chief
at Brucoe, "had the Misfortune (as he was chastising his Black

Boy) to fall down . . . and split his Skull." Mr. James Ellis "died a Martyr to Rum; for when he was not able to lift a mug to his Mouth, he made shift to suck it thro' a Pipe, and died with a Pipe and a Mug full of Bumbo close to his Pillow." Mr. William Rusling, a company writer, or clerk, died respectably of a fever. "Some few Days before he died, he desir'd, that whenever he should die, I would see that his Grave was dug six feet deep, for Fear of the Wolves eating him." The "wolves," which were hyenas, had dug up the bodies of other buried white men and eaten off their heads. Moore records dozens of other deaths on the Gambia during his five years' tour of duty. There were supposed to be eighty-six Englishmen on the river—traders, soldiers, and mechanics—but it was impossible to keep the garrison up to strength. "Sickness, occasion'd by excessive drinking . . . reduced it to a very weak condition."

The English kept sending out new recruits, with no consideration for the risks they ran. Some of them died on the day of their arrival, and half of them were dead in two years, which was regarded as the average term of life for an Englishman on the Guinea Coast. Success in the slave trade had become a fixed governmental policy, a matter of state. Sometimes, if a slaving area was rendered so dangerous by fever or native hostility that no factor would enter it, an English naval officer was sent to operate as a factor until trade could be restored. In 1771 the English factor in Sierra Leone was murdered by the warlike Ballam, who had already captured and killed the crews of several vessels. Until 1785 no white man dared to set foot in this potentially rich slaving area. In that year the British sent Lieutenant John Matthews, RN, to Sierra Leone to establish a factory. Matthews opened negotiations with the Ballam by the dramatic gesture of digging a hole and announcing impressively, "In this grave I bury all past animosities. Whoever opens it shall be subject to a palaver."

"Ya, oh' ya! Oh' fafee!" cried the natives, and the king and Matthews together filled in the hole.

That evening the Ballam brought in an old man "much bruised

with the blows he had received about the head and face." They told Matthews that the man had bewitched them into causing all the trouble and was to be regarded as a scapegoat for past misunderstandings. The man was then taken out to sea in a canoe, a stone was fastened around his neck, and he was drowned.

Matthews notes that many of the natives on the Windward Coast had as many as two or three hundred slaves—not for sale—and that the powerful Mandingos of the Sierra Leone highlands often had from seven hundred to a thousand. As in the New World, the house servants were treated better than the field hands, who were "no better than horses or oxen [while] the house-slave was in some respects considered as a member of the family." The field hands worked from before sunrise until sunset. The Mandingos were brutal to their field hands, and in 1785 there was a slave insurrection. The slaves fired the upland rice, which was dry and ready to be cut, decapitated any Mandingo they could find, and triumphantly carried the heads on poles. In order to end the insurrection, the Mandingos were forced to make terms with the rebels, exactly as the Dutch had lately done in their South American colony of Surinam.

Matthews believed that the slave trade would persist as long as the African nations remained divided against one another. "We may safely conclude," he says, "that slavery can never be abolished in a country like Africa, consisting of a prodigious number of small, independent states, perpetually at variance and under no restraining form of government."

Even by the early part of the century, the trade had become so complicated that it was no business for an amateur or a gentlemanly dilettante. So John Atkins, who described himself as a "gentleman of Plaistow," discovered to his cost in 1721. In that year two frigates, the *Swallow* and the *Weymouth*, sailed from Spithead in pursuit of Bartholomew Roberts, perhaps the greatest pirate of his century and the only one who did not touch liquor; he stayed sober and is said to have taken more than four hundred vessels. Roberts had sailed to the Guinea Coast, where he was burning slave ships and finding eager recruits among their crews. Atkins joined the pirate-hunting expedition as supercargo, taking with him a collection of trade goods he hoped to exchange for slaves.

The warships had received word that Roberts was operating off the Grain Coast, so they went to Sierra Leone, but they arrived too late; Roberts had been there before them. Sailing into port with the Jolly Roger flying—Roberts used his own design of a skeleton holding an hourglass with blood dripping from it—the pirate had ordered the fort to surrender. The commanding officer of the fort was a peppery old gentleman named Plunket, who, although he had only enough powder to fire the salutes demanded by native kings, refused to yield. It was a futile gesture, and after a few broadsides from the pirate vessel the fort was forced to strike its colors. Plunket was dragged before Roberts, who angrily demanded why he had had the audacity to resist. Plunket replied with such an inspired flow of oaths that the pirates, experts in profanity, were impressed. They decided that it would be a sin to kill a man with such an extensive vocabulary. They looted the fort, however, and captured and burned several slavers in the river. When the frigates arrived, the wrecks of the slavers were stranded on the beach.

The frigates continued southward along the coast, hoping to come up with Roberts. At this point Atkins made the discovery that he had invested in the wrong sort of trade goods; he had omitted several important items, chiefly strong liquors. His private venture was unsuccessful, but he has left us an interesting account of the trade at this period. Panyaring was the curse of it, Atkins believes. Panyaring had created such terror that even the caboceers "never care to walk even a mile or two from home without Fire-Arms." He adds, "It is not infrequent for him who sells you slaves today, to be a few days hence sold himself at some neighboring Town." Not only was panyaring wicked in itself, but the natives frequently retaliated by seizing the first white man they could lay their hands on and holding him for ransom. Atkins gives a list of white men killed or captured as a result of their having kidnaped, or of some other vessel's having kidnaped, natives to sell in the West Indies—Captain Piercy's lieutenant killed on shore; Captain Canning of the *Dove* captured and his mate held for a ransom of seventeen pounds' worth of trade goods. Trading with the natives was almost impossible on the Grain Coast and the Ivory Coast; they were afraid to approach the ships.

Atkins was not unsympathetic with the natives, but he had little use for the factors. He reported that they had "dwindled from the genteel air they brought, wear no Cane nor Snuff-Box, have lank bodies, a pale Visage and their Tongues tied." The general in command of Cape Coast Castle was not only openly living with a Negress but was wearing her charms to keep off bad luck. There was keen competition among the factors, each trying to get rid of the others. It was a standard trick to get a competitor drunk, hire a native to burst in on him with news of a big supply of cheap slaves many miles down the coast, and then rush wildly out, hallooing for canoes. The drunken competitor would cry still louder for canoes, and so the factor got rid of him.

One of the merchants whom Atkins encountered, called Old Cracker, had purchased a slave named Tomba, who had been a war chief before his capture. Tomba refused to go through the gyrations required by slavers when they were checking a slave's physical fitness. Old Cracker gave him an inhuman beating, but Tomba refused to cry out under the lash. He was a magnificent specimen, and the slaver purchased him anyhow. A few days later, farther down the coast, Atkins met this same slaver. Tomba had cost him dear. The former war chief had induced a woman slave to free him from his shackles, with four other men. He had killed three sailors before being overpowered. One of Tomba's four men followers had also been killed, and the slaver forced the other three to eat the dead man's heart and liver. He then hung up the woman slave by her thumbs and had her flogged to death. Tomba himself was too valuable to be killed.

At Axim, the first large slaving station on the Gold Coast, Atkins met the renowned caboceer John Conny. When the warships refused to pay Conny's dash, he seized a shore party filling water casks and held the sailors for ransom. The captains tried to explain to Conny that the frigates belonged to the king of England and were not ordinary merchantmen. Atkins reports that John, who knew enough English to swear, said, "By G——, me King here." The shore party was ransomed by the payment to Conny of an anchor of brandy and six ounces of gold.

The frigates, still in pursuit of Roberts, sailed on to Whydah, on the Slave Coast. There the two captains met the local king, whom Atkins describes as being "absolute as a Boar." Rumors had reached the coast of a powerful inland nation called Dahomey, which was said to be on the march southward to gain control of the slaving business, but the king of Whydah scoffed at such tales. He boasted that, "If the King of Dauhomey should invade him, he would not cut off his head but keep him alive to serve in the vilest of offices." Later, before losing his own head, the king of Whydah would bitterly regret his boast, when the terrible Dahomans conquered his kingdom and massacred most of his subjects. At the time he was more concerned with the pirate Roberts, who was interfering with the slave ships, his principal source of wealth. He offered Captain Ogle of HMS *Swallow* fifty-six pounds of gold dust if he captured Roberts. Ogle accepted his offer and continued eastward along the coast. When he finally caught up with the pirates, Roberts was killed in a fierce engagement, and the surviving members of his crew—fifty-two of them, a full pack—were taken to Cape Coast Castle and hanged on the beach, as a warning to Guinea sailors who dreamed of escaping their cruel captains by turning pirates themselves.

We have many accounts of the eighteenth-century trade by European merchants, sea captains, factors, and common seamen, but we know comparatively little about the slaves themselves and how they reacted to captivity. Few of them were taught to write English, and few of their masters bothered to learn or recount their histories. But some of the Moslem slaves from Senegambia could write in Arabic, and at least one of them, Job ben Solomon, regained his freedom because of his erudition.

Job was a Fula, born in the valley of the Senegal, where his father was a wealthy herdsman. In 1730 Job was sent to sell two slaves to an English ship then anchored in the Gambia. He was cautioned not to cross the river into Mandingo country lest he be enslaved himself. When he reached the Gambia, however, he heard that he could exchange his slaves for cows on the other side, and he yielded to the temptation of making a better bargain. Then, having disposed of the slaves, he sat down to a feast, unwisely hanging up his arms while he ate. A group of Mandingo slave hunters passed by, saw that he was defenceless, and captured him. Their king sold Job to the *Arabella*, the very ship to which he had been directed to sell his own slaves. As part of the purchase price the king received a pistol, which he hung round his neck on a string.

The *Arabella* took Job to Maryland, where he was bought by a tobacco planter and put to work in the fields. It was a torture for him to wield a heavy hoe, as he had never before done manual labor. The planter learned the facts and put Job in charge of his cattle, a task at which he did fairly well until some white boys made his life miserable by jeering at his Moslem genuflections during prayers. Job ran away, but was captured and jailed. In his despair he wrote a letter in Arabic, which was shown to Mr. Bluett, an English traveler in the colonies. Bluett carried the letter home with him and gave it to James Oglethorpe, then an official of the Royal African Company. Fascinated by the notion of an erudite slave, Oglethorpe sent it to Oxford to be translated, then purchased Job from his master and brought him to England.

Job is described as a handsome man, five feet, ten inches tall, with long curly hair. He was interviewed by Sir Hans Sloane, who found that he was an accomplished Arabic scholar and had him translate several manuscripts. Job also wrote three copies of the

Koran from memory, not bothering, after he finished the first copy, to refer to it while writing the other two. He was lionized in London, where he was taken under the patronage of the Duke of Montague and presented at court. The one request he made of his influential friends—who by now included the directors of the Royal African Company—was to be sent home.

At last, in 1734, he arrived at the mouth of the Gambia and went upstream with our old acquaintance, Francis Moore. The two men were sitting under a tree at a village called Damasensa when, Moore says, "There came by us six or seven of the very People who robb'd and made a Slave of Job about thirty Miles from hence, about three Years ago; Job, tho' a very even-temper'd Man at other times, could not contain himself when he saw them, but fell into a most terrible Passion and was for killing them with his broad Sword and Pistols, which he always took care to have about him." Moore pointed out that neither of them would escape with his life if Job killed the men. Restraining himself, Job asked them if they remembered capturing a young Fula lad a few years before. The men remembered it well because the pistol their king had received as part of the purchase price had gone off and shot him through the neck. "Job was so very much transported," Moore says, "that he immediately fell on his Knees, and returned Thanks to Mahomet for making this Man die by the very Goods for which he sold him into Slavery."

When Job reached the Fula country, he learned that his wife had married another man. He forgave her, "For, Mr. Moore," he said, "she could not help thinking I was dead, for I was gone to a Land from whence no Pholey ever yet returned; therefore she is not to be blamed, nor the Man neither." Having sold some of the presents he carried back from England, he used the proceeds to buy a woman slave and two horses; then he settled down to live among his people. When Moore went back to James Fort, Job gave him a number of letters to his noble English friends. He repaid his debt of gratitude to the Royal African Company by assuring his people that the slaves were not eaten by the white men but were well treated, a message which, Moore notes approvingly, "took away a great deal of the Horror of the Pholeys for the State of Slavery among the English."

There was another captured African who learned English so well that, after regaining his freedom and leading an adventurous life, he wrote a famous volume of memoirs. Olaudah Equiano or, to give him the name bestowed on him by his master, Gustavus Vassa, was born about 1745 in the kingdom of Benin. His father was an elder of the village and had many slaves. When the adults were working in the fields, the children, left to themselves, were told to keep lookouts in trees to watch for kidnapers. Once little Olaudah saw a man trying to carry off one of his friends and raised the alarm. The children overpowered the kidnaper and kept him tied up until their parents came home. The man was sold as a slave in his turn.

A few days later when Olaudah was playing with his sister near their home, two strangers, a man and a woman, seized the children, gagged them, and carried them off into the jungle. They were sold to different traders on the third day, and after that they saw each other only once, when two coffles happened to meet. Olaudah passed through the hands of several masters during the next few months, till at last he was put into a canoe with other slaves, paddled down a large river, and put ashore near its mouth. He says in his narrative:

> The first object which saluted my eyes when I arrived on the coast was the sea and a slave ship which was then riding at anchor and waiting for its cargo. This filled me with astonishment which was soon converted into terror which I am yet at a loss to describe and the then feelings of my mind when I was carried on board. I was immediately handled and tossed up to see if I were sound by some of the crew and I was now persuaded that I had gotten into a world of bad spirits and that they were going to kill me. Their complexions, too, differing so much from ours, their long hair, and the language they spoke (which was very different from any I had ever heard) united to form this belief. Indeed, such were the horrors of my fears that if ten thousand

worlds had been my own, I would have freely parted with them all to have exchanged my condition with that of the meanest slave in my own country. When I looked round the ship and saw a large furnace or copper boiling and a multitude of black people of every description chained together, every one of their countenances expressing dejection and sorrow, I no longer doubted my fate and, quite overpowered with horror, I fell motionless on the deck and fainted.

When I recovered, I found some black people about me. I asked if we were to be eaten by these white men with horrible looks, red faces, and long hair.

The conviction that the white men were cannibals seems to have been found almost everywhere, except among the sophisticated Gold Coast Negroes. Lieutenant Matthews reports from Sierra Leone, "I have seen some of these poor wretched beings so terrified with apprehension of their expected fate as to remain in a state of torpid insensibility for some time." But he adds that there were others of bolder constitution who "looked at a white man with amazement but without fear, examined his skin and their own, opened his breast, and felt whether the hair on his head was fast or not—and frequently burst into laughter at the uncouth appearance of a white man."

The change in the slave trade at the middle of the century was a change for the worse. There was a sudden growth in almost all the subsidiary evils that had developed from one great evil. The panyaring of natives by English sea captains was only one of these abuses. When the natives borrowed trade goods to use in obtaining slaves from the interior, they usually left "pawns" on shipboard as security. More and more captains took to sailing off with the pawns, who might be the children of caboceers. Four of the pawns sold into slavery by one vessel were the sons of Grandy King George of Old Calabar.

The Royal African Company, until its dissolution after 1750, had tried to keep on good terms with the natives, because its ships would be returning to the coast year after year. Sometimes when a native had been seized by fraud or force, the company redeemed him from his owner and sent him back to Africa at its own expense; that was meant to help in future dealings. But the private merchants, in general, were less concerned with the future. This was especially true of the small Liverpool enterprisers, the "attornies, drapers, ropers, grocers, tallow chandlers, barbers, taylors, etc.," who fitted out a single vessel on shares. Their captain, often a partner in the venture, was told to buy slaves honestly if he could, but anyhow to get them cheaply and not to waste money on his crew. Vessels were undermanned with sailors and then overloaded with slaves. Crews were overworked, underfed, and flogged at the least excuse. Trade goods exchanged for slaves were shoddy merchandise, bought as cheaply as possible. Attempts to cheat the natives, in addition to panyaring and the seizure of pawns, led to frequent palavers with the coastal tribes. Sometimes a town was bombarded to bring down the price of slaves, and the Negroes were by no means helpless or unarmed; sometimes they cannonaded back, destroying an English vessel. After 1750 the English and American newspapers often printed accounts of ships "cut off" by a slave mutiny (with smaller crews, mutinies had become more frequent) or captured and their sailors massacred by angry natives.

Some of these conditions were laggingly remedied as, over the years, ten or a dozen of the larger Liverpool houses gained control of the trade; the larger houses were less concerned with making sudden fortunes and thought more about next year's supply of human merchandise. But meanwhile the English public was learning about the abuses of the trade and was becoming concerned with the high mortality to which it led among English sailors. Two angry books about the trade were published in 1788. One was by Alexander Falconbridge, formerly a surgeon on a number of slave ships, and the other was by John Newton, a slaving captain who had entered the ministry. Then the Privy Council and afterward Parliament itself conducted a series of investigations of the trade that continued until 1791. Scores of slaving captains, their mates and surgeons, Liverpool merchants, West Indian planters, officers in the Royal Navy, Guinea factors, and common seamen were called upon to testify. An official report of the Parliamentary investigations was later published in thick folio volumes. For public convenience these were reduced to an angry "Abstract of the Evidence" by Thomas Clarkson, the abolitionist, and also to a much longer and more judicial "Abridgement," but the whole report has to be consulted as the single most complete and vivid source of information on slaving in its busiest era.

The report, called *Minutes of the Evidence*, is often quoted in these pages. First it should be said, however, that although the investigations did not lead to the immediate abolition of the English slave trade, they were a blow that eventually proved fatal. Even before they started, Parliament passed a law (1788) which limited the number of slaves a vessel could carry, depending on its tonnage: five slaves, approximately, for every three tons of burden. Another measure provided that at least one sailor should be signed on for every ten slaves in the prospective cargo. One effect of these regulations was to increase the outlay of capital for a slaving voyage, and hence to confirm the largest Liverpool houses in their quasi monopoly of the English trade. During the last years of legal slaving, the small, undermanned, overloaded vessels were from American ports, and the small, reckless, and grasping enterprisers were mostly Yankees.

From the evidence offered to Parliament, as well as from the accounts of Falconbridge and Newton, it becomes evident that the slavers had developed two new techniques for obtaining and safeguarding their cargoes. One of these methods, used chiefly on the Windward Coast, was called "boating." A Guineaman would anchor in some convenient road or harbor and then send its boats along the coast and up the rivers to buy small groups of slaves from local traders. Often the boats would be out for days or weeks at a time, their crews soaked to the skin and racked with fever. The Reverend John Newton, once known as "the pious slaver," says, "I have myself in such a boat been five or six days together without . . . a dry thread about me, sleeping or waking. . . .

The boats seldom returned without bringing some of the people ill of dangerous fevers or fluxes."

Instead of "boating," the slave ship could simply drop anchor in a river, pay the local customs duties, and wait for slaves to be brought to her by the local merchants, kidnapers, or kings. This was an old practice, and its disadvantage was that the ship would be at anchor for weeks or months. Many of the first-purchased slaves failed to survive in the heat and squalor of the ship's hold. The new technique was to build a "house" on deck where they could be confined in somewhat less discomfort. Dr. Falconbridge describes these houses as running from mast to mast, the roof being supported by the ship's booms and yards, and the walls being composed of lattice made by weaving together bamboo shoots or mangrove branches. Small openings were made in the walls so that blunderbusses and small cannons could be trained on the slaves in case of a mutiny, and food was passed in through a trapdoor in the roof.

The slaves' gain, if any, was the seamen's loss. James Stanfield, who wrote a narrative of his Guinea voyage, reports that building the house was one of the greatest hardships in the trade. The men were required to cut mangrove branches and reeds to thatch the roof while standing in muddy slime up to their waists, covered with clouds of mosquitoes and in danger of being bitten by poisonous snakes. When the slaves began to come aboard, the seamen had the daily task of cleaning up filth and blood from the floor of the house, as most of the slaves on Stanfield's vessel suffered from dysentery, or the "bloody flux." All the work was done in the intense tropical heat, with most of the men suffering from fever.

By the middle of the eighteenth century most of the slaves purchased by the English either had been captured in local wars (which had become, in large part, mere slave-raiding expeditions) or else had been kidnaped. Both techniques were highly organized and were conducted on a large scale. There were also slaves captured and sold by their own kings, sometimes—but not always—

on the pretense of their being criminals. Crimes punishable with slavery had become still easier to manufacture. As any object might be a fetish, chieftains or priests would strew the paths leading to their villages with old pitchers, and even pieces of wood that had been pronounced sacred. Anyone disturbing the objects was seized by guards hiding in the underbrush and was sold. White men were not safe from these traps. The mate of the *Brookes* was arrested and had to produce a male slave to avoid being sold himself. But these were subterfuges, and some kings—especially in Senegambia—were too proud to employ them. Captain Thomas Wilson, commanding HMS *Racehorse*, was dispatched there in 1783 to embark troops and stores from Goree. Offered a slave by the reigning Damel of Cayor, he asked the guards what crime the man had committed. One of the guards replied, "It is of no consequence and is never inquired into." C. B. Wadström, Chief Director of the Assay Office in Sweden, was in Africa on a scientific expedition from 1787 to 1788. He testified that Chief Barbesin of Senegal was reluctant to sell his own people unless drunk, "which he usually was as the French traders took care to keep him supplied with brandy."

Simple kidnaping had become much more common than sale for pretended crimes. Dr. Falconbridge says, "I have good reason to believe that of the one hundred and twenty negroes purchased for the ship to which I then belonged . . . by far the greater part, if not the whole, were kidnaped." John Douglas, a seaman on a slaver, was watching a young girl bathing when he saw two men steal out of the bushes and seize her. The girl screamed and fought, but she was beaten into submission, and the kidnapers carried her on board Douglas's ship. He testified that his captain had given orders to purchase all slaves immediately and no questions asked. Panyaring was so common that, during the Middle Passage, children used to play at kidnaping one another.

Some of the kidnapers became famous. There was Griffiths, a white man, who operated between Cape Le Hout and Apollonia for many years. Griffiths eventually made the mistake of carrying off two "pawns" from the Gold Coast and selling them. On his return, he claimed that they had died of smallpox, but the natives knew better and Griffiths at last paid the penalty for his crimes. There was Blundell Foubre, a native trader who was also a kidnaper. Falconbridge tells of seeing Foubre come alongside his ship in a canoe with a wide-eyed young man who was obviously astonished by the wonders about him. The two men came aboard, and Foubre sold his companion to the ship's captain. Later Falconbridge questioned the bewildered man, who explained that he had come from the interior and that Foubre had asked him if he had ever seen a ship. When the man said no, Foubre had generously offered to show him one. Fat Sam, called the "gold-taker," used to bring his panyared victims on board after dark. Fat Sam refused payment for his captives until just before the ship sailed, for fear that they might be redeemed by their relatives.

Most famous of all the kidnapers was Ben Johnson, a powerful Negro who operated off Piccaninni Sestus on the Windward Coast. Johnson was so energetic that he was able to kidnap enough of his fellow Africans almost to load a slave ship by himself. In 1769 he kidnaped a girl and sold her to a slaver lying in the river. A few hours later the girl's brothers came on board. They had missed their sister and had been following Johnson, but arrived too late. When they saw the girl in chains on the deck with the other slaves, they leaped into their canoe and paddled back to shore. The next day they reappeared with Johnson bound hand and foot and offered him to the captain.

"You won't buy me, whom you know to be a great trading man, will you, Captain?" begged Johnson.

"If they will sell you I will buy you, be you what you may," replied the captain, and Ben went the way he had sent so many others.

The kidnaping of Negroes by white men was called "buckra panyaring." Always a fairly common practice, it seems to have been especially prevalent after the dissolution of the Royal African Company. John Douglas, who shipped to the Gold Coast in 1771, says that while his vessel was lying off Cape Coast Castle, the captain ordered pipes, tobacco, and brandy to be laid out on the deck to entice natives. The gratings were unlaid, the slave room was cleared, and every preparation was made to receive black visitors. Canoes surrounded the ship, but only two men could be persuaded to come aboard, and they insisted on standing in the main chains. When the seamen tried to seize them, they jumped off, and all the canoes made for shore. John Bowman, a mate under Captain Strangeways, says that when his vessel was in the Sierra Leone River two Negro traders came aboard. Shortly afterward the vessel put to sea. The captain called Bowman and, pointing to the sail case, told him to look inside and "see what a fine prize we got." Inside were the two traders, dead drunk. Later they must have been very sober when they were handcuffed and put in the hold among the other slaves. The little port of Lancaster, once a rival of Liverpool, ruined her slave trade because Lancaster captains acquired such a reputation for buckra panyaring that natives refused to deal with them.

Whites and blacks cooperated in the famous case of panyaring that occurred at the mouth of the Old Calabar River. At that point there were two towns on opposite sides of the river, Old Town and New Town, each under its own king. (New Town, Old Calabar, is not to be confused with New Calabar, thirty leagues to the west.) The two Old Calabar towns were busy rivals in the slave trade, obtaining most of their merchandise from regions one or two hundred miles in the interior. Paddling up the rivers in fleets of big canoes, they would act as peaceful traders by day, buying slaves at the local fairs, and as kidnapers by night. The exports of both towns together amounted to about seven thousand slaves a year.

In 1767 there was a temporary halt in the trade, jealousy between the two towns having reached such a point that no canoes would venture up the river. Seven English ships lay at the rivermouth, waiting to be slaved and grumbling because the delay was eating into their profits. One evening the ships' captains held a meeting, and six of them agreed to a plan that would fill their empty holds. They invited the people of both towns to come aboard their vessels on a certain day, as if to reconcile them, and at the same time they agreed with the New Town people to "cut off"—that is, kill or capture—such of the Old Town People as remained on shipboard next morning.

The Old Towners came paddling out by hundreds, including their king and their caboceers. Many New Towners also came, to dispel suspicion, and the carousing lasted all night. At eight o'clock in the morning one of the ships fired a gun. At this signal the sailors assaulted the Old Town people, knocking them down with belaying pins, hacking them with cutlasses, or forcing them against the afterhouse with boarding pikes. Many jumped overboard, but the ships' guns opened fire on their canoes, and soon the river was dotted with the heads of men trying to swim ashore. Now the New Town people, who had been hiding behind a point of land, went into action. As the survivors struggled ashore, they attacked the exhausted men. The English captains had instructed them to capture, not kill, their enemies, but the New Towners went berserk, spearing dozens of Old Towners before their own king could stop them.

As for the king of Old Town, he escaped from the ship he was in by killing two sailors. He paddled toward shore in a one-man canoe until it was smashed to pieces by a six-pound shot; then he swam the rest of the way, though wounded by musket fire. The New Towners pursued him, but he reached the shelter of his palace. Of his three brothers, captured on shipboard, one was delivered to the New Towners for execution, and the other two were sold in the West Indies. It was estimated that three or four hundred Negroes died in the massacre and that as many more were enslaved. Perhaps the last victim was an Old Town grandee or caboceer named Amboe. He had brought a letter on board the *Canterbury* and then, as the carnage started, had hidden behind a medicine chest. Discovered there, he was chained among the slaves. Shortly afterward a New Town trader called Willy Honesty boarded the ship. He heard about Amboe and told the captain, "If you will give me that man, to cut off his head, I will give you the

best man in my canoe, and you shall always be slaved first ship."
The captain looked into Willy Honesty's canoe, picked his man,
and unchained and delivered the other. Amboe's head was struck
off, there in the canoe, and his body was thrown to the sharks.

The Old Town people had a partial revenge the following year,
when—in sight of Captain Colley's ship, the *Latham*—they totally
routed the New Town people, killing and wounding more than
three hundred of them. Captain Colley said in a letter that they
won their victory in spite of being outnumbered ten to one.

Although panyaring by professional kidnapers had become an
important source of slaves, it continued to rank second to wars
among nations, tribes, and villages. Most of the slavers agreed
that these wars were conducted chiefly for the purpose of obtaining captives for sale. "The slaves," says Dr. Falconbridge, "are
not prisoners of war as we understand the word war. In Africa, a
piratical expedition for making slaves is termed a war."

James Morley, for many years a seaman on slavers, testified that
"War was putting the villages in confusion and catching them as
they could." Such wars were described as being of two types, the
"grand pillage" and the "lesser pillage." Henry Dalrymple, a lieutenant in the 75th Regiment, stationed at Goree in 1779, explains
the difference by saying that the grand pillage "is executed by the
king's soldiers, from three hundred to three thousand at a time,
who attack and set fire to a village and seize the inhabitants as they
can." In the lesser pillage, "Parties lie in wait about the villages
and take off all they can surprise which is also done by individuals
who do not belong to the king but are private robbers."

Parliament was given a good account of this lesser pillage by
John Bowman, the mate of a slaver. His captain sent him up the
Scassus (Scarcies) River in Sierra Leone to operate as a factor.
Bowman's orders were to furnish any native community that would
go slave-raiding with the necessary powder and ball. Having reached
the head of navigation on the river, he found a little cluster of
native huts. Bowman explained his mission and, after the village

had discussed it for two or three days, a group of the men came to him for the ammunition plus rum and tobacco. "They were dressed in some kind of skins, with large capes and their faces painted white to make them look dreadful. They asked for a drink of rum which when given them, they went off to the number of twenty-five or thirty. After six or seven days, some of them returned with two women, and a girl six or seven years old."

The raiders reported that they had surprised a small town and managed these captures. The other inhabitants had fled, but the rest of the raiders were out looking for them. When the other raiders returned, they brought with them two men whom Bowman knew; he had traded with them on his trip up the river. These men told Bowman that the women were their wives and that they all had been surprised in their sleep by the raiders.

Bowman spent several months in this community, the "war-men" going out on raids every few days. Once Bowman joined the party to see how they obtained the slaves. After traveling all day the raiders came to a small river near a village. They hid here in the bushes until evening. When night came the war-men prepared to cross the stream, but Bowman decided to remain behind, so the others left him. Half an hour later he heard the war cry go up and knew that his men were attacking the town. Soon he saw a red glow in the night; the war-men had fired the thatched huts. At dawn they returned with a catch of some thirty men, women, and children; the prisoners were roped together with tie-tie bark and the men's hands were tied behind their backs.

Under Bowman's supervision, the little river hamlet increased to a sizable village of some fifty huts and a hundred and twenty-five inhabitants; people were flocking in to join his raiders. He was often called out at night by the townspeople to see the fires of distant villages lighting the sky as proof that the war-men were doing an efficient job. Bowman adds, "Whatever rivers I have traded in, I have usually passed burnt and desert villages and learnt from the natives in the boat with me that war had been there and the natives taken and carried to the ships."

Captain John Hall, who made two voyages to Africa on a Guinea-man in 1772 and 1776, says that when a slaver touched at Old Calabar it was the signal for the natives to go upstream in their war canoes. He had seen from three to ten canoes in a fleet, each with forty to sixty paddlers and twenty to thirty warriors armed with muskets. Each canoe had a four-pound cannon lashed on the bow. After ten days to three weeks, the canoes would return, full of slaves. Falconbridge saw a similar canoe fleet at Bonny, and once it returned with twelve hundred slaves.

The grand pillage was a more impressive affair. The surgeon of a Liverpool slaver, Robert Law, reported in his journal:

> *Sestro, Dec. 29th. 1724.* No trade to Day tho' many Traders come on board, they informed us that the People are gone to War within Land and will bring prisoners enough in two or three Days in Hopes of which we stay.
> *The 30th. Day.* No Trade yet, but our Traders came on board to Day and informed us the People had burn't four Towns of their Enemies and indeed we have seen great Smoke all the Morning a good Way up the Country so that To-morrow we expect Slaves . . . another large Ship is just come in. Yesterday came in a large Londoner.
> *The 31st.* Fair Weather but no Trade, yet we see each Night Towns burning but we hear the Sestra Men are many of them killed by the Inland Negroes so that we fear this War will be unsuccessful.
> *The 32nd.* Last Night we saw a prodigeous Fire break out about eleven o'clock and this Morning see the Town of Sestro burn't down to the Ground (it contained some Hundred Houses) so that we find their Enemies are too hard for them at present and consequently our Trade spoil'd here; so that about eleven o'clock we weighed Anchor as did likewise the three other Vessels to proceed lower down.

As can be seen, obtaining slaves either by panyaring or by wars was a protracted and uncertain business. It often involved long waits by the slavers and trusting the native kings with considerable amounts of gunpowder, bullets, and muskets. The slavers frequently complained that time meant nothing to an African and

that the chiefs had no moral standards; they might deliberately
delay slaving a vessel, since every day she remained in port they
could obtain additional "dash" and make a profit by supplying her
crew with food. Even when the chiefs did set out on a grand or
lesser pillage, they were quite capable of selling the slaves captured with the slavers' ammunition to some newly arrived vessel
that could offer them a better price, not having to make up for the
weeks of delay and the cost of the powder and lead. To expedite
the trade and make sure of receiving value for their money, the
slavers put an increasing emphasis on the use of pawns.

The understanding was that unless slaves were produced by a
certain date, the pawns would be taken in their place. Probably
nothing caused so much trouble between the slavers and the coastal
towns as the carrying off of pawns. Captain Frazer, often described
as "the only Bristol captain who didn't deserve to hang," was particularly outspoken against this practice, insisting that it delayed
the ships and caused "bad blood." On the Gambia the captain
of one of three English slavers tried to sail off with some pawns,
taking advantage of a favorable wind. But the wind changed and
he was trapped. The natives not only killed him and all his crew,
but also the crews of the other two ships, all except one young lad
whom they kept as a slave.

A typical story concerning pawns is the one told to Parliament
by James Arnold, surgeon of the brig *Ruby*, out of Bristol. "While
we were lying at the island of Bimbe," he says,

> Capt. Bibby of the *Molly*, of Liverpool, came out of the river
> Cameroons with several pawns on board belonging to King
> George, King Peter and the trader Quon. Captain Bibby had
> given them notice that he should sail for the Cape on a certain
> day and would wait there for three days before he went to sea
> and if the pawns were not redeemed by that time, he should
> carry them to the West Indies and sell them. It chanced that
> King George and the other traders were not able at that time to
> redeem their pawns and so in great haste they came to Captain
> Williams of the *Ruby*, asking him to spare them some slaves and

ivory so they might redeem the pawns which Captain Bibby had threatened to take away.

Captain Williams let them have eleven slaves and five teeth which were carried to the *Molly* and six or seven pawns were released and brought to the *Ruby* to be held as security. The next day, however, the *Molly* sailed for the West Indies having on board about thirty pawns, which so enraged the traders that they immediately left us and returned to the Cameroons. Here, they put a stop to all trade with the captains, five of whom were seized and carried away into the country where they were kept chained to trees, as we afterwards learned. It was an awkward situation and after conference, a schooner, with slaves aboard, was dispatched to overtake the *Molly* and bring back the pawns that had been carried off by Captain Bibby.

The price of slaves went up and down, depending on how successful the local wars had been and also depending on how many Guineamen were waiting for cargoes. What the slaves actually cost, delivered on shipboard, is hard to determine, first because they were bartered for merchandise, and second because of all the extra charges that slavers had to pay, including port duties, wages of native labor, brokerage fees, and presents before and after the purchase. A slave bought from a native merchant for ten pounds might cost five pounds more before he was stowed in the ship's hold. Over the years, the cost of slaves kept rising. Thus, in 1708 the average cost of a Negro delivered on shipboard was £10, and it seemed fantastically high to old sea captains who were used to paying half as much. In 1750 the cost had risen to an average of about £15, although it was lower in Calabar and Angola. By 1786, a year for which we have pretty complete figures for the Liverpool trade, the actual cost in English merchandise of a slave delivered on shipboard was £27 5s. 10d. The net sales price of a slave in the West Indies, after deducting factorage, was £40 8s. 6¾d.

As the natives grew more sophisticated, the old trade units—"bars" (of iron), "ounces" (of gold dust), and "pieces" (of cloth)—lost their original meanings, although the names persisted. In

1734 on the Gambia a "bar" might be a pound of fringe, two pounds of gunpowder, an ounce of silver, or a hundred gun flints. In Loango a "piece" might be a musket, or it might be twenty pounds of iron. Cheating the native traders was a standard practice among slavers. Newton tells how false heads were put on powder casks, how two or three yards were cut from the center of a roll of cloth, how liquor was adulterated, and how guns were made so cheaply that they burst after the first few shots. Lieutenant Storey remarks that natives without fingers and thumbs were common on the coast. Falconbridge says it was a popular observation among natives that the trade guns "kill more out of the butt than the muzzle."

James Towne, who served as carpenter on board a Guineaman in 1768, testified that the slavers "used different weights to which they gave the same appearance by casting a stone and a piece of lead alike in brass; I had such weights myself and used them in dealing for wax, teeth, etc. by order of my commanding officer whom I repeatedly saw do it himself." Such tricks were so common that when a native was accused of cheating he sometimes answered indignantly, "What do you think I am, a white man?" The slavers for their part claimed that native dealers could never be trusted and that they were not above drugging a sickly slave so he would pass inspection. Often a fine-looking Negro, "seemingly the best in the whole coffle," would drop dead a few hours after being purchased.

By the eighteenth century the coastal tribes could not meet the demand for slaves from their own population, or by warring on their neighbors, and the result was that more coffles began moving toward the coast from the deep interior. One author after another mentions the tentacles of trade that were reaching out through the continent to find new sources of supply.

For example, Francis Moore, the English factor on the Gambia (1730–1735), traveled three hundred miles upstream to get his slaves, and then they had been brought to the "feeder" factories near the river from regions much farther inland. Falconbridge says,

"The slaves are bought by the black traders at fairs, which are held for that purpose, at the distance of upwards of two hundred miles from the sea coast; and these fairs are said to be supplied from an interior part of the country. Many negroes, upon being questioned relative to the place of their nativity, have asserted that they travelled during the revolution of several moons . . . before they have reached the places where they were purchased by the black traders." Newton says, "Though a considerable number of them may have been born near the sea, I believe the bulk of them are brought from afar. I have reason to think that some travel more than a thousand miles before they reach the coast." That many of the slaves were born "more than a thousand miles" in the interior seems unlikely, considering that distances are easy to exaggerate, but it is probable that the activities of the slave hunters reached at least five hundred miles from the ocean.

We have several accounts of the great coffles, which, regardless of their origin, sometimes comprised hundreds of suffering captives and stretched for miles. In Senegambia the coffles were smaller. Francis Moore tells us that the merchants, usually Mandingo, brought down "in some Years Slaves to the Amount of 2000, most of whom they say are Prisoners taken in War: they buy them from the different Princes who take them. . . . Their Way of bringing them is, tying them by the Neck with Leather-Thongs, at about a Yard distance from each other, 30 or 40 in a String, having generally a Bundle of Corn, or an Elephant's Tooth upon each of their Heads. . . . I cannot be certain of the Number of Merchants who follow this Trade, but there may perhaps be about an Hundred, who go up into the Inland Country with the Goods, which they buy from the White Men, and with them purchasing in various Countries Gold, Slaves and Elephants Teeth."

The most detailed account of a coffle was written by Mungo Park, the great Scottish explorer, who was the first European to visit the upper reaches of the Niger. In 1795 Park went up the Gambia, then traveled east across the Senegal. He was captured by the Moors and carried into the desert, but later escaped with only a starved horse and his pocket compass; at last he came in sight of the Niger, "glittering to the morning sun, as broad as the Thames at Westminster, and flowing slowly *to the eastward*"; every European had believed that it flowed west. Having turned back toward the coast and having given away the starved horse, Park accompanied a coffle of slaves from Kamalia, in the kingdom of Manding, to the town of Jindey, on the lower Gambia, a distance of some five hundred miles.

There were seventy-three slaves, owned by several merchants, in Park's coffle. Two of the slaves, a woman and a girl, ate clay in an effort to commit suicide, but vomited it up and were severely beaten. The coffle was attacked by a swarm of bees, and one woman was stung so badly that later she had to be abandoned for the lions to eat. On another occasion the coffle was scattered by a herd of elephants, and on still another it was forced to hide in high grass to escape a band of marauders. Many of the slaves nearly died of hunger, thirst, and exhaustion, but the coffle kept on, sometimes spending the night in a prosperous town, at other times only passing the ruins of villages burned in slave raids; fording rivers that swarmed with crocodiles, crossing the Jallonka wilderness, where it huddled together at night for protection against lions, and often climbing over "wild and rocky country, everywhere rising into hills, and abounding with monkeys and wild beasts." In June 1797, at the beginning of the rainy season, the coffle at last reached tidewater on the Gambia, after two months on the road.

There was little demand for slaves at the time, no European vessel having visited the river for several months. James Fort had been abandoned, and most of the English trade had moved far southward to the Bight of Biafra and the Congo. Park's friend Karfa, the headman of the coffle, set his own slaves to making a crop while waiting for ships to arrive. Park resigned himself to a long delay, but was saved from it by the appearance of an American vessel, the *Charlestown*, Captain Charles Harris, bound for South Carolina with a cargo of a hundred and thirty Negroes. Park seized the opportunity of getting back to England by crossing the Atlantic twice. The westward voyage was costly in human lives. Five of the crew, including the surgeon, died of fever in the Gambia, and Park volunteered to take the surgeon's place. In spite of his best attentions, he lost more than twenty of the slaves, and "many of the survivors," he says, "were reduced to a very weak and emaciated condition." Still, they were more fortunate in the Middle Passage than hundreds of other black cargoes.

# 5

# The Middle Passage

See the poor native quit the Libyan shores,
Ah! not in love's delightful fetters bound!
—William Shenstone

As soon as an assortment of naked slaves was taken aboard a Guineaman, the men were shackled two by two, the right wrist and ankle of one to the left wrist and ankle of another. Then they were sent to the hold or, at the end of the eighteenth century, to the "house" that the sailors had built on deck. The women— usually regarded as fair prey for the sailors—and the children were allowed to wander by day almost anywhere on the vessel, though they spent the night between decks in other rooms than the men. All the slaves were forced to sleep without covering on bare wooden floors, which were often constructed of unplaned boards. In a stormy passage the skin over their elbows might be worn away to the bare bones.

William Bosman says, writing in 1701, "You would really wonder to see how these slaves live on board; for though their number sometimes amounts to six or seven hundred, yet by careful management of our masters of ships"—the Dutch masters, that is—"they are so regulated that it seems incredible: And in this particular our nation exceeds all other Europeans; for as the French, Portuguese and English slave-ships are always foul and stinking; on the contrary ours are for the most part clean and neat." Slavers of every nation insisted that their own vessels were the best in the trade. Thus, James Barbot, Jr., who sailed on an English ship to the Congo in 1700, was highly critical of the Portuguese. He admits that they made a great point of baptizing the slaves before taking them aboard, but then, "It is pitiful," he says, "to see how they crowd those poor wretches, six hundred and fifty or seven hundred in a ship, the men standing in the hold ty'd to stakes, the women between decks and those that are with child in the great cabin and the children in the steeridge which in that hot climate occasions an intolerable stench." This youngest Barbot adds, however, that the Portuguese provided the slaves with coarse thick mats, which were "softer for the poor wretches to lie upon than the bare decks . . . and it would be prudent to imitate the Portuguese in this point." The English never displayed that sort of prudence, and neither did they imitate the Dutch, who had special ships built for the trade, Barbot says, "very wide, lofty and airy betwixt decks, with gratings and scuttles . . . to let in more air. Some also have small ports . . . and that very much contributes to the preservation of those poor wretches who are so thick crowded together."

There were two schools of thought among the Guinea captains, called the "loose-packers" and the "tight-packers." The former argued that by giving the slaves a little more room, with better food and a certain amount of liberty, they reduced the mortality among them and received a better price for each slave in the West Indies. The tight-packers answered that although the loss of life might be greater on each of their voyages, so too were the net receipts from a larger cargo. If many of the survivors were weak and emaciated, as was often the case, they could be fattened up in a West Indian slave yard before being offered for sale. The argument between the two schools continued as long as the trade itself, but for many years after 1750 the tight-packers were in the ascendant. So great was the profit on each slave landed alive in the West Indies that hardly a captain refrained from loading his vessel to her utmost capacity. The hold of a slaving vessel was usually about five feet high. That seemed like waste space to the Guinea merchants, so they built a shelf or platform in the middle of it, extending six feet from each side of the vessel. When the bottom of the hold was completely covered with flesh, another row of slaves was packed on the platform. If there was as much as six feet of vertical space in the hold, a second platform might be installed above the first, sometimes leaving only twenty inches of headroom for the slaves; they could not sit upright during the whole voyage. The Reverend John Newton writes from personal observation:

> The cargo of a vessel of a hundred tons or a little more is calculated to purchase from 220 to 250 slaves. Their lodging rooms below the deck which are three (for the men, the boys and the women) besides a place for the sick, are sometimes more than five feet high and sometimes less; and this height is divided toward the middle for the slaves lie in two rows, one above the other, on each side of the ship, close to each other like books upon a shelf. I have known them so close that the shelf would not easily contain one more.
>
> The poor creatures, thus cramped, are likewise in irons for the most part which makes it difficult for them to turn or move or attempt to rise or to lie down without hurting themselves or each other. Every morning, perhaps, more instances than one are found of the living and the dead fastened together.

Dr. Falconbridge stated in his Parliamentary testimony that "he made the most of the room," in stowing the slaves, "and wedged them in. They had not so much room as a man in his coffin either in length or breadth. When he had to enter the slave deck, he took off his shoes to avoid crushing the slaves as he was forced to crawl over them." Taking off shoes on entering the hold seems to have been a widespread custom among surgeons. Falconbridge "had the marks on his feet where [the slaves] bit and pinched him."

In 1788 Captain Parrey of the Royal Navy was sent to measure such of the slave vessels as were then lying at Liverpool and to make a report to the House of Commons. He discovered that the captains of many slavers possessed a chart showing the dimensions of the ship's half deck, lower deck, hold, platforms, gunroom, orlop, and great cabin, in fact of every crevice into which slaves might be wedged. Miniature black figures were drawn on some of the charts to illustrate the most effective method of packing in the cargo.

On the *Brookes*, which Captain Parrey considered to be typical, every man was allowed a space six feet long by sixteen inches wide (and usually about two feet, seven inches high); every woman, a space five feet, ten inches long by sixteen inches wide; every boy, five feet by fourteen inches; every girl, four feet, six inches by twelve inches. The *Brookes* was a vessel of 320 tons. By the law of 1788 it was permitted to carry 454 slaves, and the chart, which later became famous, showed how and where 451 of them could be stowed away. Captain Parrey failed to see how the captain could find room for three more. Nevertheless, Parliament was told by reliable witnesses, including Dr. Thomas Trotter, formerly surgeon of the *Brookes*, that before the new law was passed she had carried 600 slaves on one voyage and 609 on another.

Taking on slaves was a process that might be completed in a month or two at Bonny or Luanda. On the Gold Coast, where slaves were less plentiful, it might last from six months to a year or more. Meanwhile the captain was buying Negroes, sometimes one or two a day, sometimes a hundred or more in a single lot, while haggling over each purchase.

Those months when a slaver lay at anchor off the Guinea Coast, taking on her cargo, were the most dangerous stage of her triangular voyage. Not only was her crew exposed to African fevers and the revenge of angry natives; not only was there the chance of her being taken by pirates or by a hostile man-of-war; but also there was the constant threat of a slave mutiny. Captain Thomas Phillips says, in his account of a voyage made in 1693–1694:

When our slaves are aboard we shackle the men two and two, while we lie in port, and in sight of their own country, for 'tis then they attempt to make their escape, and mutiny; to prevent which we always keep centinels upon the hatchways, and have a chest full of small arms, ready loaden and prim'd, constantly lying at hand upon the quarter-deck, together with some granada shells; and two of our quarter-deck guns, pointing on the deck thence, and two more out of the steerage, the door of which is always kept shut, and well barr'd; they are fed twice a day, at 10 in the morning, and 4 in the evening, which is the time they are aptest to mutiny, being all upon deck; therefore all that time, what of our men are not employ'd in distributing their victuals to them, and settling them, stand to their arms; and some with lighted matches at the great guns that yaun upon them, loaden with partridge, till they have done and gone down to their kennels between decks.

The danger of mutiny was greatest when all the slaves on board belonged to a single tribe, especially if it was one of the warlike tribes from the Gold Coast. On the other hand, the Gold Coast slaves despised other Negroes, and this fault of theirs proved useful to the white men. Phillips says, "We have some 30 or 40 gold coast negroes, which we buy . . . to make guardians and overseers of the Whidaw negroes, and sleep among them to keep them from quarreling; and in order, as well as to give us notice, if they can discover any caballing or plotting among them, which trust they will discharge with great diligence; . . . when we constitute a guardian, we give him a cat of nine tails as a badge of his office, which he is not a little proud of, and will exercise with great authority."

In spite of such precautions, mutinies were frequent on the coast, and some of them were successful. Even a failed mutiny might lead to heavy losses among the slaves and the sailors. James Barbot, Sr., of the *Albion-Frigate*, made the mistake of providing his slaves with knives so they could cut their meat. The slaves tore pieces of iron from the forecastle door, broke off their shackles, and killed the guard at the entrance to the hatchway. Before the mutiny was quelled, twenty-eight slaves either had been shot dead or had thrown themselves overboard. Bosman went through two mutinies. In the second of these the slaves would have mastered the ship had it not been aided by a French and an English vessel. About twenty slaves were killed. William Snelgrave survived more perils on the coast than any other Guinea captain of the early eighteenth century. Among the perils were three mutinies, one at Old Calabar, when there were four hundred slaves on his father's ship and only ten sailors not disabled by fever, and the other two on the Gold Coast. Both the Gold Coast mutinies were led by Coromantees, against hopeless odds. About the first of these he says:

> This Mutiny began at Midnight. . . . Two Men that stood Centry at the Forehatch way . . . permitted four [slaves] to go to that Place, but neglected to lay the Gratings again, as they should have done; whereupon four more Negroes came on Deck . . . and all eight fell on the two Centries who immediately called out for help. The Negroes endeavoured to get their Cutlaces from them, but the Lineyards (that is the Lines by which the Handles of the Cutlaces were fastened to the Men's Wrists) were so twisted in the Scuffle, that they could not get them off before we came to their Assistance. The Negroes perceiving several white Men coming towards them, with Arms in their Hands, quitted the Centries and jumped over the Ship's Side into the Sea. . . .
>
> After we had secured these People, I called the Linguists, and ordered them to bid the Men-Negroes between Decks be quiet; (for there was a great noise amongst them). On their being silent, I asked, "What had induced them to mutiny?" They answered, "I was a great Rogue to buy them, in order to carry them away from their own Country, and that they were resolved to regain their Liberty if possible." I replied, "That they had forfeited their Freedom before I bought them, either by Crimes or by being taken in War." . . . Then I observed to them, "That

if they should gain their Point and escape to the Shore, it would
be of no Advantage to them, because their Countrymen would
catch them, and sell them to other Ships." This served my purpose, and they seemed to be convinced of their Fault.

Mutinies were frequent during the years from 1750 to 1788,
when Liverpool merchants were trying to save money by reducing
the size of their crews. A small crew weakened by fever was no
match for the slaves, especially if it had to withstand a simultane-
ous attack from the shore. On January 11, 1769, the *Nancy* out of
Liverpool, Captain Williams, was lying at anchor off New Calabar.
She had 132 slaves on board, who managed to break their shackles
and assail the crew. The slaves were unarmed, but "it was with
great difficulty, though [the crew] attacked them sword in hand, to
make them submit." Meanwhile the natives on shore heard the
fighting and swarmed aboard the *Nancy* from their canoes. They
seized the slaves (whom they later resold to other ships, as Captain
Snelgrave had prophesied) and looted the cargo. There was a wild
scene of plunder, with black men running through the vessel,
breaching rum casks, throwing ships' biscuit and salt beef into the
canoes, and robbing the sailors of everything they possessed. Afterward they cut the cables and set the *Nancy* adrift. Another slaver
lying in the river sent a boat to rescue Captain Williams and the
surviving seamen. The vessel, however, was wrecked.

William Richardson, a young sailor who shipped on a Guineaman in 1790, tells of going to the help of a French vessel on which
the slaves had risen while it was at anchor in a bay. The English
seamen jumped into their boats and pulled hard for the Frenchman, but by the time they reached it there were "a hundred slaves
in possession of the deck and others tumbling up from below." The
French vessel had its netting rigged—a customary precaution for
slavers lying at anchor—and the nets prevented the Englishmen
from boarding. Even after they had broken through the nets, the
slaves put up a desperate resistance. "I could not but admire,"
Richardson says, "the courage of a fine young black who, though
his partner in irons lay dead at his feet, would not surrender but

fought with his billet of wood until a ball finished his existence. The others fought as well as they could but what could they do against fire-arms?"

There are fairly detailed accounts of fifty-five mutinies on slavers from 1699 to 1845, not to mention passing references to more than a hundred others. The list of ships "cut off" by the natives—often in revenge for the kidnaping of freemen—is almost as long. On the record it does not seem that Africans submitted tamely to being carried across the Atlantic like chained beasts. Edward Long, the Jamaica planter and historian, justified the cruel punishments inflicted on slaves by saying, "The many acts of violence they have committed by murdering whole crews and destroying ships when they had it in their power to do so have made these rigors wholly chargeable on their own bloody and malicious disposition which calls for the same confinement as if they were wolves or wild boars." For "wolves or wild boars" a modern reader might substitute "men who would rather die than be enslaved."

As long as a vessel lay at anchor, the slaves could dream of seizing it. If they managed to kill the crew, as they did in perhaps one mutiny out of ten, they could cut the anchor cable and let the vessel drift ashore. That opportunity was lost as soon as the vessel put to sea. Ignorant of navigation, which they regarded as white man's magic, the slaves were at the mercy of the captain. They could still die, but not with any hope of regaining their freedom.

The captain, for his part, had finished the most dangerous leg of his triangular voyage. Now he had to face only the ordinary perils of the sea, most of which were covered by his owners' insurance against fire, shipwreck, pirates and rovers, letters of mart and counter-mart, barratry, jettison, and foreign men-of-war. Among the risks not covered by insurance, the greatest was that the cargo might be swept away by disease. The underwriters refused to issue such policies, arguing that they would expose the captain to an unholy temptation. If insured against disease among his slaves, he might take no precautions against it and might try to make his profit out of the insurance.

The more days at sea, the more deaths among his cargo, and so the captain tried to cut short the next leg of his voyage. If he had shipped his slaves at Bonny or Old Calabar or any port to the southward, he might call at one of the Portuguese islands in the Gulf of Guinea for an additional supply of food and fresh water, usually enough, with what he had already, to last for three months. If he had traded on the Windward Coast, he made straight for the West Indies. Usually he had from four to five thousand nautical miles to sail—or even more, if the passage was from Angola to Virginia. The shortest passage—that from the Gambia River to Barbados—might be made in as little as three weeks, with favoring winds. If the course was much longer, and if the ship was becalmed in the doldrums or driven back by storms, it might take more than three months to cross the Atlantic, and slaves and sailors would be put on short rations long before the end of the Middle Passage.

On a canvas of heroic size, Thomas Stothard, Esq., of the Royal Academy, depicted "The Voyage of the Sable Venus from Angola to the West Indies." His painting is handsomely reproduced in the second volume of Bryan Edwards' *History of the West Indies,* where it appears beside a poem on the same allegorical subject by an unnamed Jamaican author, perhaps Edwards himself. In the painting the ship that carries the Sable Venus is an immense scallop shell, in which she sits upright on a velvet throne. Except for bracelets, anklets, and a collar of pearls, she wears nothing but a narrow embroidered girdle. Her look is soft and sensuous, and in grace she yields nothing—so the poem insists—to Botticelli's white Venus,

> In FLORENCE, where she's seen;
> Both just alike, except the white,
> No difference, no—none at night
> The beauteous dames between.

The joint message of the poem and the painting is simple to the point of coarseness: that slave women are preferable to English girls at night, being passionate and accessible; but the message is embellished with a wealth of classical details, to show the painter's learning. Two legendary dolphins draw the bark of Venus toward the West. Triton leads one of them, while blowing his wreathèd horn. Two mischievous loves gambol about the other dolphin. There are cherubs above the woolly head of Venus, fanning her with ostrich plumes. In the calm distance a grampus discharges his column of spray. Cupid, from above, is shooting an arrow at Neptune, who strides ahead bearing the Union Jack. As the poet (who calls the dolphins "winged fish") describes the idyllic scene:

> The winged fish, in purple trace
> The chariot drew; with easy grace
>     Their azure rein she guides:
> And now they fly, and now they swim;
> Now o'er the wave they lightly skim,
>     Or dart beneath the tides.

Meanwhile the Sable Venus, if she was a living woman borne from Angola to the West Indies, was roaming the deck of a ship that stank of excrement, so that, as with any slaver, "You could smell it five miles down wind." She had been torn from her husband and her children, she had been branded on the left buttock, and she had been carried to the ship bound hand and foot, lying in the bilge at the bottom of a dugout canoe. Now she was the prey of the ship's officers, in danger of being flogged to death if she resisted them. Her reward if she yielded was a handful of beads or a sailor's kerchief to tie around her waist.

Here is how she and her shipmates spent the day.

If the weather was clear, they were brought on deck at eight o'clock in the morning. The men were attached by their leg irons to the great chain that ran along the bulwarks on both sides of the ship; the women and half-grown boys were allowed to wander at will. About nine o'clock the slaves were served their first meal of the day. If they were from the Windward Coast, the fare consisted of boiled rice, millet, or cornmeal, which might be cooked with a few lumps of salt beef abstracted from the sailors' rations. If they were from the Bight of Biafra, they were fed stewed yams, but the Congos and the Angolans preferred manioc or plantains. With the food they were all given half a pint of water, served out in a pannikin.

After the morning meal came a joyless ceremony called "dancing the slaves." "Those who were in irons," says Dr. Thomas Trotter, surgeon of the *Brookes* in 1783, "were ordered to stand up and make what motions they could, leaving a passage for such as were out of irons to dance around the deck." Dancing was prescribed as a therapeutic measure, a specific against suicidal melancholy, and also against scurvy—although in the latter case it was a useless torture for men with swollen limbs. While sailors paraded the deck, each with a cat-o'-nine-tails in his right hand, the men slaves "jumped in their irons" until their ankles were bleeding flesh. One sailor told Parliament, "I was employed to dance the men, while another person danced the women." Music was provided by a slave thumping on a broken drum or an upturned kettle, or by an African banjo, if there was one aboard, or perhaps by a sailor with a bagpipe or a fiddle. Slaving captains sometimes advertised for "A person that can play on the Bagpipes, for a Guinea ship." The slaves were also told to sing. Said Dr. Claxton after his voyage in the *Young Hero*, "They sing, but not for their amusement. The captain ordered them to sing, and they sang songs of sorrow. Their sickness, fear of being beaten, their hunger, and the memory of their country, &c, are the usual subjects."

While some of the sailors were dancing the slaves, others were sent below to scrape and swab out the sleeping rooms. It was a sickening task, and it was not well performed unless the captain imposed an iron discipline. James Barbot, Sr., was proud of the discipline maintained on the *Albion-Frigate*. "We were very nice," he says, "in keeping the places where the slaves lay clean and neat, appointing some of the ship's crew to do that office constantly and thrice a week we perfumed betwixt decks with a quantity of good vinegar in pails, and red-hot iron bullets in them, to expel the bad air, after the place had been well washed and scrubbed with brooms." Captain Hugh Crow, the last legal English slaver, was famous for his housekeeping. "I always took great pains," he says, "to promote the health and comfort of all on board, by proper diet, regularity, exercise, and cleanliness, for I considered that on keeping the ship clean and orderly, which was always my hobby, the success of our voyage mainly depended." Consistently he lost fewer slaves in the Middle Passage than the other captains, some of whom had the filth in the hold cleaned out only once a week. A few left their slaves to wallow in excrement during the whole Atlantic passage.

At three or four in the afternoon the slaves were fed their second meal, often a repetition of the first. Sometimes, instead of African food, they were given horse beans, the cheapest provender from Europe. The beans were boiled to a pulp, then covered with a mixture of palm oil, flour, water, and red pepper, which the sailors called "slabber sauce." Most of the slaves detested horse beans, especially if they were used to eating yams or manioc. Instead of eating the pulp, they would, unless carefully watched, pick it up by handfuls and throw it in each other's faces. That second meal was the end of their day. As soon as it was finished they were sent below, under the guard of sailors charged with stowing them away on their bare floors and platforms. The tallest men were placed amidships, where the vessel was widest; the shorter ones were tumbled into the stern. Usually there was only room for them to sleep on their sides, "spoon fashion." Captain William Littleton told Parliament that slaves in the ships on which he sailed might lie on their backs if they wished—"though perhaps," he conceded, "it might be difficult all at the same time."

After stowing their cargo, the sailors climbed out of the hatchway, each clutching his cat-o'-nine-tails: then the hatchway gratings were closed and barred. Sometimes in the night, as the sailors lay on deck and tried to sleep, they heard from below "an howling melancholy noise, expressive of extreme anguish." When Dr. Trotter told his interpreter, a slave woman, to inquire about the cause of the noise, "she discovered it to be owing to their having dreamt they were in their own country, and finding themselves when awake, in the hold of a slave ship."

More often the noise heard by the sailors was that of quarreling among the slaves. The usual occasion for quarrels was their problem of reaching the latrines. These were inadequate and hard to find in the darkness of the crowded hold, especially by men who were ironed together in pairs.

> In each of the apartments [says Dr. Falconbridge] are placed three or four large buckets, of a conical form, nearly two feet in diameter at the bottom and only one foot at the top and in depth about twenty-eight inches, to which, when necessary, the negroes have recourse. It often happens that those who are placed at a distance from the buckets, in endeavoring to get to them, tumble over their companions, in consequence of their being shackled. These accidents, although unavoidable, are productive of continual quarrels in which some of them are always bruised. In this situation, unable to proceed and prevented from going to the tubs, they desist from the attempt; and as the necessities of nature are not to be resisted, they ease themselves as they lie.

In squalls or rainy weather, the slaves were never brought on deck. They were served their two meals in the hold, where the air became too thick and poisonous to breathe. Says Dr. Falconbridge, "For the purpose of admitting fresh air, most of the ships in the slave-trade are provided, between the decks, with five or six air-ports on each side of the ship, of about six inches in length and four in breadth; in addition to which, some few ships, but not one in twenty, have what they denominate wind-sails." These were funnels made of canvas and so placed as to direct a current of air into the hold. "But whenever the sea is rough and the rain heavy," Falconbridge continues, "it becomes necessary to shut these and every other conveyance by which the air is admitted. . . . The negroes' rooms very soon become intolerably hot. The confined air, rendered noxious by the effluvia exhaled from their bodies and by being repeatedly breathed, soon produces fevers and fluxes which generally carry off great numbers of them."

Dr. Trotter says that when tarpaulins were thrown over the gratings, the slaves would cry, "Kickeraboo, kickeraboo, we are dying, we are dying." "I have known," says Henry Ellison, a sailor before the mast, "in the Middle Passage, in rains, slaves confined below for some time. I have frequently seen them faint through heat, the steam coming through the gratings, like a furnace." Falconbridge gives one instance of their sufferings.

> Some wet and blowing weather [he says] having occasioned the port-holes to be shut and the grating to be covered, fluxes and fevers among the negroes ensued. While they were in this situation, I frequently went down among them till at length their rooms became so extremely hot as to be only bearable for a very short time. But the excessive heat was not the only thing that rendered their situation intolerable. The deck, that is, the floor of their rooms, was so covered with the blood and mucus which had proceeded from them in consequence of the flux, that it resembled a slaughter-house. . . . Numbers of the slaves having fainted they were carried upon deck where several of them died and the rest with great difficulty were restored. It had nearly proved fatal to me also. The climate was too warm to admit the wearing of any clothing but a shirt and that I had pulled off before I went down; notwithstanding which, by only continuing among them for about a quarter of an hour, I was so overcome with the heat, stench and foul air that I nearly fainted; and it was only with assistance that I could get on deck. The consequence was that I soon after fell sick of the same disorder from which I did not recover for several months.

Not surprisingly, the slaves often went mad. Falconbridge mentions a woman on the *Emilia* who had to be chained to the deck. She had lucid intervals, however, and during one of these she was sold to a planter in Jamaica. Men who went insane might be flogged to death, to make sure that they were not malingering. Some were simply clubbed on the head and thrown overboard.

While the slaves were on deck they had to be watched at all times to keep them from committing suicide. Says Captain Phillips of the *Hannibal*, "We had about 12 negroes did wilfully drown themselves, and others starv'd themselves to death; for," he explained, " 'tis their belief that when they die they return home to their own country and friends again." This belief was reported from various regions, at various periods of the trade, but it seems to have been especially prevalent among the Ibo of eastern Nigeria. In 1788, nearly a hundred years after the *Hannibal's* voyage, Ecroide Claxton was the surgeon who attended a shipload of Ibo. "Some of the slaves," he testified, "wished to die on an idea that they should then get back to their own country. The captain in order to obviate this idea, thought of an expedient viz. to cut off the heads of those who died intimating to them that if determined to go, they must return without heads. The slaves were accordingly brought up to witness the operation. One of them by a violent exertion got loose and flying to the place where the nettings had been unloosed in order to empty the tubs, he darted overboard. The ship brought to, a man was placed in the main chains to catch him which he perceiving, made signs which words cannot express expressive of his happiness in escaping. He then went down and was seen no more."

Dr. Isaac Wilson, a surgeon in the Royal Navy, made a Guinea voyage on the *Elizabeth*, Captain John Smith, who was said to be very humane. Nevertheless, Wilson was assigned the duty of whipping the slaves. "Even in the act of chastisement," Wilson says, "I have seen them look up at me with a smile, and, in their own language, say, 'presently we shall be no more.'" One woman on the *Elizabeth* found some rope yarn, which she tied to the armorer's vise; she fastened the other end round her neck and was found dead in the morning. On the *Brookes* when Thomas Trotter was her surgeon, there was a man who, after being accused of witchcraft, had been sold into slavery with his whole family. During his first night on shipboard he tried to cut his throat. Dr. Trotter sewed up the wound, but on the following night the man not only tore out the sutures but tried to cut his throat on the other side. From the ragged edges of the wound and the blood on his fingers, he seemed to have used his nails as the only available instrument. His hands were tied together after the second wound, but he then refused all food, and he died of hunger in eight or ten days.

"Upon the negroes refusing to take food," says Falconbridge, "I have seen coals of fire, glowing hot, put on a shovel and placed so near their lips as to scorch and burn them. And this has been accompanied with threats of forcing them to swallow the coals if they persisted in refusing to eat. This generally had the required effect"; but if the Negroes still refused, they were flogged day after day. Lest flogging prove ineffective, every Guineaman was provided with a special instrument called the "speculum oris," or mouth opener. It looked like a pair of dividers with notched legs and with a thumbscrew at the blunt end. The legs were closed and the notches were hammered between the slave's teeth. When the thumbscrew was tightened, the legs of the instrument separated, forcing open the slave's mouth; then food was poured into it through a funnel.

Even the speculum oris sometimes failed with a slave determined to die. Dr. Wilson reports another incident of his voyage on the *Elizabeth*, this one concerning a young man who had refused to eat for several days. Mild means were used to divert him from his resolution, "as well as promises," Wilson says, "that he should have anything he wished for; but still he refused to eat. He was then whipped with the cat but this also was ineffectual. He always kept his teeth so fast that it was impossible to get anything down. We then endeavored to introduce a Speculum Oris between his teeth but the points were too obtuse to enter and next tried a bolus knife but with the same effect. In this state he was for four or five days when he was brought up as dead to be thrown overboard. . . . I finding life still existing, repeated my endeavours though in vain and two days afterwards he was brought up again in the same state as before. . . . In his own tongue he asked for water which was given him. Upon this we began to have hopes of dissuading him from his design but he again shut his teeth as fast as ever and resolved to die and on the ninth day from his first refusal he died."

One deadly scourge of the Guinea cargoes was a phenomenon called "fixed melancholy." Even slaves who were well fed, treated with kindness, and kept under relatively sanitary conditions would often die one after another for no apparent reason; they simply had no wish to live. Fixed melancholy seems to have been especially rife among the Ibo and among the food-gathering tribes of the Gaboon, but no Negro nation was immune to it. Although the disease was noted from the earliest days of the trade, perhaps the best description of it was written by George Howe, an American medical student who shipped on an illegal slaver in 1859:

> Notwithstanding their apparent good health [Howe says] each morning three or four dead would be found, brought upon deck, taken by the arms and heels, and tossed overboard as unceremoniously as an empty bottle. Of what did they die? And [why] always at night? In the barracoons it was known that if a Negro was not amused and kept in motion, he would mope, squat down with his chin on his knees and arms clasped about his legs and in a very short time die. Among civilized races it is thought almost impossible to hold one's breath until death follows. It is thought the African can do so. They had no means of concealing anything and certainly did not kill each other. One of the duties of the slave-captains was when they found a slave sitting with knees up and head drooping, to start them up, run them about the deck, give them a small ration of rum, and divert them until in a normal condition.

It is impossible for a human being to hold his breath until he dies. Once he loses consciousness, his lungs fill with air and he recovers. The simplest explanation for the slaves' ability to "will themselves dead" is that they were in a state of shock as a result of their being carried through the terrifying surf into the totally unfamiliar surroundings of the ship. In certain conditions shock can be as fatal as physical injury. There may, however, be another explanation. The communal life of many tribes was so highly organized by a system of customs, relationships, taboos, and religious ceremonies that there was practically nothing a man or a woman could do that was not prescribed by tribal law. To separate an individual from this complex system of interrelationships and suddenly place him, naked and friendless, in a completely hostile environment was in some respects a greater shock than any amount of physical brutality.

Dr. Wilson believed that fixed melancholy was responsible for the loss of two-thirds of the slaves who died on the *Elizabeth*. "No one who had it was ever cured," he says, "whereas those who had it not and yet were ill, recovered. The symptoms are a lowness of spirits and despondency. Hence they refuse food. This only increases the symptoms. The stomach afterwards got weak. Hence the belly ached, fluxes ensued, and they were carried off." But flux, or dysentery, is an infectious disease spread chiefly by food prepared in unsanitary conditions. The slaves, after being forced to wallow in filth, were also forced to eat with their fingers. In spite of the real losses from fixed melancholy, the high death rate on Guinea ships was due to somatic more than to psychic afflictions.

Along with their human cargoes, crowded, filthy, undernourished, and terrified out of the wish to live, the ships also carried an invisible cargo of microbes, bacilli, spirochetes, viruses, and intestinal worms from one continent to another; the Middle Passage was a crossroads and marketplace of diseases. From Europe came smallpox, measles (less deadly to Africans than to American Indians), gonorrhea, and syphilis (which last Columbus's sailors had carried from America to Europe). The African diseases were yellow fever (to which the natives were more resistant than white men), dengue, blackwater fever, and malaria (which was not specifically African, but which most of the slaves carried in their bloodstreams). If anopheles mosquitoes were present, malaria spread from the slaves through any new territories to which they were carried. Other African diseases were amoebic and various forms of bacillary dysentery (all known as "the bloody flux"), Guinea worms, hookworm (possibly African in origin, but soon endemic in the warmer parts of the New World), yaws, elephantiasis, and leprosy.

The particular affliction of the white sailors after escaping from the fevers of the Guinea Coast was scurvy, a deficiency disease to which they were exposed by their monotonous rations of salt beef and sea biscuits. The daily tot of lime juice (originally lemon juice) that prevented scurvy was almost never served on merchantmen during the days of the legal slave trade, and in fact was not prescribed in the Royal Navy until 1795. Although the slaves were also subject to scurvy, they fared better in this respect than the sailors, partly because they made only one leg of the triangular voyage and partly because their rough diet was sometimes richer in vitamins. But sailors and slaves alike were swept away by smallpox and "the bloody flux," and sometimes they went blind from various forms of ophthalmia, the worst of which seems to have been a gonorrheal infection of the eyes.

Smallpox was feared more than other diseases, since the surgeons had no means of combating it until the end of the eighteenth century. One man with smallpox infected a whole vessel, unless —as sometimes happened—he was tossed overboard when the first scabs appeared. Captain Wilson of the *Briton* lost more than half his cargo of 375 slaves by not listening to his surgeon. It was the last slave brought on board who had the disease, says Henry Ellison, who made the voyage. "The doctor told Mr. Wilson it was the small-pox," Ellison continues. "He would not believe it, but said he would keep him, as he was a fine man. It soon broke out amongst the slaves. I have seen the platform one continued scab. We hauled up eight or ten slaves dead of a morning. The flesh and skin peeled off their wrists when taken hold of, being entirely mortified." But dysentery, though not so much feared, could cause as many deaths. Ellison testifies that he made two voyages on the *Nightingale*, Captain Carter. On the first voyage the slaves were so crowded that thirty boys "messed and slept in the long boat all through the Middle Passage, there being no room below"; and still the vessel lost only five or six slaves in all, out of a cargo of 270. On the second voyage, however, the *Nightingale* buried "about 150, chiefly of fevers and flux. We had 250 when we left the coast."

Dr. Claxton sailed from Bonny on the *Young Hero*, Captain Molyneux. "We had 250 slaves," he says, "of whom 132 died, chiefly of the flux. . . . The steerage and the boys' room were insufficient to receive the sick, so greatly did the disorder prevail. We were therefore obliged to place together those that were and those that were not diseased, and in consequence the disease and mortality spread more and more." The hold was swimming with blood and mucus. Toward the end of her voyage the *Young Hero* met another vessel with almost the same name—the *Hero*, Captain Wilson—and learned that she had lost 360 slaves, more than half her cargo. Most of them had died of smallpox. When moved from one place to another, they left marks of their skin and blood upon the deck, and the other surgeon told Claxton that it was "the most horrid sight he had ever seen."

The average mortality in the Middle Passage is impossible to state accurately from the surviving records. Some famous voyages were made without the loss of a single slave, as notably by Captains John Newton, William Macintosh, and Hugh Crow. On one group of nine voyages between 1766 and 1780, selected at random, the vessels carried 2362 slaves and there were no epidemics of disease. The total loss of slaves was 154, or about 6½ per cent. On another list of twenty voyages compiled by Thomas Clarkson the abolitionist, the vessels carried 7904 slaves and lost 2053, or 26 per cent. Balancing high and low figures together, the English Privy Council in 1789 arrived at an estimate of 12½ per cent for the average mortality in the Middle Passage. That comes close to the percentage reckoned long afterward from the manifests of French vessels sailing from Nantes. Between 1748 and 1782 the Nantes slavers bought 146,799 slaves and sold 127,133 on the other side of the Atlantic. The difference of 19,666 would indicate a loss of 13 per cent in the voyage.

Of course there were further losses. To the mortality in the Middle Passage, the Privy Council added 4½ per cent for the deaths of slaves in harbors before they were sold, and 33 per cent for deaths during the seasoning process, making a total of 50 per cent. If those figures are correct (U. B. Phillips, the author of *American Negro Slavery*, thinks they are somewhat high), then only one slave was added to the New World labor force for every two purchased on the Guinea Coast.

To keep the figures in perspective, it might be added that the mortality among slaves in the Middle Passage was possibly no greater than that of white indentured servants or even of free Irish, Scottish, and German immigrants in the North Atlantic crossing. On the better commanded Guineamen it was probably much less, and for a simple economic reason. There was no profit in a slaving voyage until the Negroes were landed alive and sold; therefore the better captains took care of their cargoes. If the Negroes died in spite of good care, the captains regarded their deaths as a personal affront. "No gold-finders," lamented Captain Phillips of the *Hannibal*, who lost nearly half of his cargo from the bloody flux, "can endure so much noisome slavery as they do who carry negroes; for those have some respite and satisfaction, but we endure twice the misery; and yet by their mortality our voyages are ruin'd, and we pine and fret our selves to death, to think that we should undergo so much misery, and take so much pains to so little purpose." It was different on the North Atlantic crossing, where even the hold and steerage passengers paid their fares before coming aboard, and where it was of little concern to the captain whether they lived or died.

After leaving the Portuguese island of São Thomé—if he had watered there—a slaving captain bore westward along the equator for a thousand miles, and then northwestward toward the Cape Verde Islands. This was the tedious part of the Middle Passage. Along the equator the vessel might be delayed for weeks by calms or storms; sometimes it had to return to the African coast for fresh provisions. Then, "on leaving the Gulf of Guinea," says the author of a *Universal Geography* published in the early nineteenth century, ". . . that part of the ocean must be traversed, so fatal to navigators, where long calms detain the ships under a sky charged with electric clouds, pouring down by turns torrents of rain and of fire. This *sea of thunder*, being a focus of mortal diseases, is avoided as much as possible, both in approaching the coasts of Africa and those of America." It was not until reaching the latitude of the Cape Verde Islands that the vessel fell in with the Northeast Trades and was able to make a swift passage to the West Indies.

Ecroide Claxton's ship, the *Young Hero*, was one of those delayed for weeks before reaching the trade winds. "We were so streightened for provisions," he testified, "that if we had been ten more days at sea, we must either have eaten the slaves that died, or have made the living slaves *walk the plank*," a term, he explained, that was widely used by Guinea captains. There are no authenticated records of cannibalism in the Middle Passage, but there are many accounts of slaves killed for various reasons. English captains believed that French vessels carried poison in their medicine chests, "with which they can destroy their negroes in a calm, contagious sickness, or short provisions." They told the story of a Frenchman from Brest who had a long passage and had to poison his slaves; only twenty of them reached Haiti out of five hundred. Even the cruelest English captains regarded this practice as Latin, depraved, and uncovered by their insurance policies. In an emergency they simply jettisoned part of their cargo.

The most famous case involving jettisoned slaves was that of the *Zong* out of Liverpool, Luke Collingwood master. The *Zong* had left São Thomé on September 6, 1781, with a cargo of four hundred and forty slaves and a white crew of seventeen. There was sickness aboard during a slow passage; more than sixty Negroes died, with seven of the seamen, and many of the remaining slaves were so weakened by dysentery that it was a question whether they could be sold in Jamaica. On November 29, after they had already sighted land in the West Indies, Captain Collingwood called his officers together. He announced that there were only two hundred gallons of fresh water left in the casks, not enough for the remainder of the voyage. If the slaves died of thirst or illness, he explained, the loss would fall on the owners of the vessel; but if they were thrown into the sea it would be a legal jettison, covered by insurance. "It would not be so cruel to throw the poor sick wretches into the sea," he argued, "as to suffer them to linger out a few days under the disorders to which they were afflicted."

The mate, James Kelsal, demurred at first, saying there was "no present want of water to justify such a measure," but the captain outtalked him. To quote from a legal document, "The said Luke Collingwood picked, or caused to be picked out, from the cargo of the same ship, one hundred and thirty-three slaves, all or most of whom were sick or weak, and not likely to live; and ordered the crew by turns to throw them into the sea; which most inhuman order was cruelly complied with." A first "parcel," as the sailors called them, of fifty-four slaves went overboard that same day, November 29. A second parcel, this time of forty-two, followed them on December 1, still leaving thirty-six slaves out of those condemned to be jettisoned. (One man seems to have died from natural causes.) Also on December 1 there was a heavy rain and the sailors collected six casks of water, enough to carry the vessel into port. But Collingwood stuck to his plan, and the last parcel of condemned slaves was brought on deck a few days later. Twenty-six of them were handcuffed, then swung into the sea. The last ten refused to let the sailors come near them; instead they vaulted over the bulwarks and were drowned like the others.

On December 22 the Zong dropped anchor in Kingston harbor after a passage of three months and sixteen days. Collingwood sold the remainder of his slaves, then sailed his vessel to England, where his owners claimed thirty pounds of insurance money for each of the one hundred and thirty-two jettisoned slaves. The underwriters refused to pay, and the case was taken to court. At a first trial the jury found for the owners, since "they had no doubt . . . that the case of slaves was the same as if horses had been thrown overboard." The underwriters appealed to the Court of Exchequer, and Lord Mansfield presided. After admitting that the law supported the owners of the Zong, he went on to say that "a higher law [applies to] this very shocking case." He found for the underwriters. It was the first case in which an English court ruled that a cargo of slaves could not be treated simply as merchandise.

Often a slave ship came to grief in the last few days of the Middle Passage. It might be taken by a French privateer out of Martinique, or it might disappear in a tropical hurricane, or it might be wrecked on a shoal almost in sight of its harbor. There was a famous wreck on Morant Keys off the eastern end of Jamaica; the sailors took refuge on a sandspit with a scanty store of provisions but plenty of rum, then massacred the slaves who tried to follow them. Only thirty-three Negroes survived (and were later exposed for sale in Kingston) out of about four hundred. On a few ships there was an epidemic of suicide at the last moment. Thus, when the *Prince of Orange* anchored at St. Kitts in 1737, more than a hundred Negro men jumped overboard. "Out of the whole," Captain Japhet Bird reported, "we lost 33 of as good Men Slaves as we had on board, who would not endeavour to save themselves, but resolv'd to die, and sunk directly down. Many more of them were taken up almost drown'd, some of them died since, but not the Owners Loss, they being sold before any Discovery was made of the Injury the Salt Water had done them. . . . This Misfortune was owing to one of their Countrymen, who came on board and in a joking manner told the Slaves that they were first to have their Eyes put out, and then to be eaten, with a great many other nonsensical Falsities."

These, however, were exceptional misfortunes, recounted as horror stories in the newspapers of the time. Usually the last two or three days of the Middle Passage were a comparatively happy period. All the slaves, or all but a few, might be released from their irons. When there was a remaining stock of provisions, the slaves were given bigger meals—to fatten them for market—and as much water as they could drink. Sometimes on the last day—if the ship was commanded by an easy-going captain—there was a sort of costume party on deck, with the women slaves dancing in the sailors' cast-off clothing. Then the captain was rowed ashore to arrange for the disposition of his cargo.

There were several fashions of selling the slaves. In a few instances the whole cargo was consigned to a single rich planter, or to a group of planters. More often a West Indian factor took charge of retail sales, for a commission of 15 per cent on the gross amount and 5 per cent more on the net proceeds. When the captain himself had to sell his slaves, he ferried them ashore, had them drawn up in a ragged line of march, and paraded them through town with bagpipes playing, before exposing them to buyers in the public square. J. G. Stedman, a young officer in the Scots Brigade employed as a mercenary by the Dutch in their obstinate efforts to suppress the slave revolts in Surinam, witnessed such a parade. "The whole party was," he says, ". . . a resurrection of skin and bones . . . risen from the grave or escaped from Surgeon's Hall." The slaves exposed for sale were "walking skeletons covered over with a piece of tanned leather."

But the commonest method of selling a cargo was a combination of the "scramble"—to be described presently—and the vendue or public auction "by inch of candle." First the captain, probably with the West Indian factor at his side, went over the cargo and picked out the slaves who were maimed or diseased. These were carried to a tavern and auctioned off, with a lighted candle beside the auctioneer; bids were received until an inch of candle had burned. The price of these "refuse" slaves sold at auction was usually less than half of that paid for a healthy Negro; sometimes it was as little as five or six dollars a head. "I was informed by a mulatto woman," Falconbridge says, "that she purchased a sick slave at Grenada, upon speculation, for the small sum of one dollar, as the poor wretch was apparently dying of the flux." There were some slaves who could not be sold for even a dollar, and they were often left to die on the wharfs without food or water.

There were horse traders' methods of hiding the presence of disease. Yaws, for example, could be concealed by a mixture of iron rust and gunpowder, a practice which Edward Long, the Jamaica historian, denounces as a "wicked fraud." Falconbridge tells of a Liverpool captain who "boasted of his having cheated some Jews by the following stratagem: A lot of slaves, afflicted with the flux, being about to be landed for sale, he directed the surgeon to stop the anus of each of them with oakum. . . . The Jews, when they examine them, oblige them to stand up, in order to see if there be any discharge; and when they do not perceive this appearance, they consider it as a symptom of recovery. In the present instance, such an appearance being prevented, the bargain was struck, and they were accordingly sold. But it was not long before a discovery ensued. The excruciating pain which the prevention of a discharge of such an acrimonious nature occasioned, not being to be borne by the poor wretches, the temporary obstruction was removed, and the deluded purchasers were speedily convinced of the imposition."

The healthy slaves remaining after an auction were sold by "scramble," that is, at standard prices for each man, each woman, each boy, and each girl in the cargo. The prices were agreed upon with the purchasers, who then scrambled for their pick of the slaves. During his four voyages Falconbridge was present at a number of scrambles. "In the *Emilia*," he says, "at Jamaica, the ship was darkened with sails, and covered round. The men slaves were placed on the main deck, and the women on the quarter deck. The purchasers on shore were informed a gun would be fired when they were ready to open the sale. A great number of people came on board with tallies or cards in their hands, with their own names upon them, and rushed through the barricado door with the ferocity of brutes. Some had three or four handkerchiefs tied together, to encircle as many as they thought fit for their purpose." For the slaves, many of whom thought they were about to be eaten, it was the terrifying climax of a terrifying voyage. Another of Falconbridge's ships, the *Alexander*, sold its cargo by scramble in a slave yard at Grenada. The women, he says, were frightened out of their wits. Several of them climbed over the fence and ran about Saint George's town as if they were mad. In his second voyage, while lying in Kingston harbor, he saw a sale by scramble on board the *Tyral*, Captain Macdonald. Forty or fifty of the slaves jumped overboard—"all of which, however," Falconbridge told the House of Commons, "he believes were taken up again."

# 6

# Captains and Crews

*During the time I was engaged in the slave trade I never had the least scruples as to its lawfulness.*
                                                —The Reverend John Newton

*When a Parliamentary Committee asked Henry Ellison, who had served as a seaman on eight slavers, whether "he considered it more advantageous to become a sailor or to go to gaol," he replied after some thought, "To become a sailor—I should suppose."*
                                                —No. 111, p. 377

THE CAPTAINS OF THE SLAVERS HAD TO BE FAR MORE THAN SIMPLE merchant skippers. They also had to be fighters, for the Middle Passage was as infested with privateers and pirates as it was with sharks. The slavers went heavily armed; so heavily, in fact, that when opportunity offered they often turned privateers themselves and preyed on foreign vessels. Several captains made a habit of arming their slaves in these engagements and found that the Negroes fought stoutly for their masters.

One of the most famous of these "fighting captains" was Billy Boates. Captain Billy had been abandoned as a baby in an open boat on the Liverpool dockside; hence his last name. Some benevo-

131

lent individual heard the child crying and took him to an orphanage. The boy grew up, was apprenticed to a shipmaster, and eventually came to command his own vessel. Captain Billy fought many times and made some noteworthy runs, losing only a small percentage of his slaves.

His most famous exploit occurred off the Leeward Islands in 1758, while he was in command of the *Knight*. He was ordered to surrender by a French privateer with "twelve carriage guns and full of men." Although heavily outclassed, Captain Billy armed his slaves and refused to strike. A terrific engagement followed, during which the *Knight* was boarded several times, but, as the captain expressed it, "never a Dago that got over the rail lived to return." The Frenchman was finally beaten off, and Captain Billy landed 360 of his original cargo of 398 slaves in Jamaica.

Later he retired from active duty and used his profits to outfit privateersmen. He became one of the leading merchants and shipowners in Liverpool. One of his ships captured a Spanish vessel loaded with gold. When Captain Billy heard the good news he ran through the streets of Liverpool, wildly shouting, "Billy Boates! Born a beggar, die a lord!" He died at the age of seventy-eight, not a lord, but esteemed and respected by all.

Not all slaving captains were Billy Boateses, but they had to be men who were ready for any emergency—attack, mutiny, or epidemic. Here is a letter from Barbados, February 28, 1758, written by Captain Joseph Harrison of the *Rainbow* to the vessel's owners, Messrs. Thomas Rumbold & Co., of Liverpool:

> We arrived here on the 25 inst. in company with Capt. Perkins from Bonny, and Capt. Forde from Angola whom we fell in with at St. Thomas's [São Thomé]. The packet arrived here from England the day after us. I expect to sail from hence for South Carolina in five days, having on board 225 slaves, all in good health except eight. On the 23rd. of June last, I had the misfortune to fall in with a French brig privateer, of fourteen 6-pounders, to leeward of Popo. We engaged him four hours, and were so near for above four glasses, that I expected every moment we should run on board him, as he had shot away all my running rigging

and the fluke of my small bow anchor. My standing rigging and sails were mostly cut to pieces, and the privateer was in a little better condition. Fifteen of his shot went through and through my sides, we being scarce the length of the ship from one another. I lost in the engagement my boatswain—William Jackson —Robert Williams—and Henry Williams. My first and second mates, three landsmen, and one servant wounded. The privateer being well satisfied sheered off. We were three days in repairing our rigging, etc., and on the 28th. got over the Bar of Benin and found only one vessel there, viz., a Portuguese sloop at Warree. I purchased eight slaves on the windward coast, and 261 at Benin, besides 5,400 weight of ivory. Leaving the river, Nov. 9th, we arrived at St. Thomas's Dec. 17th. from whence our three vessels sailed, Jan. 4th.

The Middle Passage, made in fifty-two days—good time from São Thomé—was a little less eventful. Still, "I have buried all my officers," Captain Harrison continued, "except my first and third mates and gunner. Having lost since left Liverpool, 25 white people and 44 negroes. The negroes rose on us after we left St. Thomas's; they killed my linguister whom I got at Benin, and we then secured them without farther loss. We have an account of five privateers being to windward of Barbadoes, by a retaken vessel brought in here this day, so that we shall run a great risk when we leave Barbadoes."

The most remarkable slaver and one of the most curious personalities of the eighteenth century, which produced many famous eccentrics, was Captain (later the Reverend) John Newton, who wrote the famous hymn "How Sweet the Name of Jesus Sounds" while waiting on the coast for a slave coffle to arrive.

Newton was born on July 24, 1725. His father was a merchant captain, a stern disciplinarian, and the boy lived in terror of him. His mother, to whom he turned for affection, died when he was seven. At ten he left school to go to sea on his father's ship. The boy kept passing through successive stages of extreme feeling: first despondency, then religious enthusiasm—before he was sixteen he had dedicated himself to the ministry four times—then a period of wild profanity and drunkenness that led to another period of despondency. During the sinful periods his oaths were so blasphemous that the sailors began to fear that God's vengeance would be visited on their ship. Newton himself saw the direct hand of God in every event. Once when a friend asked him to go rowing and Newton refused, the boat was upset and the friend was drowned. Newton interpreted this as a divine warning to mend his ways, but soon he lapsed once more.

When he was sixteen, his father despaired of being able to teach the boy and sent him to Jamaica on another ship. Newton proved to be as incorrigible with the new commander as he had been with his father. On his return to England in 1742 he met a thirteen-year-old girl named Mary Catlett and fell in love with her. Later he was to say that his passion for the girl was more like the legendary transports of Tristan for Isolde or Romeo for Juliet than like a normal romance. Rather than leave Mary he deserted his ship, but he was caught and sent back to sea.

He made other voyages, but always, when the ship reached England, he deserted in order to see his beloved Mary. The captain of a merchantman on which he served was so brutal that Newton seriously considered murdering him. He might have done so had he not been lying in his hammock one afternoon when a shipmate, admittedly joking, threatened to cut him down. Newton went into such a fury that he did not trust himself to face the shipmate and went on deck. The ship was anchored in the harbor of Madeira, and near by was a Guineaman taking on stores. Newton had heard about the dissolute lives led by the crews of most slavers, and he determined to join this one, for then, he said to himself, "I could be as abandoned as I liked." His own captain was happy to let him go.

On board the Guineaman, Newton made himself so generally hated that he knew the captain would get rid of him as soon as the vessel reached the West Indies. He therefore asked the Sierra Leone factor who supplied the ship with slaves if he could stay in

Africa as the factor's assistant. Soon the Guineaman departed, leaving Newton behind. Whatever sins he had committed, he was now punished for them. The factor had a Negro wife who delighted in humiliating the helpless young white man. She starved him, then sometimes allowed him the scraps from her own plate as a sign of condescension. Screaming with delight, she would watch him devour the scraps, but she insisted on being thanked for her beneficence. There were "few even of the negroes themselves," Newton says, ". . . but thought themselves too good to speak to me."

Then Newton contracted a fever. He lay delirious in his hut, and the factor's wife would not send him so much as a cup of water. He would have died except for the kindness of the slaves waiting to be sold, who gave him what they could spare from their meager rations. The factor had planted some lime-tree saplings. To taunt the boy he remarked sarcastically, "No doubt you'll return as captain of your ship and pluck the limes that will grow on these trees." Newton never forgot his gibe.

After Newton had recovered, he saw a ship cruising along the coast; evidently a slaver looking for a cargo. Newton made the traditional smoke-signal that meant trade, and a boat came ashore. By a remarkable coincidence, he discovered that the captain of the vessel was a friend of his father, who had been sent to find out what had happened to him. Once aboard, Newton began to drink heavily and used such foul language that the captain expressed regret at having rescued him. Then the ship encountered a series of unprecedented storms. The crew regarded Newton as a Jonah and asked that he be thrown overboard. Newton himself never doubted that the tempest had been sent to punish him for his transgressions. On March 9, 1748, a date Newton never forgot, the ship was struck by such a storm that she nearly sank. This, Newton felt, was the last convincing bit of evidence that God was determined to convert or destroy him. He became converted and never again lapsed into his old habits.

Newton reached England and went at once to see Mary Catlett, who had never been a moment out of his thoughts. He obtained her parents' consent to their marriage if he could support the girl. Newton knew of only one way to make a substantial living: the slave trade. He made his first voyage as a slaver to Sierra Leone that same year as mate of a Guineaman. The voyage was so successful that he was able to marry on his return. He was made captain of the *Duke of Argyle*, and later of the *African*. His most successful voyage was in 1753, when he reached the West Indies with the happy record of not having lost a single slave. Newton attributed his success to God's help and insisted that the crew attend a special church ceremony to return thanks.

On one of his voyages, he returned to the old barracoon at Sierra Leone and confronted the black wife of his former master. She expected the worst and she fell on her knees to beg for mercy, but, Newton says, "I forgave her being now a Christian." He did, however, have the satisfaction of being the captain of his ship and of picking limes from the factor's trees.

In 1764 Newton left the sea to enter the clergy. He went to Olney, where he spent sixteen years, first as a curate and then as vicar. Later he was made rector of Saint Mary Woolnoth in London, where he became famous as the author of hymns and sermons. He and Mary were ideally happy together. When she died Newton came close to a complete collapse, for he was unable to reconcile her death with the justice of a benevolent God. He finally decided that God had taken Mary to punish him for giving to a human being the devotion which only the Almighty should expect.

Toward the latter part of his life, Newton became a vehement anti-slavery advocate. He wrote, "Custom, example and interest had blinded my eyes. I did it ignorantly . . . I should have been overwhelmed with distress and terror if I had known or even suspected that I was acting wrongly. . . . I only thought myself bound to treat the slaves under my care with gentleness and to consult their ease and convenience so far as was consistent with the safety of the whole family of whites and blacks on board my ship." Newton died in 1807 at the advanced age of eighty-three.

The last English ship to carry a legal cargo of slaves from Africa to the West Indies was the *Kitty's Amelia* of Liverpool. Her master was Hugh Crow, who for years before that last voyage had been a fighting captain even more famous than Billy Boates. Not only his crew but his slaves, it was said, respected and loved him. It was his custom to select likely young Negroes from his cargo, arm them, and teach them to fire at a bottle hung from the yardarm; every man who hit it was given a cap and a drink of grog. If the vessel was attacked, Crow expected the slaves to help defend it, and they never disappointed him.

Crow was born on the Isle of Man in 1765 and was always extravagantly proud of being a Manxman bred to the sea. At an early age he lost one of his eyes, but the other was, according to popular report, "a piercer." He was apprenticed to a boatbuilder and went to sea as a ship's carpenter in 1782, but soon attained a mate's rating. His first voyage to Guinea was in the *Prince* out of Liverpool, in 1790. Four years later, while he was chief mate of the *Gregson*, the ship was attacked by a French privateer. The *Gregson*, with a crew of only thirty-five men, fought for two hours before striking. Together with the other English survivors, Crow was sent to a French prison camp, where conditions were so bad that two thousand prisoners died within the next few months. "We wished our color had been black," Crow says in his memoirs, ". . . so we might have attracted the notice and commanded the sympathy of Fox, Wilberforce"—the anti-slavery men—"and others of our patriotic statesmen." After escaping to England, Crow shipped out at once on another Guineaman.

Either he played in extraordinary bad luck or he was of a naturally combative disposition, for he seldom made a voyage without having to fight, often against staggering odds. When he was captain of the *Will*, he was first attacked by a fast-sailing privateer

schooner, then by three frigates in Bonny River, and finally by
a French cruiser of eighteen guns. Crow beat them all off. He
reports that after the last fight the slave women "gathered round
me and saluting me in their rude but sincere manner, thanked their
gods with tears in their eyes that we had overcome the enemy."
The Liverpool merchants were also moved, in their pecuniary
fashion: they awarded him a piece of plate.

Crow's whole career was a series of sea fights, storms, shipwrecks,
and loss of his crews to the Royal Navy. When most of his seamen
were impressed by a man-of-war, as happened more than once, he
taught the slaves how to handle the vessel. Once off Tobago he was
hailed by a large French privateer that ordered him to surrender.
"I may go down with the ship," Crow answered, "but I'll not
strike." He loaded his guns with copper dross to repel the boarders.
The battle lasted four hours, with slaves manning the guns beside
the English seamen; twelve slaves and two seamen were struck
down in the fighting. Finally the Frenchman drew off. The underwriters, who had saved the insured value of the ship and its cargo,
awarded Crow a plate valued at two hundred pounds.

Quite possibly he was the most popular captain in the trade,
not only with English merchants and underwriters but with African kings, sailors before the mast, and even to some extent the
slaves in his cargoes. He was one of the very few Guinea captains
to give his seamen and slaves a ration of lime juice to prevent
scurvy; he even made sure that they brushed their teeth. When
Wilberforce persuaded Parliament to award a hundred pounds to
every captain who landed a cargo of slaves without losing a single
man, Crow was delighted. "Many a laugh," he reports, "have I
had at Wilberforce and his party when I got my bounty."

In Africa, Crow tried to stop the human sacrifices that were part
of certain native religions. Any attempt to interfere with the
"customs," as they were called, was often fatal for a white man,
but King Pepple and King Holiday, the joint rulers of Bonny, always spoke highly of Captain Crow. King Pepple even forgave an
attack on his royal person. Once he got drunk and came aboard

Crow's ship, the *Ceres*, while Crow was laid up with a fever. Knowing the captain's weak point, the king began to taunt him with being a Manxman, saying that the islanders "were a miserable people, poor as rats, and unable to support a king." Weak as he was, the Manxman crawled out of bed, seized a stick, and pursued the king on his hands and knees, shouting, "You villain! How dare you abuse my country!"

King Pepple fled to his canoe. As he was paddled away, he kept wailing drunkenly, "Poor boy! You can't havee king!"

Crow's next-to-last voyage was on the *Mary*, a ship of five hundred tons, one of the largest in the trade. Late one evening it was overhauled by two men-of-war, one of eighteen, the other of thirty guns. The battle raged for most of the night. One man-of-war was disabled, but the other still outgunned the *Mary*. At last Crow collapsed on the deck from loss of blood. His first mate struck the colors, saying sadly, "Sir, we can do no more." Then dawn broke and Crow saw that the two men-of-war were English; they had mistaken him for a Frenchman. "If we *were* Frenchmen," said the lieutenant in command of the boarding party, "you'd have beaten us both."

On the first Sunday after the *Mary* anchored in Kingston harbor, Crow received a visit from a great number of black men and women, the men with bright-colored neckcloths, the women with long gilt earrings. They were among the slaves who had been with him in one or another of the actions in which he had been engaged on former voyages. "God bless massa!" they shouted. "How poor massa do? Long live massa, for em da fight ebery voyage." They had even composed a calypso in his honor:

> Cap'n Crow em come again,
> But em always fight and lose some mans,
> But we glad for see em now and den,
> Wid em hearty, joyful, gay . . .
> Wid em hearty, joyful, gay ara.

The *Mary* arrived in Liverpool on May 2, 1807, one day after the law abolishing the English slave trade had gone into effect. But

Crow was immediately offered command of the *Kitty's Amelia*, a ship of three hundred tons that had already received her clearance papers. After taking on further supplies and a crew of sixty men, she sailed on July 27, the last slaver to leave an English harbor. In Bonny River, where she arrived after a voyage of seven weeks, the captain had a long palaver with King Holiday. "Crow," said the king, according to the captain's memoirs, "you and me sabby each other long time, and me know you tell me true mouth; for all captains come to river tell me you king and you big man stop we trade, and s'pose dat true, what we do? For you sabby me have too much wife, it be we country fash, and have too much child . . . and we law is, s'pose some of we child go bad and we no can sell em, we father must kill dem own child; and s'pose trade be done we force kill too much child same way. But we tink trade no stop, for all we Ju-Ju man tell we so, for dem say you country no can niber pass God A'mighty."

Crow heartily agreed with his Negro collaborator. After a long delay—for there were ten or twelve ships in the river waiting to be slaved—he sailed from Bonny with "as fine a cargo of blacks, as ever had been taken from Africa," but there seemed to be a curse on this final voyage. Cargo and crew were racked with fever and dysentery. Fire broke out in the afterhold, and Crow barely kept it from reaching the powder magazine. When he finally reached Kingston, after losing fifty slaves and thirty members of his crew, including both surgeons, he found that mortality on the *Kitty's Amelia* was only half as large as on the other slavers in the harbor. There were sixteen of these, with most of their cargoes still on board, because the market for slaves was glutted. But Crow's slaves were in better condition than those on the other vessels, and he managed to sell them at a profit.

After this final voyage Crow retired to his beloved Isle of Man with a comfortable fortune. He was, however, always bitter about the abolition of the trade, arguing that "these pretended philanthropists have . . . been the indirect cause of the death of thousands, for they have caused the trade to be transferred to other nations who carry it on in defiance of our cruisers with a cruelty and disregard for life."

Possibly the most important single element in the operation of the trade was the common seamen who manned the great fleet of slavers. Although it was the factors who supplied the human merchandise and the captains who commanded the vessels, it was the seamen who made the entire venture possible.

They could be seen in Liverpool taverns or haunting the wharves of Charleston and the sugar islands: men with yellow eyeballs, cheeks sunken with fever, and backs scarred by the cat; men left behind by their ships and begging for food; men crippled by scurvy or syphilis, but some of them still capable of laying aloft in a gale and performing feats of dexterity that might have astonished a circus acrobat. No more vivid picture of the trade exists than the stories that many of the common sailors told when called upon to testify before Parliament in 1790 and 1791; it is as if a trapdoor had been opened into hell.

Their testimony makes it clear that Guinea seamen were treated almost as badly as the wretched Negroes in the hold. Some were treated worse, including the starved and neglected crew of the *Albion*, whose surgeon said that he was "only paid for attending the slaves." The captain had almost unlimited power over his men; he was forbidden by law to strike them down with a deadly weapon, but he could, in effect, condemn them to death. Captain Saltcraig of the *Lily* used to punish his men for falling sick. A sailor named John Coffee was so crippled by scurvy that he could no longer walk, and Saltcraig for punishment had him tied up in the shrouds —"whence he begged the captain to shoot him and put him out of pain. Who answered, 'No, no, do you think I'll be hanged for you?' " When Coffee was finally released, "he lay down on his bed upon the deck and in about two hours expired."

Captain John Newton, who was incapable of such cruelty, said in a letter to his adored Mary, "I am as absolute in my small dominions . . . as any potentate in Europe. If I say to one, come,

he comes; if to another, go, he flies. If I order one person to do
something, perhaps three or four will be ambitious of a share in
the service. Not a man in the ship will eat his dinner till I please
to give him leave . . . and should I stay out till midnight (which
for that reason I never do without necessity) nobody must pre-
sume to shut their eyes till they have had the honor of seeing me
again." Newton was among the best of slaving captains. So was
Hugh Crow, but he felt impelled to apologize for the savage discipline and high mortality that prevailed on most ships in the Guinea
trade.

"It must be taken into account," Crow says in his memoirs, "that
many of the individuals" composing the crews of African ships
"were the very dregs of the community. Some of them had escaped
from gaols; others were undiscovered offenders who sought to with-
draw themselves from their country, lest they should fall into the
hands of the officers of justice. These wretched beings used to flock
to Liverpool when the ships were fitting out, and after acquiring a
few sea phrases from some crimp or other, they were shipped as
ordinary seamen, though they had never been at sea in their lives.
If, when at sea, they became saucy and insubordinate, which was
generally the case, the officers were compelled to treat them with
severity; and having never been in a warm climate before, if they
took ill, they seldom recovered. . . . For my own part, I was always very lucky in procuring good crews, and consequently the
charge of great mortality could not apply to my ships."

In spite of Captain Crow's apologies, it would seem that most
of the individuals who signed on for a slaving voyage were not
outcasts or criminals; they were, in almost equal proportions, sailors down on their luck and young landsmen with romantic notions
of the Guinea trade. The sailors knew better, but they were "compelled by want," says Henry Ellison, who had survived eight
Guinea voyages, or else compelled "by getting in debt to their
landlords, when they must go on board a Guineaman, or go to
gaol." Many captains, especially those with a reputation for brutality, had a standing agreement with rooming-house landlords,

tavern-keepers, and madams of brothels to keep their vessels manned. There were also the crimps, who made a profession of tricking, drugging, or kidnaping sailors—or simply plying them with drink—until they could be carried on board a Guineaman. One method they followed was to find a tipsy sailor and offer him an advance against his pay on the next voyage. As soon as the sailor had spent the money, the crimp could have him arrested for debt and sold to any captain who needed another hand.

In the Liverpool taverns, "music, dancing, rioting, drunkenness and profane swearing were kept up from night to night," says Clarkson, the great reformer, who spent years in collecting evidence from seamen. "The young mariner, if a stranger to the port, and unacquainted with the nature of the Slave Trade, was certain to be picked up. The novelty of the voyages, the superiority of the wages in this over any other trades, and the privileges of various kinds, were set before him. . . . If these prospects did not attract him, he was plied with liquor till he became intoxicated when a bargain was made over him between the landlord and the mate." If he refused to drink, he might simply be beaten insensible. He would come to himself on shipboard, where he had no redress.

It was the custom for a Guineaman to lie at anchor in the outer harbor of an English port, sometimes for weeks, until it had assembled a crew. During this time conditions on board were not intolerable; the men had enough to eat and the mates were not allowed to mistreat them, lest they jump overboard and swim ashore. Everything changed as soon as the ship weighed anchor and passed the Black Rock of Liverpool (or the Isle of Lundy, in the Bristol trade). Sailors were reduced to their sea rations of a pound of bread and a pound of salt beef per day (with a stockfish once a week for variety). In some ships, even before the black cargo had been taken aboard, sailors were forbidden to sleep anywhere except on the open deck; and their sea chests were staved in, so that they would have no excuse for going below. Meanwhile, on every ship, one of the crew was set to work making a cat. This was defined as "An instrument of correction, which consists of a handle or stem, made of a rope about 3½ in. in circumference and about 18 in. in length, at one end of which are fastened nine branches, or tails, composed of log line, with three or more knots upon each branch." It was the knots that cut the flesh from a sailor's back. The cat was seldom used on ordinary merchantmen, but in the Guinea trade it was the principal means of enforcing discipline.

On the *Alexander*, Captain M'Taggart—says Falconbridge, who was a surgeon on the vessel—only three persons escaped being flogged, out of a crew of fifty. One man was flogged every day, until at last he jumped overboard. He was picked up by a native canoe. When asked if he wasn't afraid of being eaten by sharks, he answered, "I expected to be, but I preferred that to life on this ship." M'Taggart then stuck the man's head in a tub of water left for the women slaves to wash their hands in. "If you want drowning, he shouted, "I'll drown you myself." The cook of the *Alexander* was flogged till he was cut from his neck to the small of his back, and then his wounds were swabbed with salt water and cayenne pepper. But flogging and its various sequels were not the only means of correction. An older man, the boatswain of the same vessel, "having complained about the water allowance, one of the officers seized him and beat out several of his teeth. Then one of the pump-bolts was fixed in his mouth and kept there by a piece of rope-yarn. Being unable to spit out the blood that flowed from the wound, the man almost choked. When the gag was removed he swore that he would drown himself so he was tied to the rail after which he was fastened to the grating of the steerage." Falconbridge adds that he had always regarded the boatswain as a "quiet, inoffensive man."

Some of the captains specialized in bizarre punishments. M'Taggart, for example, had a Newfoundland dog which he set on any seaman who dared to complain. Captain Williams of the *Little Pearl* amused himself by making the black Portuguese cook swallow live cockroaches, on pain of being flogged if he refused—as he sometimes did—and of having his wounds rubbed with beef brine. Captain Noble of the *Brookes*, generally regarded as a sound captain, had twelve parakeets. When they died, he suspected a sailor of having killed them. He ordered the sailor to be lashed to the topmast for twelve days and to be fed nothing but one of the dead birds each day. Luckier than others, the man survived.

The sailors revenged themselves as they could, if not on the captain then on the slaves under their care. They stole from the ship's trading goods, carried the loot ashore, and exchanged it for rum. When they were sent "boating" for slaves up the rivers, it was impossible, Newton says, to keep them away from the rum or brandy taken along for trade; often they became too drunk to handle the oars. Another of the captain's problems was to keep the seamen from attacking women in the native villages. If the resentful villagers did not dare to kill the attackers openly, they might, on occasion, give them poisoned food.

The Guinea trade brought out the worst in masters and seamen alike. John Newton said late in life that the necessity of treating the Negroes with rigor "gradually brings a numbness upon the heart, and renders most of those who are engaged in it too indifferent to the sufferings of their fellow creatures." There were, of course, the good captains like Newton and Crow and Frazer, "the only Bristol captain who didn't deserve to hang," and there were others who tried, if less decisively, to be just to the seamen as well as kind to the slaves. Most of the Guinea captains were hard and grasping rather than deliberately cruel; their chief fault was the numbness that had fallen upon their hearts. They recognized no higher duty than that of making a profit from the voyage, for themselves and their owners, at any cost in suffering and death so long as it was paid by slaves or by common seamen.

There were some captains, however, who had been absolutely corrupted by the absolute power they exercised. After first being heartless for the sake of profits, they had learned to enjoy cruelty for its own sake, even when it cost them money by leading to the needless loss of slaves or by driving their crews to desert on the Guinea Coast, where there was work for every man. James Stanfield had the ill fortune to serve under two of these monsters successively, on the same vessel. Years later he wrote a narrative of his experience, *The Guinea Voyage* (Edinburgh, 1807).

As a young seaman in Liverpool, Stanfield was picked up by the crimps. They took him to three public houses before they could get him drunk enough to be put aboard a slaver. "We were fortunate to be in a leaky vessel," Stanfield reports—fortunate because it had to put into Lisbon for repairs and because the captain, afraid that his crew would desert, did not dare to mistreat them until they were south of the Canary Islands. Then flogging made its appearance and spread like a contagion: "scarcely an hour passed any day without flogging . . . sometimes three were tied up together."

The week's allowance of bread was distributed on Sunday, but was always gone by Tuesday. Salt beef was handed out daily, but in such small slices that the seamen did not boil it for fear of losing the meat. Water was at first doled out at the rate of three pints a day, but the allowance was reduced as they neared the African coast. Stanfield hit upon the expedient of licking dew from the captain's hencoops early in the morning; that partly satisfied his thirst until other seamen discovered the secret and licked off most of the dew. The captain never went thirsty; he had a supply of beer and wine in his cabin, besides a kettleful of water delivered each morning and evening. When the crew begged for more to eat and drink, the captain told them that the ship was so full of trade goods there was no room for other supplies. His "whole delight was in giving pain," Stanfield reports. The captain had men flogged for no other reason than to watch their struggles and listen to their screams. He had the steward flogged for giving a sick man a glass of wine. When the steward explained the circumstances, the captain had him flogged a second time for offering excuses. Then the captain died of drink while the ship was still at anchor in Benin River.

Soon afterward the two mates died, one while begging for a cup of water, the other lying in a puddle of his own filth. There was no one left to navigate the ship, which was still anchored close to the

Dutch ships trading on the Guinea coast: (A) ship; (B) Negro merchants; (C) how goods are passed from the canoes to the shore; (D) where the merchants have to pay a tax to the chief; (E) canoe being carried up the beach. (From De Bry's *Oriental Voyages*, Part Six, 1604)

The Gold Coast with some of its "castles" about 1700, after John Barbot (from Churchill's *Voyages*). "Mina" is Elmina, then a Dutch stronghold; "Cabo Corso" is Cape Coast Castle

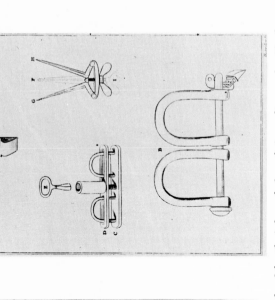

LEFT: A consignment of slaves from the Windward Coast, valued for their knowledge of rice culture, advertised for sale in a Charleston newspaper, 1766. The Laurens of the commission merchants was Henry Laurens, later president of the Continental Congress       RIGHT: Standard equipment for the Middle Passage. A is a pair of iron handcuffs by which the right wrist of one slave was padlocked to the left wrist of another. B is a pair of leg irons, also for two slaves. C, D, E is an instrument of torture, the thumbscrew. F, G, H is the speculum oris or mouth opener, for slaves who refused to eat. All these were displayed for sale in Liverpool ship chandleries. (From Clarkson's *Abolition of the Slave Trade*, 1808)

Bartering for slaves on the Gold Coast (from a colored lithograph in the Macpherson Collection, London). The seamen, but not the slaves, are drawn from first-hand observation

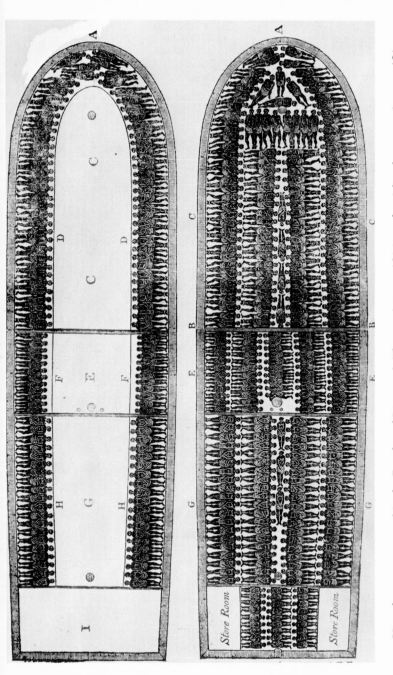

How slaves were stowed in the *Brookes* of Liverpool. The men's room (C) is to the left, and the boys' room (E) in the center. The upper illustration shows the six-foot-wide platform on which slaves were ranged "like books on a shelf"; they had not space above them to sit up. The deck itself (lower illustration) was completely covered with rows of bodies. (From Clarkson's *Abstract of the Evidence*, 1791)

"The Voyage of the Sable Venus from Angola to the West Indies" (Chapter 5),
as idealized by Thomas Stothard of the Royal Academy. (From Bryan Edwards' *History of the West Indies*)

"Flagellation of a Female Samboe Slave," drawn by William Blake as an illustration for Stedman's *Expedition against the Revolted Negroes of Suriname*. A samboe (or zambo) was the offspring of a Negro and a mulatto

The king of Dahomey leading his Amazons to war. Not having enough men to defeat the combined armies of Whydah and Popo (1728), King Trudo formed a brigade of armed women. The brigade was maintained until the French conquest of Dahomey (1892), and it was the flower of the Dahomean army. (From Archibald Dalzel, *History of Dahomy*, 1793)

AM I NOT A MAN AND A BROTHER.

Josiah Wedgwood & Sons
Peabody Museum, Salem, Mass.

A slave market in Martinique, early nineteenth century

ABOVE LEFT:
The famous Wedgwood medallion that became the seal of the Slave Emancipation Society.

BELOW LEFT:
Cape Coast Castle, 1806, with slave ships at anchor. What the artist omitted was the "terrible surf"

Ferrying slaves to the Portuguese brig *Paquito de Cabo Verde*, anchored in Bonny River. She had 676 slaves on board when captured there by the boats of HMS Scout, January 11, 1837

Peabody Museum, Salem, Mass.

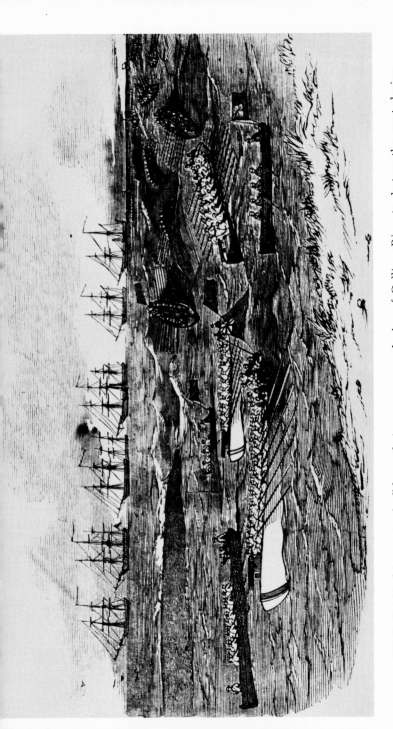

While British frigates stand offshore, their seamen cross the bar of Gallinas River to destroy the great slaving establishment founded by Pedro Blanco. (*Illustrated London News*, April 14, 1849)

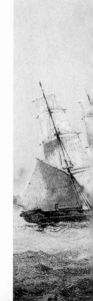

Capture of the American slave ship *Martha* (right) by the U.S. brig *Perry* (from Andrew Hull Foote, *Africa and the American Flag*)

Seamen from HMS *Dee* and *Castor* burn a group of barracoons on the East Coast. Note the stern of an Arab dhow almost hidden among the mangroves. (*Illustrated London News*, January 18, 1851)

HMS *Gorgon*, a British steam frigate attached to the East Coast Slaving Squadron

A slave coffle in the 1870s, sketched from life by an English artist. These women, captured in the Congo forest, were being driven to the east coast for sale to the Arabs, together with the merchandise they carried. Neck chains were a late development. In earlier times, when iron was more expensive, each slave in a coffle was tied by the neck to a forked log, with rope made of tie-tie bark

The Yankee clipper *Nightingale*, bought and sailed by Francis Bowen of Salem, called "the prince of slavers"

"Walking skeletons covered over with a piece of tanned leather." Slaves on the deck of the bark *Wildfire*, captured and brought into Key West, April 30, 1860. (Engraved from a daguerreotype and published in *Harper's Weekly*)

fever-ridden shore. By the time new officers arrived from Liverpool, with a new crew, only five men were left of those who had started the voyage.

The new captain was worse than his predecessor. Too ill to walk, he had himself carried round the vessel, while he amused himself by tearing at the men's faces with his long nails or cutting them with a pocket knife. When he ordered a man to be flogged, he first had him taken to the cabin and tied to his bedstead, so that he could bring his face close to the victim's and watch every detail of his suffering. On the passage to the West Indies, the vessel was swept with dysentery and both of the new mates died. The captain, however, recovered sufficiently to flog one slave to death, and he killed the cook with his own spit for having burned the roast.

Of the two complete crews that manned this hell ship, Stanfield claims there were only three survivors: himself, the carpenter, and the captain with long fingernails.

Stanfield's grim voyage was not the only one on which the seamen complained of being treated worse than the slaves. Sometimes the slaves agreed with them. Cases were reported of seamen who in squally weather, having no shelter of their own, stole down the hatchway to sleep with the Negroes in the stinking hold. Other seamen had been known to beg the Negroes for part of their rations, and often, out of pity, the Negroes would pass it up to them through the gratings. A seamen who later became a lieutenant in the Royal Navy testified that once in the *Tyger*, when dishing out rice to the slaves, he took a handful for his own use and was "unmercifully beat with a rope." He knew of many others who had done the same through hunger and had been treated in the same way.

In the Middle Passage there was never enough water for the crew. To keep them from wasting it—and also as a preventive of scurvy, which was thought to be caused by idleness—many captains adopted a cruel device. A water cask was left standing on deck with no opening except the bunghole. A gun barrel, to be used as a drinking straw, was then fastened to the topmast. A thirsty sailor had to climb the shrouds, unfasten the gun barrel, carry it down to the water cask, suck up his drink of water—making sure that the gun barrel was not used by anyone else—then carry the barrel back to the topmast. Henry Ellison testified that after the double climb he was often thirstier than before. He also said that sick men were forced to obtain water in the same fashion. One man collapsed halfway up the shrouds. Ellison and another seaman rescued him and begged the doctor to give him water. After first refusing, the doctor later gave him "a small pannikin full." The man lingered on for two days before he died.

In the earlier days of the trade, the men often mutinied and turned pirate. After 1730, however, the Guinea coast was patrolled by the Royal Navy and pirate ships had a short life. The only remaining ways to escape a brutal captain were either by desertion or else by the happy accident, for the seamen, of being impressed by a man-of-war. There was not much hope of such an accident while the slaver was in African waters. The trade was regarded as essential to English economy, and naval captains were instructed not to interfere with it by impressing seamen on the coast. Nevertheless the seamen often rowed out to warships, or swam to them through shark-infested bays, always begging to be taken aboard and threatening to turn pirate if they were turned away. The situation changed when a slaver reached the West Indies. As soon as the cargo had been landed, its seamen were subject to impressment, but by this time they were likely to be so weakened by disease that naval captains would not accept them. Captain John Samuel Smith, RN, testified that although he had boarded it might be twenty slavers in the West Indies for the purpose of impressing sailors, "he was never able to get more than two men. The principal reason was the fear of infection, having seen many of them in a very disordered and ulcerated state."

The other way of escape, desertion, was a dangerous course to adopt on the African coast. There are many records of sailors who, after taking to the jungle or being hidden by kindhearted natives, obtained passage to England on other vessels. There are more records, however, of escaped sailors who were returned to their captains, flogged, and forced to work in chains—not to mention all the others who died of starvation or fever. Captains needed every man while they were taking on slaves. They paid high rewards to natives for bringing back runaway seamen; later the rewards would be deducted from the seamen's wages. Sometimes they paid the rewards for seamen who had escaped from other vessels; any seaman would do, if he could pull a rope. As for the death rate among deserters, it was even higher than among the seamen who stayed with the ship. A possibly typical example is that of eleven men who escaped from Captain M'Taggart's *Alexander* while the vessel was lying in Bonny River. They sailed off in the longboat with half a hundredweight of bread and a small cask of water, but they missed their destination and were driven ashore. Seized by the natives, they were marched through the jungle to Old Calabar, where they were sold to Captain Burrows of the *Lyon*. Three of them died on the march; five died at Old Calabar or in the Middle Passage, and one died in the West Indies. Two got back to England, but almost at the point of death. Even after they recovered, one of the two survivors had holes in his shoulder torn by Captain M'Taggart's Newfoundland dog.

Desertion in the West Indies was a different story. After the cargo had been landed, there was no further need for a large crew. The captain, instead of paying a reward for the return of runaway sailors, would encourage, or maltreat, his men into deserting the vessel and thereby forfeiting their wages. Sometimes he sailed for Liverpool without notice, leaving half of his men behind. "It was no uncommon thing," one witness told Parliament, "for the captains to send on shore, a few hours before they sail, their lame, emaciated, and sick seamen, leaving them to perish." Those marooned Guinea sailors were such a common sight that there were special names for them in the sugar islands. At Kingston, Jamaica, where they lay on the wharves and under the cranes, they were called "wharfingers"; at smaller ports without wharves they were "beach-horners"; on Dominica they were "scowbankers." The Negroes sent to bury the dead sailors called them "po' buckra mans."

As for the mortality on shipboard, it seems to have been consistently higher among the white seamen than among the slaves. This was true at least during the second half of the eighteenth century, the period for which we have the most trustworthy statistics. Of course the slaves were carried on only one leg of the triangular voyage, so that they spent, on the average, less than half as much time on shipboard as did the seamen. They were less exposed to scurvy than the seamen were, and they were resistant— not immune—to the deadly African fevers; whereas the seamen were subject to all the diseases that spread among the slaves. Also there was the economic motive. "We are worth money," as some of the slaves used to say, and notably they were worth money to the captain, who received a "prime" of about 4 per cent on the selling price of every slave landed alive in the sugar islands. A seaman landed alive in Liverpool might be owed as much as a year's wages, and hence he was a liability. That helps to explain why the seamen were often treated as outcasts, whereas the slaves were treated like cattle, that is, with a certain rough care.

Having chosen nine slaving voyages for which there were complete figures, Thomas Clarkson prepared a table of comparative mortality:

| SHIP | | SAILORS | DIED | SLAVES | DIED |
|------|------|---------|------|--------|------|
| Royal Charlotte | 1766 | 17 | 0 | 120 | 3 |
| Royal Charlotte | 1767 | 18 | 0 | 455 | 10 |
| Molly | 1769 | 13 | 7 | 105 | 50 (ap.) |
| Ferret | 1770 | 13 | 3 | 105 | 5 |
| Surrey | 1771 | 25 | 4 | 255 | 10 |
| Three Friends | 1773 | 12 | 2 | 144 | 8 |
| Venus | 1775 | 22 | 2 | 321 | 10 |
| Harriet | 1776 | 18 | 0 | 277 | 7 |
| Camden | 1780 | 65 | 4 | 580 | 51 |
| Totals | | 203 | 22 | 2362 | 154 |

On this particular group of voyages, which seem to have been fortunate beyond the average, only 6.5 per cent of the slaves were lost, as compared with 11 per cent of the seamen. But Clarkson also prepared a more comprehensive table of deaths among Guinea seamen, based on the reports of all the Liverpool and Bristol slave ships that returned their muster rolls to the local custom houses from September 1784 to January 5, 1790. The table does not show deaths among slaves, but, for comparison, we might remember the Privy Council's estimate (1789) of 12.5 per cent as the mortality for Negroes in the Middle Passage:

| PERIODS | NUMBER OF VESSELS | ORIGINAL CREWS | DIED | BROUGHT HOME |
|---|---|---|---|---|
| 1784–1785 | 74 | 2915 | 615 | 1279 |
| 1785–1786 | 62 | 2163 | 436 | 944 |
| 1786–1787 | 66 | 2136 | 433 | 1073 |
| 1787–1788 | 68 | 2422 | 623 | 1114 |
| 1788–Jan. 5, 1790 | 80 | 2627 | 536 | 1350 |
| Totals | 350 | 12,263 | 2643 | 5760 |

The death rate shown in the table is comparable to that of British soldiers in Flanders during the First World War. More than one-fifth (21.5 per cent) of all the seamen on Liverpool and Bristol slave ships died on shipboard during the voyage, not counting the additional deaths among the 3860 seamen carried as discharged or deserted. An average slaver of the time sailed out of Liverpool or Bristol with a crew of 35 men. Of these 7 or 8 died on shipboard, 11 were left behind—either on the Guinea coast or more often in the West Indies—and only 16 or 17 returned home on the same vessel, consistently less than half of the original crew. Of those who stayed on the vessels, Clarkson says, a great number were permanently crippled, went blind, or died in the Liverpool and Bristol infirmaries. He estimates that the English slave trade employed 5000 seamen each year and that the yearly loss was 1950, or almost 40 per cent.

Sailoring of any sort was a dangerous trade in the eighteenth century, but losses on the Guinea voyage were vastly higher than in any other branch of the merchant service. On this point too Clarkson assembled figures, which he published in his essay *The Impolicy of the Slave Trade*. Out of 910 sailors on East Indiamen, 37 would die in the long voyage round the Cape of Good Hope. Out of 910 sailors in the trade direct from England to the West Indies, 21 would be lost; out of 910 in the Greenland trade, all but 9 would return. The loss *on shipboard* out of 910 sailors on Guineamen was about 200 per voyage. Sir George Young, RN, after commanding a man-of-war on four voyages to inspect forts and factories on the Guinea coast, told Parliament that the slave trade was "not a nursery but a grave for seamen."

His statement, widely quoted at the end of the eighteenth century, was a blow to the Guinea traders. English seamen were front-line troops in the never-ending wars against the French. Although they were subjected to brutal discipline, they were, in naval opinion, a resource that was not to be wasted. Meanwhile the English abolitionists were waging another war, in which their principal opponents were the Liverpool shipowners and the West Indian planters, both represented by powerful factions in Parliament. If the abolitionists had also been opposed by the Royal Navy, they could not have won their struggle for many years. But the Navy was unhappy and of divided opinions about the slave trade. That it had become a grave for seamen proved to be the most effective of all the arguments that the abolitionists were able to present.

# 7

# The Yankee Slavers

Captain Ball was a Yankee slaver,
Blow, blow, blow the man down!
He traded in niggers and loved his Saviour,
Give me some time to blow the man down.
—Stephen Vincent Benét, *John Brown's Body*

THE SLAVE TRADE AS CARRIED ON IN NEW ENGLAND VESSELS WAS different from the Liverpool trade, but this does not mean that it was, on the whole, either better or worse. It was better in one respect, that is, in the treatment of seamen. Generally speaking there was no cat-o'-nine-tails on New England vessels, and the captain's authority was a little less than absolute. He might order a seaman to be flogged with an end of rope, but first he might find it advisable to explain why the man was being punished, lest his order be disobeyed. Refusals to carry out orders, sometimes amounting to bloodless mutinies, were relatively frequent on Yankee slavers. At home the lines between social classes were less firmly

153

drawn than in eighteenth-century England, and even on shipboard there was not an impassable gulf between the captain and the ship's carpenter or even the cabin boy. They might all be farmers' sons; in the early days of the trade they might all be neighbors; and the captain was frequently reminded of what the neighbors might say. If he allowed one of his younger seamen to die of neglect, he might have to face the boy's mother in church or his father at a town meeting. One remembers Whittier's poem about a Marblehead skipper:

> Old Floyd Ireson, for his hard heart,
> Tarr'd and feather'd and carried in a cart
> By the women of Marblehead!

Scholars tell us that this is not the true story of Captain Flood (not Floyd) Ireson, who was never tarred and feathered for an act of inhumanity which, as a matter of fact, he did not commit, but nevertheless it is a true picture of New England seaport manners. As such it helps to explain why most of the Yankee skippers were afraid to be absolute tyrants over their men. Even with regard to their shiploads of slaves, they preferred not to outrage public opinion. Captain James deWolf, who belonged to the leading family of Bristol, Rhode Island, made the mistake of tossing over-board a female slave who had caught smallpox and who he feared might infect the rest of his cargo. His sailors carried the story back to Bristol, and in 1791 he was indicted for murder by a federal grand jury. The bill of indictment charges that the said James de-Wolf, "not having the fear of God before his eyes, but being moved and seduced by the instigation of the Devil . . . did feloniously, willfully and of his malice aforethought, with his hands clinch and seize in and upon the body of said Negro woman . . . and did push, cast and throw her from out of said vessel into the Sea and waters of the Ocean, whereby and where-upon she then and there instantly sank, drowned and died."

Although the warrant for James deWolf's arrest was never served, and although the case was nol-prossed in 1795, still the captain—who later became a United States senator—was not allowed to forget the story. John Brown—not the abolitionist, but the Providence merchant and banker, who had also been involved in the slave trade—wrote to a friend just before the election of 1802. "I wish it may properly be introduced to Mr. James deWolf," he said, "that it already begins to be talked of in our streets that if he don't conduct himself within the bounds of reason, the statement of his murdering his negroes in the smallpox to preserve the other part of his cargo in his passage from Africa will be echoed through the papers of the various states."

But in spite of community opinion and its effect on Yankee skippers, their slaves probably suffered more in the Middle Passage than those on the Guineamen from Liverpool. That is because the New England vessels were smaller and often unseaworthy, "so you could see daylight all around the bows under the deck," as was said of more than one slaver; and because they carried smaller crews. The slaves had to be confined in their extremely cramped quarters to keep them from seizing the vessel. If the men slaves were ever released from their shackles, it was only to work the pumps when water was flooding the hold. Mungo Park's account of his westward voyage on the ship *Charlestown*, mentioned at the end of Chapter 4, reveals some features that seem to be typical of the American trade. The *Charlestown*, Captain Charles Harris, had anchored in the Gambia River on June 15, 1797, with a cargo of rum and tobacco. Since she was the first vessel to enter the river for several months, the cargo was quickly exchanged for a hundred and thirty slaves, mostly Mandingos. The whole transaction took only two days, but then her passage down the river was delayed by contrary winds. Before she reached Goree, where she planned to take on provisions for the Middle Passage, four sailors and the surgeon had died of African fevers. She was left with hardly more than half a crew.

At Goree, in the lee of Cape Verde, provisions were scarce and the *Charlestown* was delayed for three months. She lost six or eight slaves, in addition to three who had died in the Gambia. It was

not until the beginning of October that she weighed anchor for
South Carolina, where, incidentally, the importation of slaves was
illegal at the time. Mungo Park volunteered to take the place of
the dead surgeon. The slaves, he says, "had in truth need of every
consolation in my power to bestow; not that I observed any wanton
acts of cruelty practised either by the master, or the seamen, to-
wards them; but the mode of confining and securing Negroes in
the American slave ships (owing chiefly to the weakness of their
crews) being abundantly more rigid and severe than in British
vessels employed in the same traffic, made these poor creatures
to suffer greatly, and a general sickness prevailed amongst
them. . . .

"In the midst of these distresses, the vessel, after having been
three weeks at sea, became so extremely leaky, as to require constant exertion at the pumps. It was found necessary, therefore, to
take some of the ablest Negro men out of irons, and employ them
in this labour; in which they were often worked beyond their
strength. This produced," evidently for the seamen as well as the
slaves, "a complication of miseries not easily to be described." It
also produced one of the bloodless mutinies that occurred on
American vessels: ". . . the leak continuing to gain upon us, notwithstanding our utmost exertions to clear the vessel, the seamen
insisted on bearing away for the West Indies, as affording the only
chance of saving our lives. Accordingly, after some objections on
the part of the master, we directed our course for Antigua, and
fortunately made that island in about thirty-five days after our de-
parture from Goree. Yet even at this juncture we narrowly escaped destruction; for, on approaching the northwest side of the
island, we struck on Diamond Rock, and got into St. John's
harbour with great difficulty. The vessel was afterwards condemned as unfit for sea, and the slaves, as I have heard, were
ordered to be sold for the benefit of the owners." Probably the
owners incurred a loss for the voyage, but not a heavy one, since
the surviving Negroes were worth a great deal more than the ship.

Most of the eighteenth-century New England merchants were

small businessmen, by Liverpool standards, with little capital to invest in the slave trade. They bought the cheapest vessels they could find—sometimes unseaworthy vessels like the *Charlestown*—and manned them with as few sailors as could be trusted to bring them home. They showed a preference for sloops, schooners, topsail schooners, and brigantines, as being easier to handle with a small crew. Many New England slaving vessels were smaller than the yachts that compete in the *America*'s Cup races. In 1789 the largest vessel that left Newport, Rhode Island, for the Guinea Coast was the sloop *Nancey*, of sixty tons, with a crew of five men (in addition to the captain and one or two mates). The smallest bore the same name; it was the schooner *Nancey*, of twenty tons, with a crew of four commanded by James deWolf's brother John. The other Newport vessels sailing for Africa in 1789 were the sloop *Betsey*, thirty-five tons, six men; the sloop *Dove*, twenty-two tons, seven men; the brigantine *Hope*, forty tons, nine men; and another sloop *Betsey*, forty tons, crew not specified.

Because the Yankee captains in their small vessels were shrewd and patient traders, they preferred to assemble their cargo one slave at a time—unless, as was the case with Captain Harris of the *Charlestown*, they were offered a special bargain. The more slaves they bought in separate transactions, the greater chance there was that someone would be cheated, and, as Yankees used to say, "I don't calculate it will be me." This preference for what might be called the retail trade in slaves led them to avoid Calabar and Angola, where the trade was wholesale and where Liverpool captains often bargained with the local monarchs for a whole shipload. Most of the New England vessels kept northward and looked for cargoes on the Gold Coast or the Windward Coast. There, where slaves were less plentiful, they might lie at anchor for months instead of weeks. Having smaller crews than English vessels, they were exposed to a greater danger of mutiny by the slaves and being "cut off" by free natives. The danger was greatest when many or most of the sailors had died of African fevers. In the spring of 1764 the sloop *Adventure* of New London, Captain Joseph Miller, was trading in the Sierra Leone River. Before she had finished taking on slaves, the captain died with his whole crew except one man. A local English factor sent two other white men to assist in taking care of the cargo. "While the sloop lay at anchor with her slaves," the *Georgia Gazette* reported on October 25, "and these three men on board, the natives came off, hauled the vessel ashore, and barbarously murdered the white men and plundered the whole cargo except two slaves." Items of this nature abound in the colonial newspapers, as note these two examples out of many:

> . . . as Capt. Faggot was at Anchor, off Goree, on the Coast of Africa, with 43 Slaves on board, the Slaves rose in the Night against the Crew, cut the Cable, killed the Capt, and two of the Men, but were at last overcome by the Mate and the rest of the Sailors, who went into Porto Rico. The Spaniards boarded the Brig, on Pretence of the clandestine Trade, and condemned both the Vessel and Cargo. (*Massachusetts Gazette and News Letter*, August 16, 1764.)

> By letters from Capt. Hopkins in a Brig belonging to Providence arrived here from Antigua from the Coast of Africa we learn That soon after he left the Coast, the Number of his Men being reduced by Sickness, he was obliged to permit some of the Slaves to come upon Deck to assist the People: These Slaves contrived to release the others, and the whole rose upon the People, and endeavoured to get Possession of the Vessel; but was happily prevented by the Captain and his Men, who killed, wounded and forced overboard, Eighty of them, which obliged the rest to submit. (*Newport Mercury*, November 18, 1765.)

The "Capt. Hopkins" of the second item was Esek Hopkins, master of the brig *Sally*, which was owned by the Brown brothers of Providence. He was an able and aggressive man, but he made mistakes that were costly to his employers (among whom, at a later date, was the Continental Congress). On the disastrous voyage of the *Sally* he lost part of his rum cargo by leakage, he lost most of his crew by fever, and he was obliged to sell the surviving slaves for a low price. Hopkins was luckier, however, than Captain John Nicoll of New York, who lost forty of his slaves in a shipboard insurrection (1761) and then lost his vessel and all his personal belongings to a French privateer.

Those French marauders that sailed out of Guadeloupe and Martinique were another special danger to colonial slavers, which, being small and lightly armed, could seldom put up a successful resistance. In the two years 1757 and 1758, at least fifteen vessels from the Newport slaving fleet were captured by the French, and insurance premiums rose to 25 per cent. The shipowners talked of retiring from business, but usually they bought new vessels and once more loaded them with cargoes for the Guinea Coast. The price of slaves was higher in wartime, and all past losses might be canceled off by two or three fortunate voyages.

Some of the shipowners had started in business by sending a schooner to the West Indies loaded with those prime New England products of the early days, pine lumber and salt fish. About one-fourth of the catch of the Grand Banks fishing fleet consisted of "Jamaica fish," not good enough for the Yankees. Slaves in the West Indies were given six or seven of these fish per week, almost their only protein food. On the schooner's return voyage it would be loaded with hogsheads of molasses, but it might also carry half a dozen slaves as part of its deck cargo. Most of the small Negro population of the Northern colonies was brought from the West Indies in this casual fashion, instead of being imported direct from Africa.

But the Yankee schooners, often commanded by their owners, were looking for business wherever they could find it. If the West Indian price of slaves was especially high, they might take on a cargo of rum, carry it to the Guinea Coast, and exchange it for fifty or sixty Negroes, whom they sold in the sugar islands before returning to New England. Then, after the shipowner had accumulated a little capital—perhaps not more than two thousand pounds sterling—he would send a vessel direct to Africa.

By the middle of the eighteenth century the New England slave trade was three-cornered, like the Liverpool trade, but it was simpler and even more symmetrical. Essentially it was based on three commodities: rum, slaves, and molasses. At its home port the vessel would take on a cargo consisting chiefly or entirely of rum. Thus, the sloop *Dove*, when it left Newport in 1789, carried "Sixty Punchions, Eight Tierces and four half Barrels Rum here Distilled, Likewise for Stores, Sixteen Barrels Beef and Pork and Six Casks Bread." In Africa the rum would be exchanged for as many slaves as it would buy, often at the rate of two hundred gallons per slave. The black cargo would be sold in the West Indies, and part of the proceeds would be invested in molasses, usually purchased in the French or Spanish islands, where it was cheaper. On the final leg of the voyage, the vessel would carry the molasses back to New England, to be distilled into more rum, to buy more slaves.

By 1750 there were sixty-three distilleries in Massachusetts alone, and each year they turned fifteen thousand hogsheads of molasses into about twelve thousand, five hundred hogsheads of rum. Even with the help of perhaps thirty distilleries in Rhode Island, they were unable to supply the demand. In 1752 Captain Isaac Freeman tried to get a cargo of rum for the Guinea voyage. His agent replied, "We are sorry to find you are ordering your sloop here in expectation of having her loaded with rum in about five weeks. We cannot give you encouragement of getting that quantity of rum these three months, for there are so many vessels loading for Guinea, we can't get one hogshead of rum for cash." There was supposed to be an import duty on molasses imported from the French, Spanish, or Dutch islands, but it was almost never paid. In 1763, when Parliament cut the duty in half and made a serious effort to collect it, the Massachusetts merchants protested that a tax on molasses would ruin the slave trade. It would, so they said, throw five thousand seamen out of work, would cause seven hundred ships to rot, and would seriously affect coopers, tanners, and farmers.

The little colony of Rhode Island issued its own remonstrance to the Board of Trade, as a resolution of the General Assembly.

Formerly [said the colonists], the negroes upon the [African] coast were supplied with large quantities of French brandies; but in the year 1723, some merchants in this colony first introduced the use of rum there, which, from small beginnings soon increased to the consumption of several thousand hogsheads yearly; by which the French are deprived of the sale of an equal quantity of brandy. . . . This little colony, only, for more than thirty years past, have annually sent about eighteen sail of vessels to the coast, which have carried about eighteen hundred hogsheads of rum, together with a small quantity of provisions and some other articles, which have been sold for slaves, gold dust, elephants' teeth, camwood, etc. The slaves have been sold in the English islands, in Carolina and Virginia, for bills of exchange, and the other articles have been sent to Europe; and by this trade alone, remittances have been made from this colony to Great Britain, to the value of about £40,000, yearly. . . .

There are upwards of thirty distil houses, (erected at a vast expense . . . ,) constantly employed in making rum from molasses. This distillery is the main hinge upon which the trade of the colony turns, and many hundreds of persons depend immediately upon it for a subsistence. These distil houses, for want of molasses, must be shut up, to the ruin of many families, and of our trade in general; particularly, of that to the coast of Africa, where the French will supply the natives with brandy, as they formerly did. Two thirds of our vessels will become useless, and perish upon our hands . . . and what must very sensibly affect the present and future naval power and commerce of Great Britain, a nursery of seamen, at this time consisting of twenty-two hundred, in this colony only, will be in a manner destroyed.

For a vessel to sail for Guinea without a sufficient supply of rum might prove disastrous. Captain George Scott reported to his Newport owners in 1740 that he had made a "Miserable voyage," chiefly because there was so little demand for his dry cargo. He had lost about one-fourth of his slaves by sickness, and if he had stayed on the Gold Coast until the whole cargo was sold, he would have lost them all. "I have repented a hundred times," he said, "the bying of them dry goods, had we Layed out two Thousand pound in rum . . . it would have purchased more in value than all our dry goods." Sometimes, however, the New Englanders sent more rum to the Gold Coast than the natives would purchase. That was the case in 1736, when Captain John Cahoone, Jr., also of Newport, wrote home to his owners: "I bles god I Injoy my health very well as yett: but am like to have a long and trublesom Voyge of it, for there never was so much Rum on the Coast at one time before. . . . heair is 7 sail of us Rume men that we are Ready to Devur one another; for our Case is Despart."

The principal New England slaving ports were Boston and Salem, Massachusetts; Portsmouth, New Hampshire; New London, Connecticut; and Newport, Providence, and Bristol, Rhode Island. Boston was by far the most important in the first half of the eighteenth century, and many of her leading merchants sent vessels to Guinea. Even the good Peter Faneuil, who made a gift to the Bostonians of Faneuil Hall, later famous as "the cradle of liberty," once tried a speculation in the slave trade. He provided half of the capital needed to buy and equip a vessel for a voyage to Sierra Leone; the other half was provided jointly by John Jones, his brother-in-law, and by John Cutler, who was to command the vessel. It was named the *Jolly Bachelor*, perhaps as a compliment to Faneuil himself, who had inherited his fortune from an eccentric uncle on condition that he should never marry.

Captain Cutler did not get back to Boston. He was "barbarously murdered," with two of his sailors, by a community of black Portuguese established near the mouth of the Sierra Leone River. The Portuguese also looted the vessel and carried off its cargo of seventy-five slaves; but they spared three of the sailors, who escaped to an English factory on the Banana Islands. There the factor, George Birchall, took charge of the case. He managed to recover the *Jolly Bachelor* and thirty-four of the slaves—though some of them later escaped and some died; he provided new sails and an anchor; and he even found a new captain in the person of Charles Winkham of Newport, whose own vessel had been taken by a Spanish privateer. When the *Jolly Bachelor* returned to New England with twenty remaining slaves, it was sold by court order to settle George Birchall's claim against it. The vessel brought £1300 in colonial currency and the slaves brought £1624.

The captains of Boston vessels were not renowned for their scrupulous dealings with the natives. Francis Moore tells the story of a schooner and a sloop, both owned by Captain Samuel Moore of Boston, which entered the Gambia River in 1732. The schooner, commanded by Captain Major, anchored at the town of Cassan, while the sloop, under Samuel Moore himself, went farther up the river to Yamyamacunda. At Cassan the king sent a native trader on board the schooner with a slave for sale, under the proviso that if he did not like the captain's trade goods, the slave would be returned. The goods did not come up to the king's standards, but Captain Major fell into a rage and insisted on keeping the slave. What happened next was explained by the native trader. "I did not say much to the Captain," he told Francis Moore through an interpreter, "but came home, called all my People together, told them the Case, and then we reckon'd up the many Injuries we had received from other separate Traders"—many of whom were New Englanders—"and at last we resolved to take the Scooner, which we did the next Morning. In the Action the Captain was killed, for which I am very sorry; but as for the rest of the Men which were on board the Scooner, I gave them the Boat and some Provisions, and let them go where they pleased."

The men went up the river and joined Captain Samuel Moore, who seems to have been a man of great courage and few scruples. At Yamyamacunda he was busy buying slaves with spread-eagle dollars made of pewter, which he passed off as silver. In spite of losing his schooner at Cassan, he made a very profitable voyage, but the people of Yamyamacunda were determined to be revenged on him if he ever came back. Captain Moore was not frightened. The following year he appeared in the sloop *Bumper*, and Francis Moore reports that this time, instead of pewter dollars, "he had on Board a good Number of Guns, and Hands sufficient, and it was thought he design'd either to make good Trade, or else get Satisfaction of the Natives for the Loss of his Scooner last Year at Cassan." The natives were prepared to give him a warm reception, but the Yankee was protected by James Conner, the local factor, and obtained a full cargo of slaves. It was not until the *Bumper* had left Yamyamacunda and was coming down the river that the natives attacked. There was "a very smart Engagement" that lasted from midnight till dawn. At one moment—so Captain Moore reported in a letter home—"by an unhappy contrary Wind, the River narrow, and the Vessel not answering her Helm, we fell along the Shore, the Natives rush'd on in great Numbers in order to board us, but were so received that they thought proper to Retreat." Captain Moore reached the Cape Verde Islands with the loss of only two men, one by gunshot and the other—his surgeon, "Doctor Blaney, a young Gentleman who had his Education at Harvard College"—by an African fever.

Some of the Rhode Island slavers were no more scrupulous than Captain Moore. There was, for example, a Bristol shipowner named Simeon Potter, uncle of the famous deWolf brothers. Potter said in a letter of instructions to his captain, William Earle, "Make yr. Cheaf Trade with the Blacks and Little or none with the white people if possible to be avoided." The blacks were easier to cheat. "Worter yr. Rum as much as possible," Potter continued, "and sell as much by the short mesuer as you can. Order them in the Bots to worter thear Rum likewise, as the proof will Rise by the Rum standing in ye Son." It was also Simeon Potter who declared, "Money? Why, I'd plow the sea to porridge to make money." He made a modest fortune, in the end, but it was smaller than those amassed by several other Rhode Island slave merchants. Rhode Island was the new center of the trade, and in 1770 Samuel Hopkins, pastor of the First Congregational Church in Newport, wrote that it had "enslaved more Africans than any other colony in New England." To this he added in 1774 that Newport was "the most guilty, respecting the slave trade, of any [town] on the continent, as it has been, in a great measure, built up by the blood of the poor Africans; and that the only way to escape the effects of the divine displeasure is to be sensible of the sin, repent, and reform." But Newport showed no disposition to reform. Soon it would suffer from what Dr. Hopkins must have thought were the effects of the divine displeasure, but for twenty years before the Revolution, it was America's answer to Liverpool.

Most of the Rhode Island shipowning families were concerned in the trade. Among the familiar names are those of Philip Wilkinson and Stephen d'Ayrault, Jr.; the Champlin brothers, Christopher, George, and Robert; the Wanton family, which included four governors of the colony; Esek Hopkins, afterward commander-in-chief of the Continental navy; Aaron Lopez, a great merchant renowned for his benevolence; and the four Brown brothers of Providence, "John and Josey, Nick and Mosey," as they were called by their less prosperous rivals. Moses Brown, the youngest, became a Quaker in 1773, and from that moment he worked tirelessly for the abolition of the slave trade. His example had its effect on the older brothers, and apparently John was the only one of them who, after leaving the family partnership, continued to speculate in Guinea voyages after the Revolution.

The Revolution halted the slave trade of New England. A few of the speedier Rhode Island slavers were refitted as privateers and returned with rich prizes to other ports. They could not return to Newport, which was occupied for three years by British troops. Aaron Lopez lost his thirty vessels and, with his worldwide business affairs in confusion, retired to a little Massachusetts town. The Wanton family, most of them Royalists, lost their entire fortune. The commerce of Newport never recovered from the Revolution.

After 1790 the most prominent Rhode Island family engaged in the Guinea trade was the deWolf brothers of Bristol: Charles,

James, William, John, and Levi the youngest, who retired in dis-
gust after making one voyage to Africa. James was the most
successful at shipping and selling slaves, and Charles, the oldest
brother, was the most avaricious. Once he invited Parson Wight
of the Bristol Congregational Church to his counting house.
"Parson," he said, "I've always wanted to roll in gold"; and he lay
down among the canvas sacks and wallowed. Much of the deWolf
money was invested in distilleries and later in textile mills. The
Brown brothers of Providence had already invested in spermaceti
candles (with the help of Aaron Lopez they monopolized the
trade); in an iron furnace and foundry that supplied cannon to
General Washington's army; and in the first cotton mills built
west of the Atlantic. The slave trade in New England, as in
Lancashire and the English Midlands, provided much of the
capital that helped to create the industrial revolution.

The vast majority of the slaves imported to America were landed
south of the Mason-Dixon Line. In Maryland and Virginia they
were used to cultivate corn and tobacco, the money crop. Since
the tobacco trade was stagnant during most of the eighteenth
century, there was never a brisk demand for slaves fresh from
Guinea, but they were introduced steadily in small numbers. Often
the smaller Guinea vessels sailed up and down the tidal rivers,
exchanging slaves for tobacco at plantation wharves. The larger
English vessels—usually from Bristol, which was a center of the
English tobacco trade—delivered their cargoes to commission merchants, who sold them by auction at Yorktown, West Point,
Hampton, and Bermuda Hundred. In the fourth volume of Elizabeth Donnan's *Documents Illustrative of the History of the Slave
Trade to America*, there is a list of the vessels that brought slaves
to Virginia between 1710 and 1769, with the number of slaves on
each and the origin of its cargo. After adding the figures in the list,
Melville Herskovits arrived at the total of 52,504 slaves as the importation to Virginia during those 60 years. (A few additional
thousands may have been smuggled in to avoid the Virginia im-

port duties.) As for the origin of the Virginia slaves, he reduced it to a table:

| | |
|---|---:|
| Origin given merely as "Africa" | 20,564 |
| The Gambia and Senegal | 3652 |
| "Guinea" (apparently the Windward Coast, the Gold Coast, and the Slave Coast) | 6777 |
| Calabar (mostly Ibo, Ibibio, and Efik from the Bight of Biafra) | 9224 |
| Angola (including the Congo) | 3860 |
| Madagascar | 1011 |
| Slaves brought direct from Africa | 45,088 |
| Slaves reimported from the West Indies | 7046 |
| Slaves from other North American colonies | 370 |

The 3860 Negroes from Angola were Bantus. The 1011 slaves from Madagascar provided the slight Mongoloid strain in the Virginia Negro population, and at least half of the 3652 Senegambian slaves must have been Caucasoid (or Hamitic). Of all the slaves whose African origins were specified, however, perhaps 80 per cent were "true Negroes" from West Africa. Figures for South Carolina, also listed by Miss Donnan and tabulated by Herskovits, give a somewhat different proportion. There was an eager, at times almost frantic, demand for slaves in the rice colonies, and the total listed importation into South Carolina for the years between 1733 and 1785—only 45 years in reality, since the trade was suspended during the Revolution—was 67,769 Negroes. (Miss Donnan's list for South Carolina is less complete than that for Virginia, and it does not include the overland importation of slaves from Saint Augustine, so that the real total may have been considerably higher.) As for the African sources of the South Carolina Negroes, they appear in the table on page 168.

In South Carolina a little less than 60 per cent of the slaves imported from Africa—as opposed to 80 per cent in Virginia—were "true Negroes." Charleston as a busy port was visited by more of the big Liverpool Guineamen. That explains why so many of the

| | |
|---|---:|
| Origin given merely as "Africa" | 4146 |
| From the Gambia to Sierra Leone | 12,441 |
| Windward Coast (including Sierra Leone, the Grain Coast, and the Ivory Coast) | 7757 |
| "Guinea Coast" (here apparently the Gold Coast, the Slave Coast, and Calabar) | 18,240 |
| The Congo and Angola | 22,409 |
| East Africa | 473 |
| Slaves imported from Africa | 65,466 |
| Slaves reimported from the West Indies | 2303 |

imported slaves—about 36 per cent—came from Angola or the Congo and hence were presumably Bantus. The Liverpool captains bought slaves where they were plentiful and sold them where they would bring the highest prices. Charleston prices were usually high, and the captains came to regard it as another West Indian island. The fact seems to be that Charleston, settled in part by Barbadians, long retained an island mentality; the rice planters of the neighborhood were more Carolinian than they were American.

Like the West Indians they prided themselves on being connoisseurs of Negroes. They were told by slave traders announcing auctions that the Congos and Angolans were "esteemed equal to the Gold Coast and Gambia slaves," but the planters did not agree. As connoisseurs they preferred first Gold Coast slaves, then those from the Windward Coast, many of whom had learned to cultivate rice in Africa, and then Mandingos as house servants. They objected to Ibo, who they feared would commit suicide, but such was their need for labor in the rice fields that they ended by purchasing any cargo that was offered.

Georgia, for seventeen years after its founding in 1733, was the only American colony that prohibited the importation or ownership of Negro slaves. But the prohibition was unpopular in the colony, white settlers kept moving to the Carolinas, and the law was repealed as of January 1, 1750. From that time Savannah, in respect to the slave trade, became a smaller model of Charleston. It showed the same preference for cargoes direct from the Gold or the Windward Coasts, though, being a less important market, it had to import more of its slaves in small parcels from the West Indies. As in Charleston, the slaves were consigned to commission merchants and were sold at auction, not by "scramble." As on South Carolina plantations, they were chiefly employed in the cultivation of rice, indigo, and sea-island cotton. Georgia planters long retained an unhappy memory of the time when slavery had been illegal. Perhaps this was the reason why they were afflicted more than others with a passion for buying slaves whether or not there was money to pay for them. But South Carolina planters suffered from the same malady, which came to be widely known as "Negro fever."

The colonial import trade in slaves reached its climax in the ten years (1764–1773) that followed the French and Indian War. It was a time when rice and indigo were booming crops that required more and more labor. From November 1, 1772, to September 27, 1773, more than eight thousand Negroes were landed in Charleston alone. Even Virginia, though suffering from the slow decline of its tobacco plantations, received many Guinea cargoes in 1772. There was, however, no demand for such cargoes north of the Potomac, and all the Southern colonies except Georgia had begun to complain of being overstocked with slaves. They also complained that the trade was draining money out of America for the sole benefit of English merchants.

These economic arguments against the slave trade were mingled with humanitarian feeling. Except in the rice colonies, most Americans were coming to feel that slavery was wrong in itself and would presently vanish from the continent. But first it was essential to stop the importation of slaves from Africa. The Virginia House of Burgesses, as early as 1769, adopted a nonimportation agreement. It could not be enforced at the time, owing to royal opposition, but it was readopted in later years with greater effect, and other colonies began to follow the Virginia example. In October 1774 the First Continental Congress adopted a resolution against the importation of any goods whatever from Great Britain, Ireland, or the East or West Indies. One clause of the resolution provided that "We will neither import, nor purchase any Slave imported after the First Day of *December* next; after which Time, we will wholly discontinue the Slave Trade, and will neither be concerned in it ourselves, nor will we hire our Vessels, nor sell our Commodities or Manufactures to those who are concerned in it."

Every colony but one quickly ratified the agreement. Georgia held out against it until after the Battle of Bunker Hill, but then was forced into line by patriotic feeling, and also by a threat to include Georgia among the territories with which the other twelve colonies were forbidden to trade. The "Non-Intercourse Association," as the agreement was called, had brought the slave trade to a virtual halt even before the outbreak of war, and no slave cargoes were landed as long as the fighting continued. When the trade was revived after 1783, there was a long series of legislative attempts to abolish it, often led by the Quakers, while Yankee merchants and Carolina planters banded together to defend the trade—but the struggle for abolition is a story in itself.

# 8

# The Fight to Abolish
# the Trade

*Never, never will we desist, till we have wiped away this
scandal from the Christian name; till we have released ourselves from the load of guilt under which we at present labour;
and till we have extinguished every trace of this bloody traffic,
which our posterity, looking back to the history of these en-
lightened times, will scarcely believe to have been suffered to
exist so long, a disgrace and dishonour to our country.*
—William Wilberforce, address to Parliament

*I tremble for my country when I reflect that God is just.*
—Thomas Jefferson

EVEN IN THE SEVENTEENTH CENTURY, WHEN THE RIGHT TO OWN
slaves was virtually unquestioned, some private and public doubts
were expressed about the rightness of the slave trade. Massachusetts in 1641 enacted her famous "Body of Liberties," which forbade slavery in the colony "unless it be lawful Captives taken in
just Warres, and such strangers as willingly sell themselves or are
sold to us." In 1652 Rhode Island passed a law designed to prohibit slavery for life. A slave was to be freed after ten years—or at
the age of twenty-four, if he had been taken in childhood. The
law was enforced, it would seem, for the rest of the century. In

1700 Chief Justice Sewall of Massachusetts published a famous pamphlet, *Selling of Joseph.* "These Ethiopians, as black as they are," Sewall argued, ". . . are the sons and daughters of the first Adam and brethren and sisters of the last Adam."

Among the small number of persons who agreed with Sewall at the time were not a few members of the Society of Friends. One group of these Quakers—the Germantown Meeting, in Philadelphia—had issued in 1688 what was perhaps the first American protest against slavery itself as well as the slave trade. "Now, tho they are black," the Germantown Quakers said, "we cannot conceive there is more liberty to have them slaves, as it is to have other white ones. . . . And those who steal or robb men, and those who buy or purchase them, are they not all alike?" This opinion, little by little, was adopted by the whole Society of Friends. By 1712 the Quakers were trying to prevent the importation of any more slaves into the colony. Various restrictive measures, passed by the colonial assembly, were vetoed in England by the Privy Council; but most of the Quakers simply refused to buy slaves, and many of them followed the example of John Woolman by using maple sugar instead of the cane sugar that was raised by slave labor. In 1761 the assembly, once more urged on by the Quakers, laid a duty of £10 on every slave imported into the colony. It put an effective end to the Pennsylvania trade.

Except for John Woolman, the first great figure in the fight against the slave trade was another Quaker, Anthony Benezet. He was born in France, to a Huguenot family that was forced to emigrate first to England and then to Pennsylvania. At fourteen he was converted to the Society of Friends. He does not seem to have played a prominent part in the society until the yearly meeting of 1772, at which the question of slavery arose. Some of the Quakers present still had slaves, although such ownership was frowned upon by the group, and the problem was being discussed as calmly as if it concerned the importing or exporting of cattle. Benezet could stand no more. With tears running down his cheeks, he rose and cried, "Ethiopia shall soon stretch out her hands unto God!" He made such a passionate appeal that the meeting condemned the trade by a unanimous vote.

Benezet became the friend of Benjamin Franklin and Benjamin Rush, both strong opponents of the slave trade. He corresponded with the leading British abolitionists. His books on Africa were read in England, where they inspired several of the men who finally succeeded in breaking up the trade. Thus, John Wesley copied out the first part of Benezet's *Some Historical Accounts of Guinea* and used it as material for his powerful sermons against slavery. Thomas Clarkson became a lifelong crusader after reading Benezet's *Short Account of That Part of Africa Inhabited by Negroes.* Both books were also widely read in France, with the result that Benezet served as a link uniting the anti-slavery movements on the two sides of the Atlantic.

American opposition to the slave trade had continued to grow, not only in the Northern colonies but also in Virginia and Maryland. All through the eighteenth century the Virginia House of Burgesses kept passing restrictive measures against the trade, though almost all of these were overruled by the royal governors. Maryland imposed higher and higher duties on imported slaves, and no Guinea cargoes were landed there after 1769. In New England the port of Salem instituted a petition in 1775 against importing more slaves. Boston in 1766 vainly asked permission "to prohibit the importation and purchase of slaves in the future." So many of these protests were submitted to the British government that in 1770 George III was forced to instruct the colonial legislatures: "Upon pain of the highest displeasure to assent to no law by which the importation of slaves should be in any respect prohibited or obstructed."

When the Declaration of Independence was signed, slavery was still legal in all thirteen colonies. Thomas Paine called it hypocrisy to fight for freedom while maintaining slavery. Many of the Continental leaders were slave-owners, but they were not happy about the situation. Henry Laurens, president of the Continental Congress from 1777 to 1778, had been the leading slave merchant of Charleston, but he had retired from the trade, which he had come to regard as evil. Patrick Henry owned slaves and said, "I am drawn along by the general inconvenience of living without them [but] I will not, I cannot justify it." John Adams refused to own slaves, but conceded that "It cost me thousands to employ free labor." Washington provided in his will for the emancipation of his own slaves. He once told Jefferson that it was "among his first wishes to see some plan adopted by which slavery in his country might be abolished by law." Jefferson, also a slave-owner, regretted that "this unfortunate difference of color and perhaps of faculty is a powerful obstacle to the emancipation of these people." In the first draft of the Declaration of Independence, he attempted to throw the blame on England, and specifically on George III as the real promoter of slavery and the slave trade. The draft included the following clause:

"He has waged cruel war against human nature itself, violating its most sacred rights of life and liberty in the persons of a distant people who never offended him, captivating and carrying them into slavery in another hemisphere or to incur miserable death in their transportation thither. This piratical warfare, the opprobrium of INFIDEL powers, is the warfare of the CHRISTIAN king of Great Britain. Determined to keep open a market where MEN should be bought and sold, he has prostituted his negative for suppressing every legislative attempt to prohibit or restrain this execrable commerce."

This clause was subsequently omitted, Jefferson says, "in complaisance to South Carolina and Georgia, who had never attempted to restrain the importation of slaves, and who, on the contrary, still wished to continue it. Our northern brethren also, felt a little tender under these censures; for though their people had very few slaves themselves, yet they had been pretty considerable carriers of them to others."

At the end of the Revolution, when John Jay was negotiating

with the British, he warned them not to make plans for exporting slaves to the United States, "it being the intention of the
said States entirely to prohibit the importation thereof." The
temper of American state legislatures seemed to support his warning. Bringing slaves into the state for sale had been forbidden
by Virginia in 1778 and by Maryland in 1783. Pennsylvania in
1780 passed "An Act for the gradual abolition of slavery." That
same year Massachusetts adopted a new constitution, and the
courts ruled that one of its clauses abolished slavery in the com-
monwealth. The series of restrictive measures continued after the
war. New Jersey forbade the importation of slaves in 1786, about
the same time that North Carolina was imposing a prohibitive
duty on them. Even South Carolina, the center of the import
trade, where the planters had been going deeply into debt to buy
slaves, put a ban on their importation for a five-year term beginning
in 1787. The ban was renewed several times, but it was regarded as
a purely economic measure, which the state would always be free
to rescind.

Still, Northern or Southern, most of the delegates to the Con-
stitutional Convention agreed with Roger Sherman of Connecticut
when he said "that the abolition of slavery seemed to be going on
in the United States, and that the good sense of the several states
would probably by degrees complete it." The importation of slaves
might have been forbidden by the Constitution had it not been
for the stubborn resistance of the delegates from South Carolina
and Georgia. When a resolution against the trade showed signs
of being passed over their protests, they threatened what was in
effect secession. Once again Roger Sherman spoke for many others.
"It is better," he said, "to let the Southern States import slaves
than to part with those States." A final compromise accepted by
Georgia and South Carolina was that the slave trade—described in
the Constitution as "The Migration or Importation of such Persons as any of the States now existing shall think proper to admit"
—should not be prohibited by Congress before the year 1808. Thus,
the scene was set for new battles over the trade.

Meanwhile English reformers had started the first organized attack on the trade. Their campaign was based almost entirely on the belief that slavery—no matter whether or not it yielded profits—was morally wrong.

In 1765 a young Londoner named Granville Sharp came on a Negro slave lying at the point of death in Mincing Lane. His owner, David Lisle, a lawyer from Barbados, had beaten him, then thrown him into the street to die. Sharp took the slave home and nursed him back to health. Lisle, hearing that the man had recovered, kidnaped him and sold him to the West Indies. When Sharp protested, the Barbados lawyer brought suit against him for having stolen his property.

The case aroused so much indignation that Lisle withdrew his suit, to the great disappointment of Sharp, who had been studying the finer points of English law as it related to property in slaves. The law provided that "all men" should have certain rights. Would the court—Sharp asked in another case regarding a kidnaped slave—say that a Negro was not a man? This time the court evaded the main issue by freeing the Negro on the ground that his former owner had attempted to seize him without a warrant. Sharp then found still another fugitive slave, James Somerset, and brought a test case. In 1772 Lord Chief Justice Mansfield handed down the historic decision that "as soon as any slave sets foot on English ground he becomes free."

Although this judgment abolished slavery in Great Britain, it did not affect British possessions. Neither did it prohibit the trade itself, which might have continued indefinitely had it not been for the efforts of two remarkable men, Thomas Clarkson and William Wilberforce.

In 1785 Cambridge University offered a Latin prize for the best essay on the subject *Anne liceat invitos in servitutem dare:* "Is it lawful to make slaves of others against their will?" A twenty-five-year-old student named Thomas Clarkson decided to compete for the prize. He knew nothing about the slave trade, but he procured a copy of Benezet's *Short Account* and set to work. Clarkson was the son of a clergyman in Cambridgeshire. His parents were reasonably well off, and the young man had a small private income. He was a quiet, unambitious, studious youngster whose only desire was to obtain a decent country parish and follow in the footsteps of his father. After reading Benezet's description of the trade, he was transformed into what the poet Coleridge would later call "a moral steam-engine," and what the pro-slavery element characterized as a "Jacobin white nigger."

Clarkson won the Latin prize. A few weeks later, while riding to London through Hertfordshire, he received what he considered to be a direct revelation from God, ordering him to devote his life to abolishing the trade. He dismounted, fell on his knees beside the road, and accepted his divinely appointed mission. Settling down in London, he began what at first seemed to be a one-man battle against the trade. He then discovered, however, that there was a Quaker committee which had been formed some years before to oppose the trade, and that there were a few men, notably Granville Sharp, more than willing to help in his fight. The Quaker committee had become inactive, but Clarkson reorganized it. With Sharp, Josiah Wedgwood the potter, and some other enthusiasts, he founded the Society for the Abolition of the Slave Trade in 1787. The seal of the Society was "An African . . . in chains in a supplicating posture, kneeling with one knee upon the ground, and with both hands lifted up to Heaven, and round the seal . . . the following motto . . . 'Am I not a Man and a Brother.'" Wedgwood copied the seal in china and turned out copies by the thousands.

In many respects Clarkson resembled the popular conception of a fanatical do-gooder. He was a humorless man, a poor talker, uncompromising, and a bore. Years later the artist Haydon said of him, "He is impatient, childish, simple, positive, hates contradiction [but is also] charitable and speaks affectionately of all." Physically he was a tall (six feet) and heavy man with a deeply furrowed face. He was an indefatigable worker. He visited Liverpool, Bristol, and the other slaving ports, gathering data on the trade from seamen, ships' doctors, merchants, and travelers. He started a collection of instruments used in the trade, such as leg shackles, handcuffs, thumbscrews, and the speculum oris, or mouth opener. Part of the collection is still in the museum at Wisbech, some thirty-five miles north of Cambridge. Also he made an English translation of his prize essay, which the Quakers published, and later he wrote many other pamphlets on his findings.

To interfere with the interests controlling the slave trade was a dangerous procedure. Once, in Liverpool, Clarkson was returning from his investigation of a slave ship when he saw a group of nine seamen walking down the pier toward him. One of the men had been previously pointed out to him as the murderer of a sailor who had dared to protest against a captain's brutality. Clarkson retreated, but the gang began to close in on him. There was no one else on the pier and the tide was running strong; a body thrown into the sea would never be found. Clarkson put his head down and charged like a bull. The sudden attack took the men by surprise. There were curses, a few blows, and then Clarkson broke through and escaped. The next day he was back again, oblivious to the scowls and mutterings around him, gravely jotting down fresh information.

Unlike many reformers, Clarkson realized his own limitations. He was not an orator or a national leader. His work would have to consist in collecting evidence against the trade and in performing the endless secretarial tasks that were vital to the society. Someone else would have to be the spokesman of the movement: a politician who could rouse the public by trumpeting out Clarkson's painfully acquired knowledge. But with the slave trade bringing in direct profits of £300,000 a year to the Liverpool traders alone, and with the merchants who supplied the "trade goods" used in obtaining the slaves making another £140,000—plus the West Indian sugar trade valued at six millions—opposition to slavery was political suicide. An utterly dedicated man had to be found—eloquent, politically prominent, well connected, and wealthy enough to be independent of governmental favors. There was only one man who possessed these qualifications: William Wilberforce.

Wilberforce was born in 1759 in Hull, Yorkshire, the son of a rich merchant. He was a sickly child with bad eyes and a puny frame, but he was brilliant and charming. His grandfather left him a fortune, and the boy grew up to be a prominent man about town. He was a member of the better London clubs, a friend of George Selwyn, Sheridan, Charles Fox, and William Pitt, and knew Benjamin Franklin. As was fashionable among the young bucks of the time, he was a gambler and a heavy drinker. His diary is interspersed with such notes as "won 600 pounds this evening" or "lost 100 pounds at whist." In spite of his dissipation and his physical handicaps, he impressed even casual acquaintances with his capabilities. Boswell remarked, "I thought he was a shrimp but the shrimp is a whale."

Bored with the fashionable world, Wilberforce decided at the age of twenty-one to enter Parliament. The election cost him £9000, as he paid two guineas to anyone who would vote for him. Finding Parliament even more boring than the coffeehouses, he decided to make a grand tour of the Continent, together with a Cambridge don named Isaac Milner. Mr. Milner was an early exponent of what later became known as "muscular Christianity." He was a big, powerful man, cheerfully aggressive and the antithesis of his delicate, intellectual charge. Milner converted him to Christianity of the militant type that is more concerned with fighting evil than with intoning pieties.

When Wilberforce returned to London, he resolved to resign from Parliament and enter the ministry. Pitt persuaded him to stay on, arguing that the brilliant young man could accomplish more good as a politician than as a clergyman. So Wilberforce retained his seat in Parliament, devoting much of his time to writing religious treatises and pondering the state of his soul. He also made several speeches denouncing both slavery and the slave trade, but with little result, as he relied on rhetoric more than facts to impress his listeners. Since he was, however, almost the only member of Parliament who had actively interested himself in the cause, the new Society for the Abolition of the Slave Trade decided to ask him to become its spokesman.

Clarkson was dispatched to ask Wilberforce for his help. In the presence of a great London gentleman, the country parson's son found himself tongue-tied; he mumbled a few words and rushed out of the room. Another member had to be selected as messenger, and Wilberforce gladly consented to be the society's champion.

No one could resist his charm when he chose to exert it. Wilberforce and Clarkson became close friends and worked together as an effective team, each possessing the qualities which the other lacked, and both dedicated to the same principles. Together they devised a strategy for attacking the trade. Clarkson had already collected figures showing that more than one-fifth of the sailors on Guineamen died in the course of a single voyage, and it was decided that the loss of English seamen was more likely to rouse public animosity toward the trade than the wholesale murder of any number of African Negroes. Although this was the first point to emphasize, the sufferings of the Negroes were not to be neglected. Both Clarkson and Wilberforce intended to work for the total abolition of slavery, but they agreed to confine their attacks to the trade itself, meanwhile assuring West Indian planters that domestic slavery would be untouched and that they were interested only in preventing possible slave insurrections. They would assert that stopping the trade would double or even triple the value of the slaves then held in the British islands and would enable the British planters to monopolize the West Indian slave market.

Clarkson now set out systematically to collect so much detailed evidence against the slave trade that the pro-slavery forces would be unable to refute his facts. He rode more than three thousand miles during the next few months. He discovered evidence that a sailor named Peter Green had been flogged to death because he refused his captain's Negro mistress the keys to the wine locker.

He found that another sailor, John Dean of the *Brothers*, had been chained face down to the deck and that the captain had made incisions in his bare back with red-hot tongs and then poured hot pitch over him. One man's brains had been beaten out with a double wall knot in the end of a rope. Clarkson was not content simply to accept the word of seamen who had witnessed these murders on slave ships; he double-checked the evidence, making sure that the murdered men had actually been part of the ships' complements, that they had not returned from the voyages, and that there were no records in the ships' logs of the manner of their deaths.

He soon found it increasingly difficult to obtain the kind of evidence he needed. Witnesses mysteriously disappeared or suddenly changed their minds. Tradesmen who were willing to cooperate with him had their shops boycotted. Ships' doctors who told him about the horrors of the Middle Passage were refused new berths on outgoing ships. The son of a West Indian planter who talked to Clarkson was promptly cut out of his father's will. On one occasion Clarkson traveled several hundred miles to interview a sailor who then refused to talk to him. Clarkson rode on, but received a message that the man had changed his mind. Clarkson rode back, traveling all night, only to find that although the sailor would talk, he would not allow his name to be used.

Some of the evidence uncovered was so patently incredible that Clarkson thought it had been deliberately arranged by the pro-slavery group as a trap for him. In Bristol he spoke to some sailors who told him that they were bound for Africa to pick up a cargo of seventy slaves. Clarkson obtained the dimensions of their vessel from the builder. It had been intended as a pleasure craft on the Severn and was designed for no more than six persons. The hold, where the slaves were to be stowed, was only thirty-one feet long and two feet, eight inches high. Obviously, Clarkson reasoned, the men had been instructed to tell him a ridiculous story in the hope that he would repeat it and make a fool of himself. Then, after checking with five other men, he discovered that the story was true. The slaves were to be piled on top of one another like sacks of merchandise.

Meanwhile the Abolition Society had started its public agitation against the trade. In its first 15 months it printed 26,526 reports and 51,432 books and pamphlets, many of which found eager readers. So many petitions for the abolition of the slave trade were submitted to Parliament in 1788 that the Crown appointed a committee of the Privy Council to hold hearings. Parliament itself took one legislative action. It passed a law limiting the number of slaves that a vessel could carry according to its tonnage: roughly five slaves for every three tons.

In 1789 Wilberforce, after an admirable speech, presented a series of resolutions as the basis for a future motion to abolish the trade. The resolutions led to the famous parliamentary hearings of 1790 and 1791, which examined every aspect of the purchase, transportation, sale, and treatment of Negro slaves. Abolition became a popular cause. At evening parties ladies refused to serve West Indian sugar and recited anti-slavery ballads, including Cowper's "The Negro's Complaint." Wedgwood's china seal of the Abolition Society appeared on snuff boxes, bracelets, and combs. Many grocers would not deal in rum or sugar, and Clarkson boasted that sugar revenue had fallen off by £200,000.

Already the excitement had spread to France, where a group of philosophers and liberal aristocrats had founded a Société des Amis du Noir. Clarkson set out for Paris in 1789, hoping to persuade the National Assembly to join with the British government in abolishing the trade. Having started with high anticipations, his visit ended with the first real setback to the cause. Although he enjoyed the support of Lafayette and Mirabeau, Clarkson was denounced as an English spy seeking to bankrupt French colonial possessions. The rumor circulated that he was planning to incite Negro slaves in the colonies to murder their masters.

A mulatto from Santo Domingo named Vincent Ogé was in Paris at the time. Ogé was demanding that all the slaves in the

island be freed within fifteen years; if not, he threatened to lead
a general uprising. Clarkson begged him to moderate his demands,
but Ogé refused. "I begin not to care," he said, "whether the
National Assembly will admit us or not. We will no longer continue to be held in a degraded light. We can produce as good
soldiers as those of France. If we are once forced to desperate
measures, it will be in vain that thousands are sent across the
Atlantic to bring us back to our former state." Words like these
infuriated the French. When Mirabeau introduced a bill to abolish
the slave trade, the National Assembly refused to pass it—unless
Parliament first abolished the trade. As not a few members of
Parliament had already indicated that they would not vote to
abolish the trade unless the French did, Clarkson was helpless.

Having returned to England, Clarkson was accused of being a
Jacobin, the eighteenth-century equivalent of being called a Com-
munist. In attacking the slave trade, his enemies said, he was up-
holding the claims of an inferior class against their masters and
hence was supporting the French doctrine of the rights of man.
He was also accused of being a French spy.

In April 1791 a motion was finally made in the House of Commons to prohibit the importation of slaves into the British West
Indies. Wilberforce shone in the debate that followed, but the
ruling classes, disturbed by the French Revolution, had become less
sympathetic to reforms. Also they were rendered fearful by signs
of unrest in the sugar islands. Ogé had returned to Santo Domingo,
had taken arms with a few followers, and, when he surrendered,
had been broken on the wheel. There had been slave revolts in
Martinique and in the British island of Dominica. After the
long investigation of the slave trade, the motion against it was
defeated by the discouraging vote of 163 to 88.

Clarkson and Wilberforce resumed their campaign. By this time
a new revolt had broken out in Santo Domingo, with massacres
of the planters, and the pro-slavery forces were thoroughly aroused.
Wilberforce was challenged to duels. Gangs of thugs attempted
to waylay him, and he was forced to hire guards. The rumor

circulated that he had a Negro mistress. West Indian planters and Liverpool merchants raised a campaign fund of £10,000 to fight the anti-slave-trade bill in Parliament. Witnesses were rushed to London from the West Indies and Africa prepared to swear that the trade was a benevolent institution dedicated solely to civilizing the primitive Africans. The Abolition Society had lost most of its wealthy supporters, but meanwhile it was gaining new adherents among the industrial workers of the north and among the Nonconformists, moved by the example of John Wesley. When Wilberforce raised the motion for abolition a second time, in 1792, it was supported by 312 petitions from England, 187 from Scotland, and 20 from Wales.

In an impassioned speech Wilberforce urged his fellow members to put moral responsibilities above economic considerations. A Mr. Henniker answered him by reading a letter from the King of Dahomey to George I in which the Dahoman had boasted of ornamenting the pavement and walls of his palace with the heads of his prisoners. Slave traders testified to the notorious "customs" and to the wholesale sacrifice of captives. Wilberforce, however, was now ready to answer this argument. Pretending great incredulity, he insisted that primitive savages armed only with spears and shields could not possibly overrun whole nations and capture thousands of their fellow Africans. The slave traders retorted that the Dahoman army was well equipped with muskets and even cannon, adding that a sentimentalist who had never been to Africa and obviously knew nothing of the facts was presumptuous to propose laws concerning the trade. Wilberforce then demanded to know from what source the native kingdoms obtained their firearms.

The slave traders took refuge in describing the happy life led by Negroes in the Middle Passage. The slaves had abundant food, ample room, and plenty of air; when on deck, they danced and made merry. The voyage was "one of the happiest periods of a Negro's life." One witness added, in the flush of his enthusiasm, "When the sailors are flogged, it is always done out of hearing of the Africans so as not to disturb them." With the blundering remarks of his opponents to help him, Wilberforce came somewhat nearer to success. This time Commons adopted an amendment to defer the abolition of the trade, but it then passed the emasculated bill. It was permitted to die in the House of Lords. Thus, after five years of desperate exertion by the Abolition Society, the only tangible result had been the law to limit the number of slaves that a vessel might carry, and this had been passed at the first session of Parliament that discussed the trade.

After 1792 political life in Great Britain entered a period of extreme conservatism. Revolutionary France was now the enemy, but British soldiers were also fighting the revolted slaves in Santo Domingo, where forty thousand of the soldiers died in four years, mostly of fever. Anyone demanding rights for Negroes was regarded in conservative circles as coming close to treason. Wilberforce did not flinch; he kept introducing his motions against the slave trade in each new session of Commons, where they were always defeated. The Abolition Society could find little money to carry on its work. Nevertheless it had created a lasting image of the slave trade in the public mind, and its work was meeting with a somewhat less violent opposition now that the West Indian planters were losing their influence in Parliament. As for the Liverpool merchants, they had become more interested in profits from wartime shipping and privateering than they were in the Guinea trade.

A new ministry, under Grenville and Fox, took office in 1806. Fox, easy-going as he was, had been a lifelong opponent of slavery. In June he brought forward a resolution "that effectual measures should be taken for the abolition of the African slave trade"; it was passed by a large majority. Fox died in September, but early the following spring Grenville presented to the House of Lords a bill providing that "all manner of dealing and trading in the Purchase, Sale, Barter or Transfer of Slaves . . . is hereby utterly abolished." It was passed by both houses, and Wilberforce collapsed weeping in his chair. He is said to have received the greatest ovation ever heard in Parliament.

The new law enacted that no slaver could clear from a British port after May 1, 1807, and that no slave could be landed in a British possession after March 1, 1808. The only penalties provided were fines and confiscations, but the British were by now determined to suppress the trade. When contraband slaves began to be landed in the colonies, another law was adopted in 1811, by terms of which slave trading became a felony punishable by transportation. The new penalty proved effective, and from that time British ships played almost no part in the trade. If, as sometimes happened, a British seaman was captured on board a slaver, he would try to escape English justice by claiming to be an American.

The Americans had proved to be less hesitant than the British in passing laws against the slave trade, but they were also less hesitant in breaking them. When the Constitution was ratified, the importation of slaves was legal in Georgia and was technically legal in North Carolina, but at the cost of prohibitive duty. Everywhere else it was a violation of state law. Many states, including Rhode Island, Massachusetts, and Connecticut, which owned most of the slave ships, had forbidden their citizens to engage in the trade. Nevertheless it had been revived illegally and had begun to flourish. In 1789 a shipowner of Bristol, England, asserted in a petition to the government that "Since the restrictions laid on the trade to Africa by British legislation, no less than 40 sail of vessels have been fitted out for the Coast in the States of New England." "An Ethiopian," said William Ellery, "could as soon change the color of his skin as a Newport merchant could be induced to change so lucrative a trade as that in slaves." Actually the Rhode Island trade had moved from Newport to Bristol, but it would soon be larger than ever. In 1797 Zachary Macaulay, an early governor of Sierra Leone (and father of the historian), reported in sorrow, "During the last year, the number of American slavers on the coast has increased to an unprecedented degree."

As for the American import trade in slaves—as distinguished from the carrying trade—it was affected after 1790 by two contrary

forces operating on Southern opinion: the fear of Negro insurrection and the hope of immense profits from slavery. The fear
resulted from the slave revolt in western Santo Domingo, or Haiti,
renewed in 1791 after the suppression of Vincent Ogé's hopeless
uprising; it continued until a final massacre of the whites by
Dessalines in 1804. Whereas the British at home were merely
disturbed by the far-away revolt, the Southern planters feared that
their own lives were at stake. There was a general feeling that
Negroes from Haiti must not be allowed to enter the country, and
the legal precautions were extended to Negroes from other West
Indian islands, on the ground that they might have been affected
by the Haitian example. Every state south of Maryland was afraid
of what would happen if the white population came to be vastly
outnumbered by the slaves. Largely as a result of this fear, even
Georgia prohibited the importation of foreign Negroes in 1798.

But the fear had already begun to be counterbalanced by the
intense demand for labor that was due to the invention of the
cotton gin in 1793. Before that time it had taken a Negro woman
all day to clean the seeds from a single pound of cotton staple. Eli
Whitney's original invention, a hand-turned gin, made it possible
for one person to clean fifty pounds of cotton a day, and the first
power-driven gins cleaned a thousand pounds. Never before had a
single invention released such tremendous economic forces. Everybody in the South wanted to grow cotton, and the plantation system rapidly spread from the coastal lowlands to the red clay hills
of the Piedmont, then to the Alabama Black Belt, and then to the
Mississippi Valley. The exportation of cotton rose from 138,000
pounds in 1792 to 6,276,000 pounds in 1795 and 17,790,000 pounds
in 1800, while the price of slaves rose with the demand for cotton.

South of the Virginia line, state laws against importing slaves
began to be openly violated. We have noted that the vessel on
which Mungo Park sailed from the Gambia in 1797 made no secret
of its being bound for South Carolina. A young man from upstate
New York named Joseph Hawkins, who had come to Charleston
to seek his fortune, shipped as supercargo on board a slaver in

December 1793, and again no secret was made of the voyage. The slaver, a square-rigged ship called the *Charleston*, assembled a cargo of five hundred Negroes in the Rio Pongo and the Rio Nuñez, north of Sierra Leone. On the return voyage there was an epidemic of ophthalmia among the cargo and the crew. Hawkins contracted it, but after eleven days he began to recover. Then, in trying to see whether a pursuing man-of-war was hostile, he strained his eyes and suddenly went blind. He never regained his sight. Some years later he dictated his memoirs to an amanuensis, but he does not tell us how or where the cargo of slaves was landed.

A few of the missing details about the American trade are supplied in a letter dated January 7, 1802. It was written by Captain Charles Clark of the Rhode Island brig *Nancy* and was addressed to the owner of the brig, James deWolf, who was engaged by that time in the wholesale smuggling of slaves into South Carolina. "When I wrote you before," Captain Clark reported, "I was bound out of the city after my cargo, which had been on the beach to the northward of Charleston. I found them all well, and much better than I expected, for the weather was very cold. They had no clothes, and no shelter except the sand hills and cedar trees, and no person to take care of them. I arrived in Charleston with them on the 14th Decr. without being troubled. . . . I sailed with 70 cargo, and lost 4 of them; but they are all very good and will bring the highest price, that is, from $350 up to $500. I don't see that the Trade stops much, for they come in town 2 or 3 hundred some nights. I believe there has been landed since New Years as much as 500 slaves. . . . I left on the [African] Coast 14 vessels belonging to the U. States, a great part of them for Charleston."

Finally these violations of the law became so flagrant, and there was such a loud complaint from up-country cotton planters, who did not get a chance to buy the smuggled slaves, that the South Carolina trade was reopened at the end of 1803. For the next four years Charleston was one of the great slaving ports of the world. It seemed that almost all the white population was infected with Negro fever. Everyone with sufficient capital dreamed of outfitting a ship for the Guinea trade, or at least of sending out a few hogsheads of rum or tobacco as a personal venture, while poorer citizens shipped as sailors before the mast. From all the cotton states, planters flocked in to buy slaves in Charleston. Ship chandleries flourished as never before, and there was a new demand for chains, shackles, cheap cotton goods, and quarter-barrels of gunpower "suitable for the African trade."

Meanwhile the book trade suffered. Ebenezer Thomas of Massachusetts had opened a bookshop in Charleston, and his business had doubled or tripled every year. In November 1803 he had just returned from a trip abroad with the largest importation of books so far made into the United States.

> I had only got them opened [Thomas says in his memoirs] and arranged for sale three days, when news arrived from Columbia, that the legislature, then in session, had opened the port for the importation of slaves from Africa. The news had not been five hours in the city, before two large British Guineamen, that had been laying off and on the port for several days, expecting it, came up to town; and from that day my business began to decline. . . . A great change at once took place in every thing. Vessels were fitted out in numbers, for the coast of Africa, and as fast as they returned, their cargoes were bought up with avidity, not only consuming the large funds that had been accumulating, but all that could be procured, and finally exhausting credit. . . . Those who had been in the habit of indulging in every luxury, and paying for it at the moment, took credit for a bundle of quills and a ream of paper. For myself, I was upwards of five years disposing of my large stock, at a sacrifice of more than one half.

The total number of slaving vessels that landed their cargoes in Charleston from 1804 to 1807 was 202. Of these 70 were from British ports (usually Liverpool), 61 were from Charleston itself (though some of these had Yankee owners), and 59 were from Rhode Island. The total importation of slaves from Africa, by figures presented to the United States Senate, was 39,075. The importation had increased year by year, from 5386 in 1804 to

15,676 in 1807, a year in which 95 slaving vessels entered the harbor. They were crowding in to land their final cargoes while the traffic was legal. By then most Americans were ashamed of the slave trade and eager to end it. A bill to abolish the trade had been signed by President Jefferson on March 2, 1807, just three weeks before the abolition law was enacted in Great Britain. In the United States the law took effect on January 1, 1808, the earliest date permitted by the Constitution. Already the slavers were planning how to evade it. They started almost immediately, but they were hampered by Jefferson's embargo on American shipping, and later the trade was brought to a complete halt by the fighting at sea with England. After the War of 1812 it was resumed on a large scale. The two centers of the contraband trade were to be Georgia and the new state of Louisiana, where Negro fever raged as nowhere else in the country.

# 9

# Contraband

*Trying to stop the slave trade with cruisers is like trying to stop a river by building a dam across its mouth.*
—A British officer in the slave squadron

WHEN THE BRITISH ACT OUTLAWING THE TRADE WAS PASSED IN A spirit of high idealism, Parliament had ignored the practical problems it would raise. The reformers had supposed that the African rulers, once freed from exploitation by the slavers, would cheerfully turn to constructive pursuits. They had supposed that other nations were as sincere in their desire to stop the trade as was Great Britain. They had taken for granted that there were natural resources throughout West Africa which would immediately interest merchants after the trade had been prohibited. Finally they had never doubted that British naval skill would make it a simple problem to patrol four thousand miles of coastline with the forces

—usually consisting of a few slow frigates—that could be spared from other urgent missions.

From the beginning there were doubts at the Admiralty. Still, Great Britain had, as it were, given her word to abolish the trade and had in fact abolished it in her own possessions. She now set about the task of suppressing it everywhere, with dogged persistence and a rather pathetic conviction that her efforts would be appreciated. A few other nations followed her, and Denmark in fact had led the way by abolishing the trade in Danish possessions after 1802. Sweden abolished it in 1813 and the Netherlands in 1814. During the next three years Portugal and Spain—at British insistence—agreed to abolish the trade north of the equator, and France abolished it completely in 1818, though at first she did not make a serious effort to control smuggling.

Even the British effort was started on a small scale. After the Abolition Act was passed in 1807, Great Britain sent the frigate *Solebay* and the sloop *Derwent* to the Guinea Coast to see that it was enforced. The vessels were small, old, and completely incapable of handling the situation. In 1810 the Admiralty sent four other vessels. These were also small and old, but they caused so much trouble among the slavers that London was besieged with protests from almost every allied or neutral nation in which slavery was still legal. Slowly and regretfully Great Britain was forced to realize that what had seemed a simple humanitarian gesture would involve a long and costly struggle in which her every act would be misinterpreted by her friends as well as her enemies, and in which slavers would take advantage of every international dispute.

The half-century that followed the British abolition of the trade became, in fact, the great "romantic" period of the slave trade. In response to what many persons honestly believed was a despotic act to curtail free intercourse among nations, scores of sleek, fast vessels with hollow-ground bows and capable of carrying an enormous press of sail came sliding down the ways of Baltimore and New England shipyards. They were manned by experienced seamen,

American, French, Spanish, and Portuguese, who feared neither God nor a frigate's broadside and whose boast was that they "would rather fight an Englishman than eat when they were hungry." To many of the slaveholders whose prosperity depended on a constant supply of fresh Negroes, these men were gallant buccaneers striking back at oppression. To those interested in the fate of the Africans, they were pirates more brutal than Blackbeard and monsters who made the old-time slavers look like respectable businessmen.

The Society for the Abolition of the Slave Trade had taken for granted that simply enacting a law against an evil would cause the evil to disappear. They were encouraged by the fact that the British themselves are a remarkably law-abiding people and, indeed, as a matter of record, there were surprisingly few attempts on the part of British captains to continue the trade. At home the battle was now for the complete abolition of slavery, under the leadership of a new Anti-Slavery Society, founded in 1823. Clarkson and Wilberforce were both vice-presidents of the society, but by then they were both old men, and Clarkson in particular had never wholly recovered from a stroke he suffered during the heat of the earlier battle. He worked on, however, until his death in 1846, "the slave of the slaves."

Wilberforce fought as fiercely against slavery in the colonies as he had fought against the trade. He once said wearily, "I am sick of battle, but I'll not leave my poor slaves in the lurch." When he stood for Parliament in 1807, as an independent, he was opposed by two wealthy men, Lord Milton for the Whigs and Lascelles for the Tories. Both adopted the platform: "Let us turn our attention to other matters besides the lot of the African." Both spent enormous sums on their campaigns, buying up wagons, coaches, and other means of transportation to keep Wilberforce's supporters from reaching the polls. An army of poor weavers and mill workers, the very people who would be ruined by a cotton shortage, marched on York chanting, "Wilberforce to a man." Re-elected as always, he remained in Parliament until his retirement in 1825. He died in 1833, just a month before Parliament passed a bill abolishing slavery in all the British possessions.

The task of serving as Parliamentary spokesman for the Anti-Slavery Society had already been assumed, at Wilberforce's request, by Thomas Fowell Buxton, who was still in his thirties. Buxton, among his many charitable activities, initiated a disastrous attempt at African colonization, but he also did his best to combat the illegal revival of the slave trade. In 1840, however, he was forced to admit: "The traffic has not been extinguished, has not diminished, but the numbers exported have increased. The destruction of human life has been fearfully augmented and the numbers exported from Africa are, as compared with the year 1807, as two to one and the annual loss of life [in the Middle Passage] has risen from 17% to 25%."

What had happened during the intervening years to revive the outlawed trade?

1. The demand for slaves had greatly increased, and this in spite of the fact that their importation had been legally prohibited in the whole Western Hemisphere. Factually as well as legally, importation had ceased in the Northern states, in the border states, in almost all the West Indian islands except Cuba, and in all the Latin American countries except Brazil. But Cuba alone was almost as big a market as the whole hemisphere had formerly been. Last and largest of the sugar islands, Cuba was expanding and multiplying her plantations year by year, and her demand for slave labor seemed to be endless. A British commission reported in 1836 that sixty thousand slaves had been landed in Cuba during that one year. Most of them stayed on the island, but some of them— nobody knows how many—were re-exported to the cotton states.

In Brazil the plantation crops were sugar, tobacco, cotton, and increasingly coffee, for which the demand was growing year by year. New areas were being opened to settlement, and thousands of strong-backed laborers were needed to clear the land. Slaves were also used, and used up, in the copper mines. Brazil had signed a treaty prohibiting the importation of slaves after 1829, but she did not pretend to enforce it. The British Foreign Office estimated that thirty-seven thousand Negroes were imported during the year after the treaty was signed. By 1830 the British consul at Rio was reporting that at least a hundred thousand Negroes had been landed in a period of eighteen months. Of these fifty thousand had arrived in the first six months of 1830.

In the United States it was cotton that created the demand for slaves. For all the other plantation crops there was an ample supply of labor—or even a surplus, as in the case of Virginia tobacco—but King Cotton demanded a larger and larger retinue. By 1850 almost 60 per cent of the slaves in the country were employed in growing this one crop, which had come to furnish, in terms of value, almost two-thirds of American exports. The market for cotton seemed to be unlimited. In England the development of the power loom and the invention of the ring spinning frame in 1828 had revolutionized the weaving and spinning of cotton almost as much as Whitney's cotton gin had revolutionized the production of cotton lint. Mills in England and New England could sell larger and larger amounts of cheap cotton cloth at tremendous profits. In 1822 the American cotton crop was half a million bales; by 1860 it was almost five million bales.

To produce more cotton the planters needed a continuous supply of cheap new land and cheap labor. The new land was to the west, and by 1840 they were already pushing up the Red River Valley into Indian Territory and were clearing new plantations in the Republic of Texas. The labor could partly be supplied from the worn-out plantations of the Eastern seaboard, and especially from Maryland, Virginia, North Carolina, and Kentucky, where the slave population was increasing more rapidly than it could be utilized. Those four states, with Delaware and Tennessee, were opposed to any reopening of the slave trade, since it would lower the value of their own human property. Planters in the Deep South had divided feelings about the trade. For a long time most of them were ashamed to support it openly, but still they needed slaves and were grateful for the shiploads smuggled in from Cuba or Africa.

The contraband trade into the cotton states reached an early climax in the years that followed the War of 1812. Nobody counted the smuggled slaves, but their number was generally estimated as between ten and twenty thousand a year. In 1819 a bank panic reduced the demand for African labor. The following year was that of the Missouri Compromise, when concessions were being made by the South as well as the North. One of the Southern concessions was a bill to define slave trading as piracy, punishable by death. Most of the men representing the cotton states in Congress voted against the bill, but, lacking the support of the border states, they did not try seriously to defeat it. Even so the bill had a stormy reception. Stanton of Rhode Island declared, "I cannot believe that a man ought to be hung for only stealing a Negro." One of Stanton's leading constituents was General George deWolf of Bristol, son of the Charles who had wallowed in gold, and now the only deWolf engaged in the trade. General George's schooners had been carrying many a stolen Negro across the Atlantic.

Smith of South Carolina taunted the Northern representatives with the known fact that most of the slave ships came from Northern ports. "Pharaoh," he said, "was drowned in the Red Sea for pursuing the Israelites, but our Northern friends are better seamen than Pharaoh and calculate to elude the vengeance of heaven." Nevertheless the bill was passed, and it had at least a temporary effect on the smuggling of slaves into the cotton states, as well as on the traffic from Guinea to Cuba under the American flag. General deWolf and other Rhode Island merchants withdrew from the trade, having little wish to be hanged. The courts, however, displayed no zealous desire to enforce the law, and nobody went to the scaffold for only stealing Negroes. Little by little the American trade revived, to meet the constantly rising demand, until it reached another climax after 1850.

2. If legal measures against the trade had not interfered with the demand for slave labor, neither had they abolished the supply. Nobody had put a stop to the intertribal wars and marauding expeditions on the Guinea coast, so that there were always captives waiting to be sold. English factors had withdrawn from the coast, but they had been replaced by renegade Frenchmen, Spaniards, Portuguese, and mulattoes: the so-called "mongos," named after a native word for "king." Some of the mongos ruled over what were in effect little kingdoms on the Windward Coast. As for the coastal tribes and towns, a few of them had turned to exporting palm oil, but most of them were still dependent on the slave trade as their principal source of the firearms they needed for survival. Testifying before a Parliamentary committee in 1830, a British sea captain quoted one monarch as saying, "We want three things: viz., powder, ball, and brandy, and we have three things to sell, viz., men, women, and children." The kings were not intimidated by a mere British frigate cruising offshore. Prince Jack of Cabinda expressed a common attitude when he told Captain Matson, "One time we tink Englishmen be almost same as God-almighty; now we tink he be same as other white men . . . all same as we." As long as the slavers would buy, the kings would sell.

3. The slavers continued to buy because the illegal trade yielded enormous profits from any successful voyage. As with bootlegging during Prohibition, there was the possibility of making a fortune almost overnight. Negro fever raged intermittently in the cotton states, and each attack of it was apparently worse than the preceding one. Thus in 1805 a "prime field hand," the highest category of unskilled labor, was said to be worth $500. In 1825 the same type of man might bring as much as $1500, and in 1860 he might bring $2500, although this was well above the average price. In 1853 the *Anderson* (South Carolina) *Gazette* reported, "Boys weighing about 50 lbs. can be sold for about $500," and the *Wilmington* (North Carolina) *Journal* observed, "This species of property is at

least 30% higher now than it was last January. What Negroes will bring next January, it is impossible for mortal man to say." Negro fever must have raged that year, and it raged again in January 1860, when, we read in the *Charleston Mercury*, "A minister who paid $3500 for a slave," probably one with some special skill like cabinetmaking or bricklaying, "was offered $4000 for him a few minutes later." In the same year ten-year-old boys sold for $1545 in Georgia, and speculators who imported slaves into Texas counted on making a profit of at least 200 per cent.

Meanwhile the cost of slaves in Africa had dropped after 1807. During the next half-century it varied from time to time and from place to place, but it remained, on the whole, substantially lower than it had been when the trade was legal. Captains expected to pay from $25 to $50 apiece for their slaves, in gold doubloons or merchandise. The cost might be even less if British frigates were cruising in the neighborhood or if intertribal wars had overcrowded the barracoons. In 1847 the Ashanti were selling able-bodied men for $10, the price of an old musket. The same men delivered in Cuba might bring, at the time, $625 each. That was an exceptional case, but slavers usually counted on selling each "piece of India" for ten times as much as it had cost them.

In his book *Twenty Years of an African Slaver*, Captain Theodore Canot gives us the balance sheet of a successful slaving voyage. Canot had established himself as a factor on the Rio Pongo, in what is now the Republic of Guinea. In 1827 he loaded the schooner *La Fortuna* with 220 slaves consigned to Havana. Only three of them died in the Middle Passage, and the voyage yielded a profit of 104 per cent to the vessel's Cuban owners. On the opposite page is an itemized list of expenditures and receipts.

Canot had sold his slaves to *La Fortuna* for a little less than $50 apiece, a high price for the time. The owners of *La Fortuna* sold them in Havana for $357 apiece, or more than seven times what they cost. It was a fortunate voyage for all concerned, except the slaves. To even the balance sheet, however, Canot next loaded the forty-ton pilot boat *Aerostatico* for the same owners, and she dis-

EXPENSES OUT

| | |
|---|---|
| Buying and fitting out a 90-ton schooner | $6200 |
| Provisions for crew and slaves | 1115 |
| Cargo (to be exchanged for slaves) | 10,900 |
| Advance on wages | 1340 |
| Hush money | 200 |
| | 19,755 |
| Commission on this at 5% | 987 |
| Total expenses out | $20,742 |

EXPENSES BACK

| | |
|---|---|
| Head money on slaves (for officers of schooner) | $3492 |
| Wages, officers and crew | 2938 |
| Total expenses back | $6430 |

EXPENSES IN HAVANA

| | |
|---|---|
| Bribes to government officers (at $8 per slave) | $1736 |
| Factor's commission | 5565 |
| Consignees' commission | 3873 |
| 217 slave dresses (at $2 each) | 434 |
| Extra expenses of all kinds, say | 1200 |
| Total expenses in Havana | $12,808 |
| Total of all expenses | $39,980 |

RETURNS

| | |
|---|---|
| Vessel sold at auction | $3950 |
| Proceeds of 217 slaves | 77,469 |
| Total returns | $81,419 |
| Total expenses | $39,980 |
| Net profit on voyage | $41,439 |

appeared at sea with her crew and her cargo of slaves. The risks of the illegal slave trade were almost as high as the profits, but determined men were always willing to disregard the first for the sake of the second.

4. Naval technology favored the slavers until the very last years of the illegal trade. Before that time the naval craft assigned to the African station were mostly veterans of the wars against Napoleon,

stoutly built and heavily armed for their size but comparatively slow sailors. More and more of the slaving vessels were newly built in American yards and were able to show their heels to any warship. They were called "clippers" at the time, because of their speed, their sharp bows, and their lean hulls, but most of them were topsail schooners or brigs. They were the greyhounds of the sea—or rather the whippets—and they were not luxury liners. Macgregor Laird reported, after his expedition to the Niger in 1832–1834, "Instead of the large and commodious vessels [formerly used in the trade] we have by our interference forced the slavers to use a class of vessel, well-known to naval men as American clippers, of the very worst description that could have been imagined for the purpose, every quality being sacrificed for speed."

It was not until the British squadron had managed to capture some of the newly built slavers that it had vessels fast enough to prove really effective. One of the first clippers to be taken was the *Black Joke* in 1828; another was the *Fair Rosamond* in 1830. The West African squadron took eleven prizes from 1830 to 1832, nine of which were captured by these two vessels. Meanwhile the slavers were buying still faster vessels from Baltimore and New England shipyards. One of them, the *Socorro*, was "a magnificent ship with slender, raking masts and an enormous spread of sail, which could be further increased by all sorts of sky sails, studding sails, etc." The *Diligente* of 1839 is described in H. I. Chapelle's *The Baltimore Clipper* as having long, straight, clean lines, her sheer very slight, her lower yards greater in length than half the deck, and "the head spars tremendous for this size craft and the whole design marked by extreme dimensions." Still later some of the China tea clippers, fastest of all, made their last voyages as slave ships, notably the *Nightingale* in 1859 and the *Sunny South* in 1860. Such vessels could be captured only when they lay at anchor. Once at sea in a fair breeze, they could outdistance even the new steam frigates.

5. Perhaps the greatest obstacle to the suppression of the trade was the fact that slaving was carried on by outlaws of all nations,

in vessels that hailed from many ports. The international complications appeared to be insoluble. Great Britain was the only nation that maintained an effective naval squadron in West African waters, and she had driven her own vessels out of the trade. Under international law, however, she could not detain vessels of other nations, and she could not even board a slaver that flew the American flag. The Foreign Office, sincerely bent on suppressing the trade, kept trying to negotiate treaties providing for a limited right of search on the high seas. Such treaties were signed by Portugal and Spain in 1817 (but with the provision that no Portuguese or Spanish vessel could be searched south of the equator), by the Netherlands in 1818, by Sweden in 1824, and by France in 1831. The United States refused to sign.

Slavers took full advantage of the confused situation, and it became almost impossible to decide the nationality of any vessel engaged in the trade. Canot tells the story of his voyage as second in command of the *San Pablo*, a trim Brazil-built brig outfitted in the Danish island of Saint Thomas by a French captain. After loading a cargo of slaves in East Africa, it set sail for Cuba but was overhauled by a small British man-of-war. Canot went into the cabin to ask the advice of the captain, who was dying of dysentery. Pointing to one of his drawers, the captain told him to take out its contents. "I handed him three flags," Canot says, "which he carefully unrolled, and displayed the ensigns of Spain, Denmark, and Portugal, in each of which I found a set of papers suitable for the *San Pablo*. In a feeble voice he desired me to select a nationality; and, when I chose the Spanish, he grasped my hand, pointed to the door, and bade me not to surrender."

It was Canot's seamanship, not his flag, that saved the *San Pablo*, but on other occasions the flag—especially if it was American— proved to be ample protection for a slaver. If pursued by a warship, it might run up a series of flags, hoping that one or another would cause the chase to be discontinued. Even when this ruse was unsuccessful, the captain could sometimes avoid condemnation by selling the vessel to any American sailor on board for one dollar.

The legal complications that ensued in a prize court were such that the case was usually dropped. Slavers then adopted the practice of carrying a single American passenger, whose only function was taking command of the vessel if it was boarded by an English cruiser. This man was called the *capitano de bandiera*, or captain of the flag. One such captain was a tailor; another was a grog-shop keeper.

There was a good reason why naval officers could often be stopped by these transparent subterfuges. If the officers transgressed any of the numerous laws or treaties that governed the seizure of slave ships, they could be sued for damages by the slaver. In 1835 Commander Meredith of HMS *Pelorus* found a vessel loading slaves at the mouth of the New Calabar River. He came in to seize her, but the vessel had time to unload her cargo on the beach. As soon as the *Pelorus* moved away, the slaver reloaded with Negroes. The game continued for several hours, until at last Commander Meredith lost his patience and seized the once again empty vessel. The commission at Sierra Leone ruled that he had behaved illegally, and the slaving captain collected damages of £1800 from Meredith himself.

Although much of the illegal slave trade was conducted under the American flag, the United States government did very little toward the suppression of slaving on the African coast. It did more, but not a great deal more, to prevent the smuggling of slaves into the seaboard cotton states. From time to time a few smugglers would be taken, but, as the collector of customs at Mobile reported in 1820, "this was owing rather to accident, than any well-timed arrangement." The collector added, "From the Chandalier Islands to the Perdido river," a distance of more than a hundred miles, "including the coast, and numerous other islands, we have only a small boat, with four men and an inspector, to oppose the whole confederacy of smugglers and pirates."

The Perdido River was the boundary of Spanish Florida, purchased by the United States in 1819 but not occupied until 1821.

Before that time Florida provided a secure base for the contraband trade. Until 1818 a slave ferry operated regularly between Havana and Pensacola. "I soon learned," says Richard Drake in his *Revelations of a Slave Smuggler*, "how readily, and at what profits, the Florida negroes were sold into the neighboring American States. The *kaffle*, under charge of negro drivers, was to strike up the Escambia River, and thence cross the boundary into Georgia, where some of our wild Africans were mixed with various squads of native blacks, and driven inland, till sold off, singly or by couples, on the road. . . . Florida was a sort of nursery for slave-breeders, and many American citizens grew rich by trafficking in Guinea negroes, and smuggling them continually, in small parties, through the southern United States."

One of the citizens trying to grow rich was a governor of Georgia, David B. Mitchell, who estimated in 1817 that twenty thousand slaves were smuggled into his state from Florida every year. Also in 1817 he resigned his office to accept an appointment as Indian agent to the Creek nation, whose fertile lands in Georgia were being occupied by white planters. One reason for his making the change was discovered four years later. Ex-Governor Mitchell had been using his new office as a means of concealing his principal occupation, which was that of smuggling newly landed Africans from Florida into the Creek lands.

The collector at Mobile referred to "the whole confederacy of smugglers and pirates." During and after the War of 1812, many enterprising persons combined the two professions. The most famous of them was Jean Laffite, who operated an emporium for stolen goods on an island in Barataria Bay, south of New Orleans. He made a practice of capturing slave ships in the West Indies and selling their cargoes at auction. His Barataria enterprise was destroyed in 1814 by a federal expeditionary force, but the following year Laffite himself received a presidential pardon in reward for his services at the Battle of New Orleans. Another haunt of slave smugglers and pirates was Amelia Island, on the east coast of Florida near the Georgia line, where a renegade Frenchman named Louis Aury maintained his own government with the help of a printing press. Aury's pirates made the mistake of capturing too many American vessels, and his island was seized by a federal force in 1817.

Laffite, in the meantime, had opened another emporium at Galveston, supplied by a whole buccaneering fleet. James Bowie, creator of the Bowie knife, bought slaves from Laffite at a dollar a pound, or an average of $140 apiece, then smuggled them to markets in the cotton states, where he received from $500 to $1000 for each of them. Although the Galveston establishment was then in Mexico, it was captured by an American warship in 1821, and Laffite sailed off into the Caribbean, where he disappeared from history.

The business of smuggling slaves declined for a number of years, but it was grandly revived after 1830. Although the Rhode Island merchants had retired from the trade, and General deWolf had gone bankrupt in 1825, new capital was forthcoming from New York, which became a home base for the slaving fleet. Other centers of the maritime trade were Baltimore, New Orleans, Boston, and Portland, Maine. Texas, an independent but loosely governed republic after 1836, was a convenient area for landing slaves. In 1837 the British consul in Havana reported on the "highest authority" that 15,000 slaves had recently been smuggled into Texas. It was thought that many of them were destined for the great slave market in New Orleans.

In 1840 Richard Drake, by then an old hand at smuggling, was put in charge of a slave depot on one of the Bay Islands off the coast of Honduras. The depot was owned by a joint-stock company which was, Drake says, "connected with leading American and Spanish mercantile houses and our island was visited almost weekly by agents from Cuba, New York, Baltimore, Philadelphia or New Orleans. During the Mexican War we had about 1600 slaves in good condition and were receiving and shipping constantly. The seasoned and instructed slaves were taken to Texas, overland, and to Cuba in sailing boats. As no squad contained more than half a dozen, no difficulty was found in posting them to the United States without discovery and generally without suspicion. . . . The Bay Island plantation sent ventures weekly to the Florida Keys. Slaves were taken into the great American swamps, and there kept till wanted for the market. Hundreds were sold as captured runaways from the Florida wilderness." Drake remained on the Bay Island until 1853. "I could tell curious stories," he says, ". . . of this business of smuggling Bozal negroes into the United States. It is growing more profitable every year, and if you should hang all the Yankee merchants engaged in it, hundreds would fill their places."

During all these years the British had continued their efforts to suppress the Atlantic slave trade at its source. One of their most difficult problems, first and last, was what to do about slavers that flew the American flag. For a short period after the War of 1812, some of their naval commanders had a simple answer: they boarded the slavers and took them to Sierra Leone. At this a roar of rage went up from Congress, the newspapers, New England shipping interests, and even private citizens who felt that American sovereignty had been infringed. John Quincy Adams, then Secretary of State, sent a strongly worded letter to our minister in London on November 2, 1818. "The admission of a right," he said, "in the officers of foreign ships of war to enter and search the vessels of the United States in time of peace under any circumstances whatever would meet with universal repugnance in the public opinion of this country." Later when Canning, the British Foreign Secretary, asked whether Adams could conceive of a more atrocious evil than the slave trade, he answered tartly, "Yes, admitting the right of search by foreign officers of our vessels upon the sea in time of peace, for that would be making slaves of ourselves."

But Adams was sincerely opposed to the trade, and he concurred with one British suggestion. If we refused to permit British cruisers to board American vessels, the Foreign Office asked, why did we not send our own ships to do the work? Our answer in 1820 was to dispatch four United States warships to West Africa. One of them was the *Cyane,* a twenty-gun sloop which we had captured during the War of 1812. Under the Union Jack she had been assigned to the West African station, where she was still remembered by the crews of her sister ships. To judge from the gloating letters of American officers, the *Cyane* had been selected for her new mission as a means of irritating the British squadron.

The American press and public had been denying that American vessels were taking part in the trade, and it was expected that the little American squadron would prove that the British claims were fraudulent. Unfortunately the squadron found that the British had been understating the extent of American participation. On April 10, 1820, at the mouth of the Gallinas River, the *Cyane* sighted seven sail, which at once put out to sea. A smart breeze was blowing, and for an hour both pursuer and pursued raced along the coast under "clouds of canvas," as Captain Trenchard of the *Cyane* reported. But at seven in the morning the wind dropped and the *Cyane* sent out her boats after the becalmed slavers. One was the *Endymion*, a schooner, and as the *Cyane*'s cutter approached her, the slaver's captain and crew tried to escape in her boat. After a long rowing race, the boat was overhauled, and it was then discovered that the *Endymion*'s captain was Alexander McKim, a former United States midshipman ("as per Naval Register 1820"). Of the seven prizes, six were completely outfitted as slavers and one as either a slaver's armed escort or a pirate. Later Captain Trenchard reported, "All the vessels hovering on this coast are similar in respect to size, fitments, and general appearance; sharp built and no doubt American vessels . . . in general, topsail schooners."

On May 27, 1821, Lieutenant Stockton of the USS *Alligator* captured four schooners at Tradetown, near Cape Mesurado. There was no doubt that they were slavers; in fact while one vessel, *La Daphnée*, had a prize crew on board, canoes carrying slaves came out from shore and tried to load her. When the canoemen saw the bluejackets, they hastily jumped overboard. But now the United States found herself in exactly the same position toward the slavers as that of Great Britain. Both the *Cyane* and the *Alligator* sent their prizes to New York, but the Spanish government protested against the seizure of vessels at Gallinas registered in the names of Spanish citizens, and the French government made a similar protest over the slavers captured at Tradetown. Since the United States would not allow the British to seize a vessel flying the American flag, Adams was forced to acknowledge the justice of these protests and release the vessels. The American squadron was ordered to take only bona-fide American slavers.

Suddenly there were no bona-fide American slavers. The *Cyane* sadly reported: "We have made ten captures; some by fair sailing, others by boat and stratagem. Although they are evidently owned by Americans, they are so completely covered by Spanish papers that it is impossible to condemn them. The slave trade is carried on to a very great extent. There are probably not less than 300 vessels on the Coast engaged in the trade, each having two or three sets of papers." As a result of these difficulties the American squadron was withdrawn three years after it had been sent out, and the United States broke off its agreement with Great Britain to keep a naval force on the African coast.

Great Britain made two more efforts, in 1824 and in 1831–1834, to obtain at least a limited right of search. The first of these efforts was based on a proposal made by Adams, and it had the approbation of President Monroe. It took the form of a treaty providing that both nations would recognize the slave trade "as piracy under the law of nations, namely: that, although seizable by the officers and authorities of every nation, they should be triable only by the tribunals of the slave trading vessel." The treaty was laid before the Senate, where it was so crippled by amendments that the British refused to accept it. In 1831 Great Britain and France signed an agreement by which each nation granted the other a geographically limited right of search. Both nations tried to persuade the United States to join in the agreement, but the Executive would not submit the project to Congress—"from an apprehension," the British minister reported, "of alarming the Southern States." Already the South could be alarmed by even a distant threat to slave property. Great Britain then offered to sign the proposed treaty of 1824 as amended by the Senate, but the offer was refused by John Forsyth of Georgia, the new Secretary of State. He informed the British minister that the United States had determined not to become "a party of any Convention on the subject of the Slave Trade."

From that time more and more slavers began to fly the American flag. They were safe till they reached the coast of Africa, they were safe while loading their cargo, and they were safe on the return voyage unless they happened to meet an American warship, in which case they simply hoisted a Spanish flag. Usually they had provided themselves with the necessary papers. When a United States vessel was sold in a foreign port, the register of the vessel was not transferred, but a "sea-letter"—a transcript of the bill of sale—could be given by the consul as a substitute. From 1834 to 1836 N. P. Trist, the American consul in Havana, openly issued sea-letters to any slave ships requesting them. Commander A. H. Foote of the United States Navy believed that "two-thirds of the slavers on the African Coast claiming American nationality have been provided with these sea-letters."

Although it had now been outlawed by every Western nation, the slave trade was booming again. T. F. Buxton, writing in 1839, asserted that the trade had increased from 100,000 slaves a year, in the days when it was legal, to 200,000 a year, of whom 150,000 were carried across the Atlantic and 50,000 went to the Arab world. The more conservative Foreign Office reckoned the number of slaves exported to the New World in 1835 at 135,000. And still the West African squadron continued its apparently hopeless battle against the slavers.

The total mortality of slaves in the Middle Passage had probably increased. We have to say "probably" because the only figures we have are those of single voyages in which the death rate differed widely from ship to ship. Most of the illegal slavers submitted no figures, except to their secret owners, and more of them than ever before were lost at sea with everyone on board. We know that clipper-built vessels were not designed to carry hundreds of human beings in their narrow holds. We know that many of them had no slave decks, but simply piled their Negroes on the water casks like bales of merchandise. We also know, however, that some of them made very swift voyages from the Windward Coast to Cuba and delivered almost all their merchandise in prime condition.

The case was different when the slaver was making a longer voyage—say from Mozambique around the Cape of Good Hope— or when it was becalmed in the horse latitudes. Then the human beings piled in the hold were subject to epidemics of measles, smallpox, dysentery, or ophthalmia, and sometimes, when the gratings had to be closed in stormy weather, they perished of suffocation. During the last voyage of the *San Pablo*, under its assortment of flags, the hatches were covered during a twenty-day gale that raged south of the Cape of Good Hope. Smallpox raged in the hold, and the dead had to be left there among the living. By something close to a miracle, there were 497 survivors out of the 800 slaves who had been shipped in Mozambique. A French brig, the *Rôdeur*, had a more terrifying voyage in 1819, which became famous in the annals of French medicine. The *Rôdeur* was not overloaded—she was a vessel of about 200 tons and carried only 162 slaves—but she was delayed in the belt of fitful winds near the equator: the doldrums. Five weeks out of Bonny River, each slave was reduced to an allowance of half a cup of water per day.

A contagious disease of the eyes broke out in the hold; one slave after another went blind. The captain had thirty-nine of the first victims thrown overboard—to save the rest, he said—but the disease spread to the crew, and soon every white man on board was blind except one sailor, who steered the vessel as best he could. One day he brought her within hailing distance of a Spanish slaver, the *Leon*, which was yawing with all sails set. The crew of the *Leon* swarmed to the rail and begged for help, saying that every soul on board was blind. With no help to be given, the *Leon* disappeared over the horizon and was never heard of again. The

*Rôdeur* finally reached Guadeloupe after a voyage of seventy-seven days and landed the miserable remnant of her cargo. The steersman, who held out to the end, went blind after he came ashore.

The additional sufferings of the slaves carried across the Atlantic as contraband were not entirely the result of epidemics or overcrowding. The legal definition of a slaver was "a ship carrying slaves." For a long time British naval officers were instructed that they could not detain a vessel, or carry her into port, "except on the single and simple fact of slaves found on board." This was a cruel temptation to slaving captains, who sometimes tried to avoid arrest by a mass drowning of every slave in the cargo.

The most famous story of the sort, but not the best authenticated, is that of the brig *Brillante*, commanded by a man named Homans, one of the very few English captains in the illegal trade. In ten voyages the *Brillante* was said to have landed five thousand Negroes in Cuba. An English cruiser that attacked her was so badly cut up that she had to be abandoned. On another occasion the boats from a sloop-of-war tried to board the *Brillante*, but she drove them off with great slaughter. Her luck ran out, however, and she was finally trapped and surrounded by four British cruisers.

At this point the sun set and the wind died down. The story is that Homans set his bower anchor ready for dropping; then he hauled the anchor chain out through the hawsehole and stretched it round the ship outside the rail by means of slender stops. To the chain he bound every slave on board, to the number of about six hundred, all piled up along the rail. When he heard the cruisers' boats approaching, he gave an order and the anchor dropped into the sea, carrying with it all six hundred slaves. The British tars heard a confusion of cries, but when they boarded the *Brillante* they found only the smell of slaves and the hot caldrons where their evening meal had been cooked; there was not a living Negro on board. Homans stood on the deck and jeered at them before sailing away.

That is the often printed story, and it lacks some essential details. What was the date of the massacre and what were the names of the four British cruisers? Where is their report to the British Admiralty? The whole story may be a fabrication, but the *Brillante* became a legend on the coast, and there are fully authenticated examples of other slavers who tried to "turn the trick" as Captain Homans had. Thus, in 1832 the *Black Joke*, already mentioned, surprised two slavers, the *Rapido* and the *Regulo*, at the mouth of Bonny River and sent out its tenders to intercept them. The slavers had no time to attach their cargo to the anchor chain, so they began tossing the Negroes overboard, manacled in pairs. Not all of them sank, but there were always sharks at the mouth of the Bonny, grown fat on the bodies tossed into the river from the barracoons. A race developed between the tenders and the slavers, with the tenders trying to board the two vessels before the last Negroes were thrown over the side. The *Regulo* was overhauled while she still had 212 slaves on board out of an original 450. The *Rapido* managed to get rid of the last of her slaves as the boarding party approached. Two of the slaves, however, were saved from the sharks by the tenders' crews, and it was decided by the commission at Sierra Leone that, as the slaves could swear they had been on board, the *Rapido* was legally a slaver. Both vessels were condemned.

The British cruiser *Medina* boarded a suspected vessel off the Gallinas River and found no slaves on board. After releasing the vessel, the British officers learned that her captain had been keeping a mulatto girl in his cabin. He was really fond of the girl, and he kept her for some time after the cruiser appeared, but he knew that he would lose his vessel if she was found. At the last moment he tied her to a kedge anchor and dropped her overboard. There are dozens of similar stories in British naval papers and in the records of slaving cases that were tried in United States courts. It was not until 1839 that the British law was amended to remove the temptation to homicide. Beginning with that year a vessel could be condemned if the naval officers, on boarding her, found a slave deck, shackles, or other "clear proof" that she was a slaver. "Clear proof" included the presence of hatches with open gratings, more water casks than would be needed by the crew, and the type of trade goods used in bartering for slaves. This was known as the "equipment clause," and it proved of great convenience to the West African Squadron.

Usually the squadron consisted of a dozen or more vessels and year by year it lost more men by disease, and sometimes from gunshot wounds, than any other squadron in the British Navy. It also captured many slavers, but never enough of them to discourage the others. The best moment for taking a slaver was when the slaves were being ferried aboard. If a cruiser surprised her in this situation—lying close inshore, her sails furled, and her cargo partly in and partly out of the vessel—she could not put up a fight. The slavers tried to reduce the risk, and the process of loading slaves, which formerly had taken days or weeks, was brought down to a matter of hours. Not only did the vessel herself maintain a lookout for warships, but the factor also dispatched sharp-eyed natives with telescopes to watchtowers built on the highest points of land. If a strange sail was sighted, the lookouts fired a gun or ran up a flag. The slaver then slipped her anchor and ran for her life.

Later, if she encountered an English cruiser at sea, the slaver clapped on every inch of canvas her yards would hold. Sometimes the chase ended disastrously for all concerned. HMS *Redwing* was pursuing two slavers off the coast of Africa in 1827 when a squall blew up. All three vessels were carrying a tremendous press of canvas, but in spite of the weather the slavers dared not and the *Redwing* would not lower sail. Slavers and warship together disappeared into the squall and were never seen again.

If a slaver was overtaken, she often fought in preference to hauling down her false colors. The *Paz*, a noted slaver sailing under the American flag, beat off the *Princess Charlotte* after killing several of her men. The *Camperdown* not only destroyed two sloops-of-war—the *Rambler* and the *Trial*, belonging to the newly formed navy of Sierra Leone—but enslaved their Negro crews and sold them in the West Indies. The *Velos Passageira* had twenty guns and a crew of a hundred and fifty men. While carrying 555 slaves, she was taken by the British sloop-of-war *Primrose*, but not until forty-six of her men had been killed by the cruiser's short-range fire.

Late one evening in 1829, the little British cruiser *Pickle* sighted a strange vessel heading for Cuba and gave chase. The *Pickle* was a topsail schooner with a crew of thirty-nine, and her armament consisted of one eighteen-pounder and two eight-pound carronades. The wind was light that evening, but the *Pickle* wet her sails and managed to overhaul the stranger. She fired a warning shot and then, securing all sails except the square topsail, came alongside. Lieutenant McHardy, in command of the *Pickle*, reports: "We reserved fire till we were close on her larboard quarter. The scene was now splendid beyond description. The moon had set and a light breeze was blowing. We could just distinguish the figure of the long, low, black vessel we were engaging as she moved around us, except when by the occasional blazes from her sides on the discharge of her guns, she was distinctly visible. The action continued within pistol shot for an hour and twenty minutes, at the end of which we had the satisfaction of seeing the slaver's mainmast fall."

The captured slaver was the *Boladora*, which carried sixteen guns and a crew of sixty-two, so that the *Pickle* had been outgunned and outmanned. There were three hundred and fifty slaves in the *Boladora*'s hold. The British put her surviving sailors in irons and stowed them on the slave deck until the two vessels reached Havana.

In spite of captures like these, the trade was now increasing year by year. More and more of the slavers flew the American flag, and the British officers were often discouraged. What increased their sense of frustration was that capturing a slaver might be an inadvertent act of cruelty to the slaves on board. These had to be carried to Sierra Leone before being set free, and many of them died on the voyage. In a report to a committee of the House of Commons (1830), Lieutenant Tringham told how his ship had captured a Spanish slaver in the West Indies with 480 slaves on board; 110 of them had died on the long passage to Sierra Leone. Tringham believed that, on the average, 44 per cent of the slaves taken by cruisers died before reaching African soil. In 1833 the *Snake* captured a slaver off the coast of Brazil. She tried to land the slaves at Rio, but the Brazilian authorities refused to let them come ashore, and the *Snake* was forced to convoy her prize to Sierra Leone. Before the end of the long voyage, the Negroes were "in a state that moved the heart of even the slave crew." Only 240 survived out of 430. On the *Flor de Loando*, also captured off Brazil, the voyage back to Africa took five months. Out of 289 slaves there were only 40 survivors.

The cost of Great Britain's attempt to suppress the slave trade, besides being high in terms of human life, was also high in pecuniary terms, even for the richest nation in the world. By 1840 Great Britain had spent £940,000 on prize money to the men of the anti-slaving squadron and £330,000 on courts to try cases involving slavers. That was only a fraction of the total outlay. Great Britain had also paid subsidies to Spain, Portugal, and Brazil to outlaw the trade, had bribed many native kings, and was supporting a community of former slaves in Sierra Leone. The total bill came close to the enormous sum, for the time, of £15,000,000. Saddled with this burden, the British government—or at least the British representatives on the African coast and in the West Indies—became impatient of legal niceties. The French, who had granted the right of search, complained that their honest merchantmen were being captured and sent with prize crews to Sierra Leone, where they were detained until their voyages were ruined—all this to the profit of their British competitors. The Americans, who were further than ever from granting the right, complained that the protection of their flag was being disregarded.

In 1839 two slavers, the *Eagle* and the *Clara*, were taken at Whydah by the British cruiser *Buzzard*, although they were flying the American flag. On examination of the vessels' papers, they were found to be Spanish. The United States, however, contested their seizure on the ground that the British cruiser could not tell whether or not the vessels were American until she had boarded them; therefore the act of boarding was illegal. The court at Sierra

Leone allowed the vessels to go free in preference to offending the United States.

The case roused an angry outcry on both sides of the Atlantic. Great Britain demanded whether the United States took the position that any slaver of any nationality had merely to run up the American flag to be safe from capture. Yes, replied the United States, for otherwise any peaceful American vessel could be stopped and boarded by British cruisers. In his first annual message to Congress (December 1841), President Tyler stated, "American citizens prosecuting a lawful commerce in the African seas under the flag of their country are not responsible for the abuses or unlawful use of that flag by others." The situation became critical when, also in 1841, Lewis Cass, the American minister to France, issued his famous pamphlet, *An Examination of the Right of Search.* Cass protested against having "our flag violated to see if it has been abused." "Who can doubt," he continued, "but that the English cruisers, stationed upon that distant coast with an unlimited right of search and discretionary authority to take possession of all vessels frequenting those seas will seriously interrupt the trade of all nations by sending in their vessels for trial under very slight pretense?" He offered an excellent summary of the American position, but it was not calculated to end the dispute. Indeed, as a result of President Tyler's message and Cass's pamphlet, the situation grew so strained that the American minister in London wrote to Washington, "There seems to be a general impression that war is inevitable."

# 10

# The Roaring Eighteen-Forties

*It was in Valparaiso I fell in with Captain Moore.*
*He commanded the clipper Flying Cloud, sailing out of Tramore.*
*'Twas there I did agree with him on a slavery voyage to go,*
*To the burning shores of Africa where the sugarcane do grow.*

*The Flying Cloud was a clipper ship, five hundred tons or more.*
*She could easily sail around any ship sailing out of Tramore.*
*I often saw this gallant ship, with wind abaft the beam,*
*With royals and stun's'ls set aloft taking sixteen from the reel.*

*We started then upon a voyage with a full cargo of slaves.*
*It would have been better for those poor souls to be going to*
*their graves.*
*The plague and fever came on board, swept half of them away.*
*We dragged their bodies to the rails and threw them in the sea.*

*We were often chased by men-of-war, liners and frigates too;*
*But to overhaul the Flying Cloud was a thing they never could do,*
*Until at last astern of us, where the cannon roar so loud.*
*A feat that they never could do was overhaul the Flying Cloud.*

> —"The *Flying Cloud*," said to be based on the experiences
> of the pirate-slaver Benito de Soto. "Tramore" may have
> been a corrupted form of "Baltimore"

THERE WERE TWO SLAVE MUTINIES IN 1839–1841 WHICH, WITH THEIR
many sequels, aggravated the diplomatic crisis over the slave trade.
The first of these was the famous *Amistad* mutiny of 1839. The
*Amistad* was a schooner that sailed from Havana on June 27 of

that year, with a cargo of fifty-two slaves bound—or so the owners claimed—for the little Cuban port of Guanaja. One of the slaves was a true *ladino*, born in Cuba, but the other fifty-one had just been illegally imported from Guinea. Among them was a man called Cinque, the son of a village headman, who had been sold for debt to the famous slave trader Pedro Blanco. Incited by Cinque, the slaves armed themselves with machetes that had been carelessly stored in the hold; they killed the captain and the cook, sent the two sailors ashore in the boat, and ordered the two remaining white men—both slave merchants—to steer them to Africa.

Cinque knew only that Africa lay to the east, and he stood with his machete raised over the steersman's head to make sure that the bowsprit of the *Amistad* was pointed toward the rising sun. But Cinque could not read the stars, and at night and in overcast weather the *Amistad* sailed toward the United States. After seven weeks of tacking eastward by day and northwestward by night, she reached the vicinity of Montauk, Long Island, where some of the slaves went ashore, stark naked but with handfuls of gold doubloons, to buy provisions and water. The United States brig *Washington* happened to be cruising in those waters. The *Washington* seized both schooner and slaves and carried them to New London, Connecticut, where the *Amistad* was libeled for salvage.

That was the beginning of a case which would, at various times, occupy the close attention of the Spanish government, the American Secretary of State, three Presidents, the Supreme Court, and both houses of Congress. The Spanish government demanded that the slaves be returned to Cuba for speedy trial as mutineers and murderers. The Secretary of State was John Forsyth of Georgia, who had no sympathy with revolted slaves. In his effort to comply with the Spanish demand, he had the support of President Van Buren, who was apparently under pressure from some respected New York City merchants. Perhaps these were really part owners of the schooner and her cargo. Richard Drake, in his *Revelations of a Slave Smuggler*, speaks of the *Amistad* as belonging to a joint-stock slave-smuggling company "connected with leading American and Spanish mercantile houses." He claims—though Drake is not to be trusted—that she was secretly consigned to the slave-fattening farm he managed off the coast of Honduras.

Meanwhile the slaves were being held in custody of the courts, which were not swayed by presidential wishes. Abolitionists had entered the case and had engaged distinguished counsel. It was John Quincy Adams who spoke for Cinque and his comrades before the Supreme Court in 1841, in a case that was now called "the trial of one President by another." The court ruled that the fifty-one Guinea Negroes on board the *Amistad* had been introduced into Cuba illegally, and hence had never been slaves in the eyes of the law; they had the right to use force in regaining their freedom. Only the *ladino* had legally been a slave from birth and could be returned to Cuba. Suddenly the *ladino* was spirited away by abolitionists and disappeared into the Underground Railway. Cinque and his comrades were sent back to Africa, accompanied by a group of clergymen who hoped to use them as the nucleus of a missionary movement. But the former slaves displayed no interest in such a movement, and Cinque himself is said to have used his knowledge of the trade to start a factory and become a slave trader.

That was by no means the end of the case. The Spanish government appealed for an indemnity to be paid to the Cuban owners of the slaves, and the Spanish claim was debated in more than one session of Congress. President Buchanan, as late as 1858, was vainly recommending that the claim be paid.

The second slave mutiny with international repercussions was on an American coasting schooner, the *Creole*, in the autumn of 1841. The *Creole* had sailed for New Orleans from Hampton Roads, Virginia, with a cargo of 135 slaves, but she did not reach her destination. One of the slaves, Madison Washington, was a determined man who had escaped from a Virginia plantation and had lived for some time in the North; then he came back to Virginia to rescue his wife. Having been recaptured there, he was on his way to New Orleans to be sold as a "cane hand," the worst of fates for a Virginia slave. Ten days out of Hampton Roads, Washington led a slave mutiny and seized the vessel after a struggle in which one white man was killed. He then compelled the crew to sail the *Creole* into Nassau harbor, where the mutineers came under the protection of British law. The United States demanded their return, but Great Britain refused to surrender them, on the ground that a slave was free as soon as he set foot on British soil. In this case, which had angry echoes in Congress, Great Britain had the moral support of the Supreme Court's decision regarding the revolted slaves on the *Amistad*. That seemed unfair to Southern congressmen, and the *Creole* did not improve the tense relations between the two countries.

It was hardly conceivable, however, that the United States would go to war to protect the slave trade. A solution of sorts was found in the Webster-Ashburton Treaty of 1842, which, besides ending a boundary dispute between the United States and Canada, provided for the "final suppression" of the slave trade. The trade was to be suppressed by the "joint cruising" of American and British warships off the coast of Africa. Then, if a slaver hoisted American colors, she could be pursued by the American ship, and if she showed any other flag, she could be pursued by the British.

Both the letter and the spirit of the treaty were disregarded from the beginning. Article 8 of the treaty provided that the United States and England should each "maintain in service, on the coast of Africa, a sufficient and adequate squadron or naval force of vessels, of suitable numbers and descriptions, to carry in all not less than eighty guns, to enforce, separately and respectively, the laws, rights, and obligations of each of the two countries for the suppression of the slave trade." In 1843 the United States sent only a token force of two ships with thirty guns. From that time until 1857, the American squadron never consisted of more than seven ships, and the average was less than five. The British squadron, on the other hand, never numbered less than twelve and averaged twenty. In addition, the American squadron was based on Cape Verde, a thousand miles from the slave-trading area. A short time after a ship reached her station, she was forced to return to her base for want of provisions.

The fact is that the American ships were sent not primarily to suppress the trade but, as the orders of Commander M. C. Perry in command of the squadron read in 1843, "to assert the rights and prevent the abuse of the flag." In any case, the attempt to patrol four thousand miles of African coast with two vessels was manifestly absurd, and Perry does not seem to have taken his duties seriously. He reported to the Secretary of the Navy in September 1843, "I cannot hear of any American vessels being engaged in the transportation of slaves; nor do I believe there has been one so engaged for several years." Yet his own reports show that he had been notified by the British squadron of at least two American slavers (the *Illinois* and the *Shakespeare*) which had picked up cargoes of slaves that summer.

The case of the *Illinois* is a good example of the difficulties under which the British cruisers operated. The *Illinois* was discovered at Whydah by a British cruiser. The British boarded her but found that she had American papers and so could not be seized. Her captain then took 430 slaves aboard and set sail. She encountered the same British cruiser, which was lying offshore, but now the captain of the *Illinois*, supposing his enemy had sailed down the coast, concluded that the ship was one of the American frigates, and so he hoisted the Spanish flag. As the right of search had been agreed upon between Great Britain and Spain, the British cruiser gave chase. The *Illinois* saw her mistake, promptly hauled down the Spanish flag and raised the stars and stripes, so the cruiser was helpless. But then the slaver ran aground. The cruiser sent her boats to help the stranded vessel, but could not board her as long as she was flying the American flag.

Not even such scrupulous observation of the law could convince many Americans that perfidious Albion was not up to her old tricks of 1812. The *Washington Globe* editorialized (February 22,

1843) that if a British captain was entitled to establish the identity of a vessel, "may he not insist on the propriety of the verification of the nationality of the seamen? And, if he finds naturalized American sailors whom he chooses to make his prey, will he not find law enough . . . to seize them as soon as he would Africans on board a slaver?"

The American squadron did make a few captures. In 1845, the American slaver *Pons* was blockaded at Cabinda by the British cruiser *Cygnet* in consort with the American frigate *Yorktown*. As the *Pons* had not as yet loaded any slaves, neither warship could take her. After twenty days the American captain of the *Pons* "sold" the ship to a Portuguese member of her crew, who became her new captain. She then took on 903 slaves and put to sea. On sighting the *Yorktown* she mistook her for the British cruiser and hoisted the American flag, with the result that the *Yorktown* was able to board her. The *Pons*'s new captain argued that the vessel belonged to him. He had neglected, however, to destroy her papers, which showed that she was of American registry, and so she became a legal prize.

The slaves in the *Pons*'s hold were so tightly packed that eighteen of them were already dead when the boarders opened the hatches. "There was no slave deck," the American naval officer reported, "and upwards of 850 were piled almost in bulk on the water casks below." It was impossible to land the slaves at Cabinda, where the local king would simply have sold them to the next slaver. They had to be taken to Liberia, a two weeks' sail during which a hundred and fifty of them died. Eight more died in the harbor before they could be landed.

In March 1845, the USS *Truxton* found HMS *Ardent* blockading the mouth of the Rio Pongo. There was a slaving schooner in the river, but the *Ardent* had not been able to touch her, since she was flying the American flag. The *Truxton* sent her boats up the river, and the schooner, mistaking their nationality, ran up the stars and stripes. So did the boats, whose crews then boarded her. She was the *Spitfire* out of New Orleans and had stowed 346 slaves.

Sometimes a slaver was taken only by a stroke of luck. In 1850 the American frigate *Perry* sighted a ship named the *Martha*, whose port, "New York," was clearly painted on her stern. As the *Perry* was flying no flag, the *Martha* hoisted the American colors at a venture. The *Perry* responded by sending a boat to board her. When the *Martha*'s captain saw the American uniforms, he hurriedly lowered the flag and hoisted the Brazilian colors. He was now technically immune from seizure, but a sharp-eyed member of the boat's crew saw a desk flung over the *Martha*'s side. The desk was retrieved and was found to contain the ship's papers, showing her American registry.

When the boarding party clambered over the *Martha*'s side, they were confronted by a Portuguese who claimed to be the ship's captain and demanded by what right the United States violated the rights of Portugal. The *Martha*, however, was well known to the blockading squadron, and her American captain was discovered, dressed as an ordinary seaman, standing among the rest of the crew. This, together with the possession of the ship's American papers, was enough to cause her to be taken as a prize to New York. The ship was condemned, but her American captain was released on $3000 bail, which he promptly forfeited.

There were other captures too, but the American squadron, in addition to being far too small, was operating under almost insurmountable legal handicaps. As the United States refused to allow its vessels to be searched by the warships of any foreign power, it followed that American cruisers could search a vessel only if it was flying the American flag. Slaves had to be found on board; the mere fact that she was fitted out as a slaver was not enough under American law. Hence a slaver would sail for Africa under the American flag, which protected her from being searched by the British and condemned under the "equipment clause"; she could ship her slaves, and she could then make a run for it, showing any colors except American. Hawthorne's friend Horatio Bridge, who served on the west coast in 1843, ends his *Journal of an African Cruiser* with the sad comment: "The foregoing journal of our cruise records not the capture of a single slave-vessel [during that period] either by our own ship or any other belonging to the American Squadron. What slaver would show the United States' flag with slaves in his hold?"

The attitude of American officials, many of whom were Southerners and in sympathy with the slavers, did little to encourage the squadron. Between 1842 and 1853 the squadron took only nine slavers, and these were released on nominal bail or were tried and punished with small fines. John Young Mason, the Secretary of the Navy in 1846, actually rebuked Commander Read in command of the squadron for making the captures, as in some cases the slavers had managed to disembark their slaves before being boarded or had Spanish, Portuguese, or Brazilian papers. Read angrily replied that, in the future, "nothing but the actual appearance of slaves on board and papers showing the vessel to be an American will induce them [the ships in his squadron] to make captures."

John Quincy Adams, whose angry denial of the British right of search has already been quoted, now wrote bitterly (July 29, 1844) that he suffered "shame for the honour and good name of my country whose government [has made] a false and treacherous pretense of co-operating with Great Britain for the suppression of one of the forms of this execrable system of slavery."

In the course of time joint cruising became a farce. A British officer complained in 1857, "For nearly three years there has been no American cruiser in these waters [the Bight of Benin] where a valuable and extensive American commerce is carried on. I cannot, therefore, but think that this continued absence of foreign cruisers looks as if they were intentionally withdrawn and as if the government did not care to take measures to prevent the American flag being used to cover Slave Trade transactions." The chaplain of the 1855–1857 American squadron reported, "Joint cruising has been from the first in spirit and letter dead. The flagships of the American and British squadron met but once and were two miles apart. The following communications were held [by signal flags]:

" 'Anything to communicate?'
" 'Nothing to communicate.' "

Even Great Britain was less single-minded in her efforts to suppress the trade than may have appeared from this narrative. Most
of the Prime Ministers and Foreign Secretaries worked hard at the
problem: Canning and Palmerston distinguished themselves by
their zeal; but the Admiralty hung back. It was inclined to believe
that the whole blockade was at best a "benevolent crotchet" and
at worst a sinful waste of men and ships. Looking back at the 1840s
and 1850s, Palmerston wrote angrily in 1862: "No First Lord and
no Board of Admiralty have ever felt any interest in the suppression
of the Slave Trade or taken of their own free will any steps to-
wards its accomplishment and whatever they have done in com-
pliance with the wishes of others they have done grudgingly and
imperfectly. If there was a particularly old slow-going tub in the
Navy she was sure to be sent to the coast of Africa to try to catch
the fast sailing American clippers; and if there was an officer
notoriously addicted to drinking, he was sent to a station where
rum is a deadly poison."

Duty in the slave squadron was unpopular, combining as it did
a maximum of risk and discomfort with a minimum of shore leave.
If the crews spent a single night on shore, they were likely to come
down with a variety of ailments ranging from mild dysentery to
yellow fever. Prize money was awarded for the capture of a slaver,
but only if the capture was ruled to be legal by the court in Sierra
Leone. The rulings of the court depended on what was by now a
large collection of treaties, often hard to interpret, so that a naval
officer could never be sure of what he was legally entitled to do.
In 1833, for example, France and Great Britain had signed an
agreement permitting the right of search between the latitudes of
15 degrees north and 10 degrees south and between the longitudes
of 0 degrees and 30 degrees west. In 1841 the limits of the permissible area were changed to 32 degrees north and 45 degrees
south by agreement among Britain, Austria, Prussia, and Russia,

but France refused to sign the new compact. For a time other countries acknowledged the right of search north of the equator but not south of it. If a slaver pursued by a cruiser could cross one of these invisible lines, she was safe from pursuit. Of course she was usually safe—though not from all naval commanders—if she raised the American flag.

Usually a slaver depended first on her spread of canvas and then, if overhauled, on a pretense of legality, but sometimes she chose to fight it out with the cruiser, broadside for broadside. We read in *Journal of an African Cruiser:* "Fell in with British brig-of-war, *Ferret.* Our captain went on board and was told that she had been engaged with a large slaver four days ago. Previous to the action, the slave-ship went to Gallenas where the *Ferret's* pinnace was at anchor. She ran alongside [but the slaver] had three guns out on a side and her waist full of musketeers—a superiority of force in view of which the pinnace did not dare to attack her and the ship took off nine hundred or a thousand slaves and went off unmolested. At sea, she encountered the *Ferret* and was fired into repeatedly by that vessel but succeeded in making her escape. She was under Portuguese colors but is said to have been the American ship *Crawford.*"

The engagement between the *Crawford* and the *Ferret* took place in 1843, a year by which the conflict between cruisers and heavily armed slavers had taken on the aspect of a naval war. Slaving crews were told when signing on that they had to be prepared to fight, or they would lose their pay. "Wages shall not be due," reads the contract between one crew and the respectable owner of the slaver, "in event of capture by a vessel of equal force nor even in the event of capture by one of superior force unless after an obstinate defense, and in that case the wages of those who will not fight shall be forfeited and divided among the brave defenders."

The naval war became embittered after the affair of HMS *Wasp* in 1845. The *Wasp* had captured two Brazilian slavers, the *Felicidade* and the *Echo,* off the west coast of Africa and had put prize crews on them. The *Echo* had four hundred slaves on board. None was found on the *Felicidade*, but she was fully equipped for the trade, and so the prize crews set sail for Sierra Leone while the *Wasp* returned to her patrol.

The two prizes parted company, and the *Echo* went on to her destination. On the *Felicidade* the prize crew consisted of Midshipman Palmer and nine seamen, who were standing guard over twenty-one Brazilians. Three of the prize crew were asleep and Palmer was taking a bath when the Brazilians attacked them. The sleeping men were knifed; Palmer and the others were thrown over the side. The *Felicidade* then hoisted Brazilian colors and headed for the Slave Coast, but she was stopped by a British man-of-war, the *Star*. The boarding party found bloodstains on her deck and a book in which one of the prize crew had written his name. A Negro servant on the *Felicidade* broke down and confessed the killings. Only ten of the Brazilians had taken part in the mutiny, and these were carried to England and tried for murder.

The court ruled that, as the *Felicidade* had no slaves on board, and as Brazil had never signed a treaty containing the equipment clause, the original capture of the vessel had been illegal. The crew, therefore, had been entitled to regain possession of the *Felicidade* by any means in their power. The defendants were acquitted and sent back to Brazil.

As a result of the *Wasp* case, as it was called, British crews on the African station lost all their lingering tolerance toward slavers. Officers led boarding parties with the watchword of "Remember the *Felicidade!*" There was no mercy for those who resisted them. Captured slaving crews, instead of being carried to Sierra Leone, were simply marooned on the African coast, where many of them were killed by the natives or perished in the jungle.

These measures had their effect, and there were not so many sea fights after the *Wasp* affair, but still there were a few. In January 1848 the boats of HMS *Philomel* and HMS *Dart* gave chase to a slaver that mounted an eighteen-pound cannon. The *Dart's* boats were driven off, but the *Philomel's* boats, commanded by Lieutenant Wharton, came in under the lee of the slaver's mizzenmast, so that the gun could not be trained on them. But the slaver loaded her gun with scrap metal, and though she must have riddled her own mast, she wounded seven of the bluejackets. Meanwhile the *Dart's* boats returned to the attack, and the slaver was taken. Wharton found that because her two lookouts had failed to sight the cruiser, her captain had shot them both.

The problem of suppressing the trade would have been much easier from the beginning if the blockading squadron had possessed the right to land shore parties on African soil and liberate the slaves in the barracoons. They did not possess the right, for the reason that the barracoons and the slaves they contained were regarded as being under control of the local African kings, who were independent sovereigns. Great Britain, still without African possessions of any importance except Sierra Leone and the Cape of Good Hope, had sworn to respect their territorial rights. Most of the factories along the coast had been taken over by individuals— usually half-caste Portuguese—who were ostensibly in the employment of the local king. To interfere with these slave brokers was, under law, an act of aggression against the officials of a friendly power.

The Foreign Office made many efforts to persuade local monarchs to abandon the trade. Between 1841 and 1850 Great Britain signed forty-two treaties with various African kings. It would be pointless to list them, since the kings paid no more attention to treaties than did the citizens of Spain, Portugal, Brazil, France, or the United States. One of the first was with King Pepple of Bonny in 1841; for a subsidy of $10,000 a year the king agreed to abandon the slave trade. Bonny continued, however, to be a favorite shipping station for slavers. The kings of Ashanti and Dahomey did not bother with evasions. When Great Britain sent a commission to King Gezo of Dahomey in 1850 to beg him to stop selling slaves, his answer was to present his best compliments to the Queen of England. "The presents which she has sent him," he said regarding a gift of umbrellas, "are very acceptable and good

for the face." As for the slave trade, "He cannot see that he and
his people can do without it. He begs the Queen of England to put
a stop to the slave trade everywhere else and allow him to continue
it. . . . He hopes the Queen will send him some good Tower
guns and blunderbusses and plenty of them to enable him to make
war."

Much later the suppression of the slave trade would be the justification that was offered—at first quite sincerely—by the English
and the French for conquering most of the African continent. It
was the English who would overcome the brave Ashanti, and the
French who would occupy Dahomey after defeating and disband-
ing the famous brigade of women—the Amazons—who were the
best soldiers of the kingdom.

On the other side of the Atlantic, the Foreign Office was trying
hard to obtain help from the Brazilians and from the Spanish overlords of Cuba in suppressing the trade. Brazil in 1826 had signed
a treaty stipulating that she would import no more slaves after
1829, but the treaty was never observed. The British tried to
maintain a blockade of the long coastline, but until the end of the
1840s slaves were coming through in vast and probably increasing
numbers. The Cuban trade was outlawed in the same fashion, by
a treaty that the Spanish navy made no attempt to enforce. Here
again without assistance from other nations, the British tried to
prevent the landing of slaves, but not with great success. Captain
Canot tells us how the slavers evaded them.

A wild, uninhabited portion of the coast [he says] where some
little bay or sheltering nook exists, is commonly selected by the
captain and his confederates. As soon as the vessel is driven close
to the beach and anchored, her boats are packed with slaves,
while the craft is quickly dismantled to avoid detection from sea
or land. The busy skiffs are hurried to and fro incessantly till the
cargo is entirely ashore, when the secured gang, led by the captain
and escorted by armed sailors, is rapidly marched to the nearest
plantation. There it is safe from the rapacity of local magistrates
who, if they have a chance, imitate their superior by exacting
"gratifications."

In the meantime, a courier has been dispatched to the owners in Havana, Matanzas, or Santiago de Cuba, who immediately post to the plantation with clothes for the slaves and gold for the crew. Preparations are quickly made through brokers for the sale of the blacks.

Canot says that, as an additional precaution, the slave ships were often burned as soon as the slaves were disembarked. The odor of the slaves always remained in the hold, and this was sometimes considered enough evidence to have the ship seized by a cruiser and to convict the crew of piracy. The profits of the trade were so great that the value of the ship was considered an unimportant item.

Concerning the Cuban officials, Canot says: "While the brokers are selling the blacks at the depot, it is not unusual for their owner or his agent to be found knocking at the door of the Captain-General's secretary. It is even said that the Captain-General himself is sometimes present and after a familiar chat about the happy landing of 'the contraband' as the traffic is amiably called, the requisite rouleaux are insinuated into the official desk under the intense smoke of a cigarillo."

Canot's statement is amply confirmed from other sources. It was a recognized fact, says Mathieson in his *British Slavery and Its Abolition*, that during an earlier period, from 1820 to 1825, "The Captain-General of Cuba denied the Trade but received a tax of three pounds ten shillings on each Negro and under the windows of his official residence were two barracoons holding from 1500 to 1000 slaves . . . almost always full."

The fabulous profits of the illegal trade attracted not only the scum of the Atlantic seaports but also men of desperate courage and great ingenuity. In contrast with the small factors of the preceding century—like poor Nicholas Owen, living as miserably as the slaves he bargained for—there were now merchants with crowded barracoons and harems stocked with native princesses. Some of these "mongos," as they were called, enjoyed an almost

regal power over the surrounding tribes. One of the most interesting was John Ormond, known in the trade as "Mongo John."

Ormond's father was a Liverpool slaving captain and his mother
was the daughter of a native king—probably belonging to the
Susu, a branch of the great Mandingo family. His father took him
to England and gave him a little schooling but never acknowledged
him as his son. Left destitute by the father's death, Ormond became a sailor and served five years on a man-of-war. He then
made his way to Africa, where he was recognized by his mother
and made a prince of the tribe.

Before 1820 the banks of the Rio Pongo, in what is now the
Republic of Guinea, were divided among a number of petty states
at constant war with one another. After establishing himself as
leader of his own tribe, Ormond conquered his neighbors one after
another, and even won recognition as overlord from some of the
Mandingo villages along the upper reaches of the river. The tribute
he exacted from them was paid in slaves. He then built a system
of barracoons and issued a proclamation that he was open for
business. During the next few years Mongo John became famous
in the slave trade. His barracoons seldom held fewer than a thousand slaves, and he could produce five thousand in a few weeks'
time. He had his own private army, maintained a harem said to
consist of a thousand women—actually there seem to have been
thirty or forty—and was thought to enjoy a yearly income of some
$200,000.

Canot, who worked as a clerk for Ormond in the middle 1820s,
describes him as "a stout, burly, black-eyed, broad-shouldered,
short-necked man." Probably as the result of a venereal infection,
he had become impotent, and his wives openly took lovers. He
began drinking heavily, neglected his business, and could no
longer hold his monopoly of the coastal trade. One evening in
1828, after drinking a bottle of trade rum, Mongo John burst into
his harem with two loaded pistols, swearing to shoot two of the
women who had boasted of their unfaithfulness. But he was so
far gone in liquor that he collapsed on the floor, and the women

crowded round him, taunting him with his impotence. In an agony of shame and rage, Ormond shot himself.

Canot tried to take over his business, but the mongo's African relatives hired a local wizard to burn down Canot's factory. After Ormond's death the great man-merchant on the Windward Coast was Pedro Blanco, who maintained a flourishing establishment northwest of Monrovia, at the mouth of the Gallinas River. Don Pedro, as everybody called him, hailed from Málaga and had arrived on the coast as captain of a Spanish slaver. Finding that he could not obtain a cargo, he sent his vessel to Cuba with a mere hundred slaves, barely enough to pay the crew's wages, and stayed on the coast with the remainder of his trade goods. His purpose was to accumulate enough slaves in his barracoons to fill the hold of any slaver on a day's notice. In older days, when the trade was legal, slavers had been willing to wait for their cargoes, but now, with British frigates on patrol outside the bar, every moment's delay was dangerous. There was little delay at the mouth of the Gallinas once Don Pedro had built his barracoons, and soon the river was filled with brigs and topsail schooners.

Don Pedro had chosen an admirable site for illegal trading, because of the dangerous bar at the mouth of the river and because of the single winding channel, known only to native pilots. Slaves were provided in large numbers by—but not from—the Vai, a powerful Mohammedan nation that had once held aloof from slave trading. Seduced by Don Pedro's rum and gunpowder, the Vai moved into the coastal region and began attacking their weaker neighbors. Don Pedro kept a stock of more than a thousand slaves in ten or a dozen barracoons on a series of marshy islands. On another island, near the mouth of the Gallinas, he had his business headquarters, run by a general manager with the assistance of two cashiers, five bookkeepers, and ten clerks, all Europeans. On still another island was a sort of palace, where he lived in barbaric splendor with only his sister for company, and on still another was his harem, a compound in the native fashion with a separate hut for each of his many wives. Don Pedro, however, had the reputation of being a temperate man, and he was better educated than his business rivals. Once, for the wager of a slave, he recited the Lord's Prayer in Latin; then he gave the slave to a captain whose ship had been captured by an English cruiser. More and more of those cruisers were patrolling the mouth of the Gallinas, and in 1839 Don Pedro retired from business with a fortune that was said to be close to a million dollars.

In the 1840s the greatest and perhaps the last of the mongos was Francisco Feliz da Souza, known to the natives as Cha-Cha. He monopolized the trade of the Slave Coast from his headquarters at Whydah. Because he was a vassal and friend of King Gezo of Dahomey, the English cruisers did not attack his barracoons. For the same reason he could depend on a steady supply of slaves. It is said that on one occasion he put 1170 Negroes on board a slaver within three hours. On other occasions, when he had to wait for the slaves to be marched down from Abomey, he would detain the slaving captains in his palace while their vessels cruised offshore, out of sight of the cruisers. He entertained them lavishly and introduced them to his gambling establishments, where they often lost the value of their trade goods and absolved him from the duty of furnishing them with slaves. Cha-Cha also had a collection of European prostitutes, some of whom were technically his wives, and some of whom he offered as gifts to visiting captains. When Richard Drake was in Whydah, Cha-Cha offered him a wife. "You shall have French, Spanish, Greek, Circassian, English, Dutch, Italian, Asiatic, African, or American," he said, laughing.

Da Souza, to give him his real name, was a Brazilian of mixed blood, born near Rio de Janeiro. He deserted from the Brazilian army, in which he had been a noncommissioned officer, and deserted again from the crew of a slaver when it reached the African coast. He prospered there through his talent for intrigue and his quickness at learning languages, including Spanish, English, Ewe, and Yoruba. It was said that he had helped to put King Gezo on his throne. When da Souza died in May 1849, a boy and a girl were decapitated and buried with him, to be his servant and his wife in the other world. Three slaves were killed on the beach. Commander Forbes of the Royal Navy, who visited Whydah five months later, tells us that the funeral honors continued into October. "The town," Forbes says in his book, *Dahomey and the Dahomans*, "is still in a ferment. Three hundred of the Amazons are daily in the square, firing and dancing; bands of Fetiche people parade the streets, headed by guinea-fowls, ducks, goats, pigeons, and pigs, on poles, alive, for sacrifice. Much rum is distributed, and all night there is shouting, firing, and dancing." Many of da Souza's descendants still live in Whydah (now Ouidah), and they used to boast of their ancestry.

Two of the slave smugglers have left us detailed accounts of their lives in the illegal trade. One of these men was the previously mentioned Richard (or Philip) Drake; there is some uncertainty about his given name, as there is about other features of his story. We meet him almost on his deathbed. One day in 1856, the Reverend Henry West of the Protestant Home Mission Society was visiting a sailors' rooming house when he found a gray-haired man lying sick on the top floor. The roof leaked, West says, and "the filthy rags which constituted his bed were reeking with puddled water." Delirious, the man was babbling of Africa with its line of brown beaches, green jungles, and vast lagoons. Then he thought that he was once again in the Middle Passage and shouted orders to his crew while directing the handling of invisible slaves. The old man was about to be evicted, but West paid his rent so he could die in peace.

He lived for three months more, and he left his memoirs to the clergyman, who published them in 1860. *Revelations of a Slave Smuggler* is a book to be approached with caution. Either Drake or his editor was bent on producing an anti-slavery tract, and much of it has to be dismissed as lurid fiction. But Drake was unquestionably familiar with the slave trade, especially the American end of it, and many of his statements can be verified from independent sources.

Born in an English mill town that he calls Stockford, Drake lost both his parents and was sent to the workhouse at the age of four. At ten he was put to work in a cotton mill. At twelve, while employed by a cushion maker, he lost two fingers in a machine and was discharged as useless. The parish overseers decided to ship him off to an uncle who, it had been discovered, was living across the sea in Boston. With his worldly goods tied up in an old Spitalfields handkerchief, Drake said goodby to the overseers, who warned him, "Never forget old England."

He was sent aboard the packet ship *Polly*, of Waterford, where he was put in the steerage among some four hundred and fifty Irish emigrants. Fifty years later Drake remembered that the *Polly* was "as bad as any slaver that ever skulked the 'Middle Passage' with battened-down hatches." Food and water ran short when she was driven off her course. Both dysentery and typhus raged in the steerage. "One day when I had crawled to the deck," Drake says, "and lay on a coil of chain near the capstan, I counted thirty corpses that were hauled up during the morning and thrown overboard. Most of the bodies were women with their long hair tangled in their filthy garments. . . . When we made the first light, off Cape Ann, we had 186 left out of 450 odd passengers and some of these died before landing."

Drake himself was saved by the kindness of a poor Irish family. In Boston nobody knew his uncle, but the boy found work as an apothecary's apprentice. When the uncle finally appeared, more than two years later, it turned out that he was the captain of a vessel being outfitted for a slaving voyage, and Drake went with him to Africa. Drake was captured by the natives and finally rescued by a Bristol captain; it was three years before he could rejoin his uncle. By then it was 1808 and Great Britain had abolished the trade, but Drake and his uncle passed themselves off as Spaniards so they could go on with the business of buying and selling Negroes. At one time they had a factory on the Windward Coast, north of Cape Palmas, from which Drake claims that they shipped seventy-two thousand slaves in five years.

Some of the wilder adventures described in his book have the air of being invented either by old Trader Drake himself or else by the Reverend Mr. West in his eagerness to expose the full horror of the slave trade. Drake's account of his later years, however, is much more realistic and is confirmed at some points by other witnesses. In 1840 he was hired by a syndicate of American and Spanish merchants to supervise their "farms," at first in Brazil and later, as has already been mentioned, on one of the Bay Islands off the coast of Honduras. The Bay Island farm was a New World barracoon, where slaves fresh from Africa were fattened and taught a few words of English before being marketed in small consignments to the cotton states; that was a safer procedure than attempting to land a whole Guinea cargo direct on American soil. Drake might have ended his days happily on the farm, but he went to Baltimore in 1853 with money for a firm in New York City. He spent the money on a drunken spree and was committed to the city workhouse. Later he begged his way to New York, and he concludes his story by saying, "There I shall end my miserable life. May God forgive me for my crimes and have mercy on me hereafter."

The most famous of all the illegal slavers, though not the most successful, was Captain Theodore Canot, known to the natives for his fiery temper; they called him "Mr. Gunpowder." His personal narrative, *Twenty Years of an African Slaver*, was written in 1853–1854 with the help of a then prominent Baltimore journalist, Brantz Mayer, and it has since been reprinted many times in many languages, besides providing material for scores of novels in which Canot is the villain or the hero. His own book is a headlong adventure story, marred here and there by boasting and self-justification, but generally accurate; indeed, it has been confirmed at many points by naval and legal records, English, French, and American.

Théophile Conneau—to give him his real name, which he disguises in the narrative—was born in Alessandria, Italy, in 1804. His mother was Italian, but his father was a paymaster general in Napoleon's army. There were two boys in the family, besides four girls, and the older brother, Dr. Henri Conneau, later became the private physician of Napoleon III. Théophile went to sea as a cabin boy on—so he says—an American vessel and spent some years in Salem; that part of his story has not been confirmed. At any rate he learned to speak fluent English—in addition to Italian, French, and Spanish—and he received his mate's certificate after studying navigation. Later he was on a Dutch vessel captured (and the rest of the crew massacred) by Cuban pirates, with whom he spent several months, and he made a cruise on board a Colombian privateer. In 1826 he found himself in Havana without a ship. Attracted by the trim lines of a slaver, he made his first voyage to Africa as mate of the *Aerostatico*, and according to naval records—which contradict his own narrative at some points where it was advantageous for him to conceal the truth—he spent the next twenty-five (not twenty) years in the trade.

During those years he practiced almost every branch of the slaving business on both sides of the Atlantic. He was for two years a slave merchant on the Rio Pongo, the rival and would-be successor of Mongo John. After his factory was burned, he was left with just enough money to buy a condemned schooner from the court at Sierra Leone. Having no trade goods to exchange for slaves, he hijacked the human cargo of a slaver anchored in the Rio Nuñez and set sail for Cuba. His excuse was that the mate of the slaver had poisoned the captain; Canot was acting as the instrument of justice. The venture was successful, and so were some of the voyages that followed; but then his finest vessel, an American-built clipper, was seized by the French colonial authorities, and Canot himself was condemned to ten years of detention in the prison at Brest. Pardoned at length by King Louis Philippe, a fellow Mason, he returned to the African coast without a sou. He went to work for Pedro Blanco, first at Gallinas and then in a semi-independent factory that flourished until Don Pedro, the Rothschild of the coast, retired in 1839.

After Don Pedro's retirement nothing went right for Canot. He bought a tract of land at Cape Mount in Liberia—the deed from King Fana Toro is still extant—and tried to live as an honest planter, but the plantation was a failure and his commercial ventures miscarried. He began trading in slaves again, and the British sent a landing party to destroy his establishment. In 1847 he was seized on board an American slaver and sent to New York for trial. Released on bail, he went to Brazil and was there in 1849 when a British squadron destroyed every slaver it found on the Brazilian coast. Penniless again, he appears to have taken service as supercargo of the American slaving brig *Chatsworth*. The brig was captured at Ambriz by Commodore Foote while she was preparing to ship several hundred Negroes, but this time Canot escaped; he had gone ashore to inspect the slaves. In 1853 he appeared in Baltimore, cadging for drinks in the waterfront saloons, "a perfect wreck."

But that wasn't the end of his story. Before his book appeared, Canot, who was always a brilliant talker, managed to court and win a young American girl of good family, Elisa McKinley of Philadelphia. He took his bride to France, where, under his real name —and through the influence of his brother, the court physician— he was appointed collector of the port of Nouméa in New Caledonia. Invalided home in 1857, he took an apartment in the rue de Rivoli, and he was intriguing to be named civil governor of New Caledonia when he died of a heart attack in 1860. His widow, who became a friend of the Empress Eugénie, survived him by seventy-two years. When she was in her nineties she used to let it be understood that she was the sister of President McKinley. It was a curious sequel to a story that included piracy, murder, prison, and hijacking slaves on the Guinea Coast.

Canot was a remarkable man, brave, astute, engaging, and unscrupulous. If he had lived in Renaissance Italy he would have been a famous *condottiere*—perhaps a lieutenant of the Sforzas, for he always did best when second in command. His relative failure in the slave trade was due to his being born ten years too late. He excelled in the trade as it was conducted during the 1820s and 1830s: in small fast brigs or schooners that could outsail or outwit the British cruisers and safely land their cargoes of perhaps two hundred slaves. By the 1840s, when Canot had reached what might have been his prosperous years, the contraband trade required more capital than he could raise. It was being conducted in larger and larger vessels, and in some cases by syndicates with connections on four continents. Canot was reduced to shipping as a supercargo and even, in the end, to living within the law.

The British Navy had adopted measures that proved effective against the small enterprisers of slaving. One of the most effective was dispatching landing parties to burn the coastal barracoons. Whether the measure had now become legal remained for a long time the subject of arguments in the courts. In 1840 Captain Joseph Denman of the West African Squadron received orders from the governor of Sierra Leone to rescue a Negro woman and her child, citizens of Sierra Leone, who had been captured by the king of Gallinas and were to be sold as slaves. The governor meant that Denman was to go ashore and make representations to the king that the mother and child were to be released. But Denman had been cruising along the coast for months, in sight of barracoons full of slaves that he was unable to touch, knowing all the time that slave ships would rush in to take them aboard as soon as the cruisers sailed off for provisions. His patience at an end, he put a liberal construction on his orders. He landed his boats' crews on the islands in the river, burned the barracoons, and forced the king to put his mark on a paper giving Denman authority to liberate all the slaves.

The principal factor at Gallinas after the retirement of Pedro Blanco was a Señor Buron, who brought suit against Denman for destroying his property. The suit dragged for eight years in the British courts, which did not make a final ruling as regards the legality of burning a slave-trading establishment that belonged to a Spanish subject. The court did rule, however, that Denman was not subject to the suit for damages, and this verdict relieved the apprehensions of other naval officers. Contraband traders, including our friend Canot, found that it was no longer possible to build factories within sight of any waters that the cruisers could navigate.

At the end of the 1840s the British also took steps to close what was then the richest transatlantic market for slaves, the Empire of Brazil. In spite of having outlawed the trade by a treaty that was to have taken effect in 1829, Brazil was still importing fifty or sixty thousand slaves a year. Finally, in 1849, the British government dispatched Admiral Reynolds with a squadron of six vessels and with orders to break up the Brazilian trade. He was authorized to seize and burn any slaver he found in Brazilian territorial waters, whether offshore, in port, or up a river. As Canot learned to his cost, Reynolds obeyed his orders with ruthless efficiency. He burned three slavers in the harbor of Rio de Janeiro. Proceeding up the coast, he sent his vessels into every river and inlet that could shelter a vessel. In the Parangua River they destroyed four more slavers. Angry crowds protested to Paulino, the Brazilian Foreign Minister, but he could only reply, "When a powerful nation like Great Britain is evidently in earnest, what can Brazil do?"

Palmerston was able to tell Parliament in 1851 that the Brazilian slave trade was ended. In 1853 the Slaving Squadron reported its conviction that no more slaves were being imported into Brazil, and the squadron was withdrawn. It seems that the trade was later revived to some extent. W. Cope Devereux, on board the British paddle-wheel frigate *Gorgon* in 1860, writes of seeing in the harbor of Rio "several clipper-built, suspicious-looking vessels, all legs and wings, long-lined hulls, short, stout lower masts, immense backstays and top-gallant masts with impudent skysail-yards across. By the number of this kind of craft I should imagine that the Brazilians are still doing a large trade in human beings." These American-built craft disappeared from Rio during the Civil War. Occasional cargoes of slaves may have been landed in Brazil as late as 1880, but it would seem that the trade was never resumed on a large scale.

The Cuban trade, however, continued to flourish after 1850, and more and more slavers were claiming the protection of the American flag. With the manifest failure of joint cruising, much of the British public was becoming discouraged. There were pleas to Parliament to call home the West African Squadron and abandon the dream of suppressing the slave trade. The *Spectator* once called it "this costly failure . . . this deadly farce." The *Morning Chronicle* echoed: "A cruel, hopeless and absurd experiment." In Parliament William Hutt protested, "England is annually weeded of her best and bravest in order to carry on this idle and mischievous project of stopping the foreign Slave Trade." At times the project seemed doomed, especially when the slavers transferred more and more of their operations to East Africa in order to avoid the West African Squadron.

# II

# Slave Catching in the Indian Ocean

*I have known children bought for less corn than would go into one of our hats and you may easily imagine where they are bought so cheaply and where they fetch so large a price on the coast, it pays the slave-dealer to collect as many as he can. It is like sending a large block of ice; you know that a certain amount will melt away but that which remains will be quite sufficient for your wants.*
     —The Reverend Horace Waller, before the House of Commons, 1871

THE ISLAND OF ZANZIBAR LIES TWENTY-FOUR MILES OFF THE COAST of East Africa, opposite Tanganyika, like a giant crocodile carved from green jade. It was a perfect slave depot, close enough to the mainland to serve as a base for raids up and down the coast and yet surrounded by a natural moat wide enough to prevent counter raids by mainland canoes. The island is also in the direct line of the northeast monsoons, which blow from the Arabian coast from December to March. Just as the West Coast traders used the trade winds to carry them to Cuba, so the Arab dhows used the monsoons to bring them to Zanzibar for their cargoes of slaves. From April to October, the monsoons conveniently reverse themselves and blow from a southwest direction, so the laden dhows could sail north again with their human cargoes. By the same token, the American clippers could use the spring monsoons to sail up the east coast from the Cape of Good Hope, pick up their slave cargoes, and return on the wings of the winter monsoons.

By 1840 Zanzibar had become the world's greatest slaving emporium. In its famous slave market there stood side by side fresh-caught cannibals from the Congo, fierce Somali from the deserts, four-foot pygmies from beyond the Mountains of the Moon, and giant seven-foot Watusi. Even white slaves were offered for sale. In *Memoirs of an Arabian Princess* (London, 1888) a lady of the court says that a really accomplished, blond Circassian slave girl brought $5000. The sight of the slave market so infuriated English sailors that their officers did not allow them shore leave in Zanzibar.

Zanzibar has been known almost throughout history. Sinbad the Sailor mentions going to what seems to have been Zanzibar on his seventh voyage, looking for ivory. A Greek manuscript called the "Periplus of the Erythraean Sea," written in 60 A.D., definitely speaks of the island and says that ivory and a "superior type of slave" came from there. The words "slaves and ivory" were almost always used in speaking of Zanzibar. The East African elephants are renowned for their heavy ivory, and the only practical way of bringing it to the coast was by slave porters. In the interior ivory was so common that stockades and chiefs' houses were built of it. Slave-traders could overpower a village, load the villagers with their own ivory, and march them to the coast, where slaves and ivory were sold together.

The Arabs filtered down the coast as early as the tenth century. In 1503 the Portuguese, following in the wake of Vasco da Gama, began to occupy the Arabized coastal towns and Zanzibar; in the north they penetrated Abyssinia and in the south, after 1600, they became overlords of the fabulous kingdom of Monomotapa in what is now Rhodesia. Eventually they abandoned the interior, but they maintained a series of forts along the coast that served as slaving factories. In 1730 the Oman Arabs, sailing south in a fleet of dhows, expelled the Portuguese from Zanzibar and the coast as far south as Mozambique, which the Portuguese continued to hold. Zanzibar and the coastal towns became a province of Oman.

Gradually the Arab slavers spread out through the whole of East Africa—eventually penetrating as far as Lake Victoria and the Congo—and sent back a steady procession of coffles, some of them containing three to four thousand slaves. Many of the huge coffles were destined for the great clearing-house at Zanzibar. By 1832 Zanzibar had become so important that the Sultan of Muscat transferred his capital to the island, so that Oman became virtually a province of Zanzibar. The sultan's annual income was computed then at $75,000; thirty years later it was $270,000. By 1857 the slave trade had grown to such an extent that Livingstone was lamenting, "The interior is drained of all its working men. . . . Africa is bleeding out her life's blood at every pore." V. L. Cameron, the first European known to have crossed Africa, believed that "the slave trade will die a natural death from the total destruction of the population." Sir Bartle Frere estimated the annual drain of human lives as a result of the trade at more than a million.

From the early days of the trade, adventurous American slavers had rounded the Cape of Good Hope in search of better and cheaper sources of slaves. In 1678 Governor Bradstreet of Massachusetts reported that a shipment of slaves from East Africa had arrived, and there are similar records from New York and Virginia. In 1683 the Royal African Company was alarmed that the trade from Madagascar would hurt the west coast, "900 slaves having been brought in within two months." In 1721 the company decided to establish its own factory in Delagoa Bay, on the southeast coast of Africa. The company returned two African princes who had been captured there by a slaver, in the hope that this gesture would win them the sympathy of the local kings.

By the beginning of the nineteenth century American slavers

were regularly trading along the east coast. In 1804 the *Charleston Courier* advertised: "On Wednesday, the 18th instant, will commence the sale of the Cargo of the ship *Horizon* at Frink's Wharf, consisting of 243 Mozambique slaves. The character of the Slaves from the East Coast of Africa is now so well known that it is unnecessary to mention the decided preference they have over all other Negroes." The *Horizon*, incidentally, had left Mozambique with a cargo of 543 slaves, but had been stopped by a French cruiser for trading in French waters and held for a month, during which period 300 of the slaves had died. In 1806 the *Courier* advertised: "Will be opened tomorrow the 1st of May on board off Gadsden's Wharf the sale of 230 Prime Slaves imported on the ship *Gustavia*, Captain Hill, from Zanquebar [Zanzibar], on the eastern coast of Africa, being natives of Gondo, Mocoa and Swabaytie [Swahili] nations." Another advertisement mentioned "94 boys from Natal. Better for working than those of Madagascar being stronger and blacker."

After the British blockade began in 1807, an increasing number of slavers dared the long passage round the Cape to find waters where there were no British cruisers. In 1812 the British Captain Lynn was complaining, "Americans visit Mozambique every year in the months of June and July and smuggle slaves to Brazil and Spanish America." The British chargé d'affaires at Rio in 1817 reported that four ships had come in, bringing 1880 slaves from Mozambique. The next year there were eight ships, bringing 2416 east-coast slaves.

In 1819 the American Captain Forbes sailed north and "discovered" Zanzibar. Although American ships had been to the island at least as early as 1806, this was before the Arab safaris had begun to send slaves by the tens of thousands to the island. Forbes raced back to report this bonanza in an area safe from British cruisers. After that, the rush was on.

In 1831 the English Captain Isaacs was bitterly commenting on Lamu, a small port on the mainland north of Zanzibar: "Few have visited it except the enterprising Americans whose star-spangled banner may be seen streaming in the wind where other nations would not deign to traffic." An American consulate was established at Zanzibar in 1836, several years before the British had a representative there. The American ivory trade with Zanzibar alone amounted to $300,000 a year. As late as 1858 there were twenty-four American ships in the Zanzibar harbor as against three British.

So many of the ships hailed from Salem that the Zanzibarians thought all white men came from this one New England town. English officers discovered to their indignation that Great Britain was considered to be a suburb of Salem. The Americans traded for slaves and ivory with a cheap calico turned out in vast quantities by the New England cotton mills, and even today cotton cloth is called "Americani" in Zanzibar. British, French, and German accounts of this period speak with amazement of the United States' failure to take advantage of the situation and seize the island as an American protectorate, thus monopolizing its wealth in ivory and slaves.

There are no records of how many American ships were engaged in trading along the East African coast or how many of them were slavers. It was illegal to transport slaves in American vessels, and none of them would admit to carrying contraband. The first British cruiser did not appear in the area until 1811, and then only to protect territories gained along the southeast coast as a result of the Napoleonic Wars. There are no records of the capture of slavers until the 1820s, when two English officers, Moresby and Owens, set out to suppress the slave trade as had been attempted on the west coast. Even then there is the confusing problem of the nationality of the ships involved. All we have to guide us are isolated statements left by British officers, Portuguese and French officials, and the slavers themselves.

In 1810 the Portuguese governor of Mozambique was accused by officials in Lisbon of having pocketed $400,000 in bribes from slavers. The governor had unquestionably managed to save this sum, and his annual salary amounted to $6000. His only defense was that one of his subordinates, whose salary was only $1500 a year, had pocketed even more. Milburn, in *Oriental Commerce*, believes that 10,000 slaves a year were sold from the port of Mozambique alone. From Quelimane, another port in Portuguese territory, we have proof of slave exports from the port records. They show that from 1814 to 1819, 12,500 slaves were shipped, and that of this number 7,497 were destined for the Western Hemisphere. At that time the trade, if conducted in Portuguese vessels, was still legal south of the equator. By 1823 the number of slaves shipped from Quelimane had increased to ten thousand a year.

How many of them went out on American slavers? We do not know, but there are indications that the trade was extensive. On January 20, 1837, HMS *Dolphin* captured the American ship *Incomprehensible* off the Cape of Good Hope with 800 slaves on board, and that was not an isolated example. General Rigby, the British representative in Zanzibar, wrote in 1858, "Another large American ship, also under Spanish colours, shipped 1200 slaves for conveyance to Cuba." Even at the end of the 1850s, very few vessels in the west-coast trade were carrying such a numerous cargo. In 1859 the general wrote again, "I have received authentic information that a large American ship under Spanish colours shipped 1200 Negroes for conveyance to Cuba from a bay a few miles to the south of Eboo." As late as August 1860, HMS *Brisk* captured a large American vessel with 846 slaves in the hold.

The voyage from Mozambique was much longer than from the west coast, and the mortality among the slaves was correspondingly higher. At one time the brig *Leao* shipped 855 slaves at Quelimane and sailed for Brazil. Smallpox broke out, and the captain threw thirty infected slaves overboard. That stopped the smallpox, but it was followed by an epidemic of measles, almost equally fatal to Africans. Before the brig reached Rio, another 253 slaves had died, and the rest were so weak they had to be carried ashore. The following record of east-coast slavers captured during the 1830s—from T. F. Buxton's *African Slave Trade*—gives a picture of the casualties involved:

| | SHIPPED | DIED |
|---|---|---|
| *Cintra* | 970 | 214 |
| *Brillante* | 621 | 214 |
| *Commodore* | 685 | 300 |
| *Explorador* | 560 | 300 |

Slaves were cheaper on the east coast, and slaving captains said they could make a profit on the voyage if they landed half of their cargo alive.

To judge from the accounts of British naval officers, most of the ships in the east-coast trade were built in American shipyards, but were later transferred to Spanish, Portuguese, or Brazilian ownership. Sometimes the transfer was nominal and took the simple form of signing on a Brazilian or Cuban supercargo who, in case of trouble, could pose as the captain or the owner, or both. As the voyage back with slaves was dangerous and dirty work, it was a common practice for an American crew to sail a ship to East Africa, turn her over to a Portuguese crew, and then take passage back to New York or Baltimore on an honest merchantman to pick up another ship. But the American crew might be bribed or browbeaten into sailing home with a black cargo, and it might be dangerous for them to resist. At that time the authority of the captain was still regarded as absolute, under law, and the courts were likely to hold that his orders had to be obeyed even when they were clearly illegal.

An outstanding example comes from the African west coast. In 1848 the American ship *Mary Ann* sailed for the Niger, supposedly for palm oil, but on reaching the coast her captain announced that she would ship a cargo of slaves. The crew refused to violate the federal law against the slave trade, and as the captain would not yield, they seized the ship. Finding no American frigate to which they could surrender on the African coast, they sailed the

*Mary Ann* back to New York and turned her over to the port authorities. They were promptly arrested for mutiny, but the court found mitigating circumstances and dismissed them with the loss of a year's pay.

On the east coast there was at least one occasion on which an American crew had to be rescued from their officers by a British frigate. Lieutenant Barnard describes the incident in his book, *Three Years' Cruise in the Mozambique Channel.*

> In another branch of the river [he says] a barque was discovered and on being boarded the mate and several of the crew came forward and asked for protection against the captain, who they declared had brought them there against their will to carry on the slave trade, and was about, they were afraid, to make away with them and replace them by Brazilians who had been smuggled on board after the ship left Rio.
>
> This barque was the *Lucy Penniman*, which on a former occasion brought cargo to purchase 5000 slaves at Quillimane, and in the present instance had been loaded with goods for the purpose of obtaining cargoes for three vessels, two of which actually escaped from this river. She was placed in charge of Mr. Chase, the American Consul at the Cape, and she was eventually given up to her owners, and has, I dare say, long ere this found her way to the same profitable waters where the chances of escape are so many. In fact, with American colours she runs no risk, if the captain and crew are true to each other.

The slavers made comparatively few voyages to southeast Africa during the winter months, but with the spring monsoon they raced up the coast to Zanzibar. They were most often sighted between March and November, says W. Cope Devereux in describing his long cruise on HMS *Gorgon.* "At the end of this time," he adds, "Portuguese and Yankee clippers sneak up the Mozambique [Channel] with the last drain of the S.W. monsoon without much fear of being captured by our slow men-of-war."

Simply that a vessel had a foreign name, a foreign captain, and was under foreign registry did not mean that she was not

American. Lieutenant Barnard describes one instance among many. "Paulo Roderigue," he tells us, "the captain of the *Defensivo*, and the shipper of 1800 slaves at Delagoa Bay, was again expected for 800 blacks which were in readiness. He was to have two American brigs under their own colours, one of which was to be delivered over to the slave-dealers, whilst the other was to take both American crews on board, touch at Quillimane with money to pay the authorities who have been in the habit of conniving at the slave trade, and return to Rio. So you may easily conceive what little chance there is of putting down this detestable traffic whilst the star-spangled banner, that boasted flag of liberty, waves over and protects the miscreants, to put down whom England has expended so many hundreds of lives of her bravest and so many millions of treasure. Look at the results!"

In 1807 the population of Zanzibar was five thousand. By 1856 it had increased to sixty thousand. What had been originally little more than a fishing village became a cat's-cradle of tiny alleys, tunnels, and bylanes often so narrow that a man could stand in the center and touch the walls on either side with his extended hands, and almost completely roofed over by balconies hanging to the sides of the houses like swallows' nests. Great carved doors made of teak and ornamented with foot-long brass spikes protected the homes of the wealthy Arabs, while outside the city the sultans built vast palaces, surrounded by high walls enclosing gardens shaded by mango and palm trees, where the ladies of the royal harem wandered by the fountains with their pet gazelles, peacocks, and slaves.

Zanzibar was one of the most cosmopolitan cities in the world. Dr. Rushenberger, surgeon on the American ship *Peacock*, which visited Zanzibar in 1836, says that the streets were crowded with "Negroes armed with spears, Arabs bearing swords, dirks and shields, and Banians (East Indians) under high red turbans." There were also English officers from the Slaving Squadron, Dutch spice traders, French, Portuguese, and German merchants, and the hard-faced Yankee slavers.

The heart of Zanzibar was the slave market. Through this one market twenty thousand slaves a year changed hands. It was an unpaved oblong court about fifty yards by thirty yards. Along one side ran a high stone wall, and in front of this wall the most valuable slaves were exhibited, pretty young girls to be sold as *shauri* (concubines). The girls were always carefully coiffured, painted, and dressed in fine clothes and jewelry, which the dealers retained after they were sold. A handsome, well-trained young Negro girl might bring as much as $500. In the center of the court was a great flame banyan tree with roots like flying buttresses, and here stood the less important slaves.

Captain G. L. Sulivan, an officer from the Slaving Squadron established off Zanzibar in the 1850s, describes the market at that time in his book, *Dhow Chasing in Zanzibar Waters:*

> The first thing that meets the eye is a number of slaves arranged in a semi-circle in the center of the square. Most of them are standing up but some are sitting on the ground; in fact, utterly incapable of standing, miserable, emaciated skeletons on whom disease and starvation has placed its fatal mark. Inside this semi-circle are half-a-dozen Arabs talking together, examining the slaves, discussing their points and estimating their value just as farmers examine and value cattle at an English fair or market. Near the middle of the square are groups of children, some not more than five years old, looking old already. They sit in silence or rise up when required, they utter few words amongst themselves for they have long lost parents and friends and those in the same position sitting around them are utter strangers, often foreigners, to them.
>
> In another portion of the square are a number of women, their bodies painted, and their figures exposed with barely a yard of cloth around their hips, with rows of girls from the age of twelve and upwards exposed to the examination of Arabs and subject to inexpressible indignities by the dealers. We saw several Arab slave-dealers around these poor creatures; they were in treaty for the purchase of three or four women who had been made to take off the only rag of a garment which they wore.

Devereux of the *Gorgon* describes the market in 1860. It was full, he says; "fierce Arabs, Turks, and Abyssinians are busy with their bargains. First lot, a row of little children of about five years, valued at two dollars. Second lot, girls of ten; price from five to ten dollars. Third, youths of nineteen, stout fellows worth from four to twelve dollars. Fourth, worn-out women and old men. These latter are sold cheaply, about a dollar each, being on their last legs. Nearly all are half asleep, their poor old heads dropping from sheer fatigue and their poor persecuted bodies as dry as a chip."

Although Great Britain had been sending occasional cruisers to Mozambique, it was not until 1842 that she began to take a serious interest in the east-coast slavers. In that year Palmerston forced Portugal to sign the equipment clause (permitting a vessel to be seized as a slaver if she was equipped to carry slaves, regardless of whether any slaves were actually on board) and established a Court of Mixed Commissions on the Cape of Good Hope to try cases. Also in 1842 the *Cleopatra* was sent to the east coast to suppress the trade, and she was soon followed by three other patrol vessels, the *Lily*, the *Sappho*, and the *Bittern*. The captains of these frigates reported that as long as the Sultan of Zanzibar was able to legalize the trade, they could do little to stop it.

In 1822 Captain Moresby had persuaded the sultan to sign a treaty forbidding "all external traffic in slaves to Christians," but the Arab dhows could still carry slaves from the mainland to Zanzibar, and also along the coast as long as they stayed in the sultan's territorial waters. Since the sultan controlled the coast as far north as the Persian Gulf, this meant that the trade to Arabia was still legal. It also meant that any Christian slaver could pick up a cargo almost anywhere along the coast, since there were scores of barracoons and since the local dealers were not too scrupulous about obeying the sultan's orders.

The British then began to force a series of treaties on successive sultans, designed to give the cruisers increasing power to seize slavers, both Arab and foreign. In 1847 Hamerton, the British representative in Zanzibar, arranged a treaty prohibiting the slave trade except between Zanzibar and the mainland. That is, slaves could be shipped to Zanzibar itself, but could not be exported from there. This treaty remained in force until 1873, but it proved to be of little use in suppressing the trade. As long as slaves could be held in barracoons along the coast—ostensibly awaiting shipment to Zanzibar—there was no way the British squadron could control the slavers' activities. The coast of East Africa is riddled with innumerable little bays, inlets, rivers, and clusters of tiny islands. The cruisers could not patrol the entire area, especially as the squadron never numbered more than seven ships. The slavers found that it was even quite possible to load slaves from Zanzibar itself in spite of the squadron, since the island had become one great barracoon, where an almost unlimited supply of slaves was constantly available.

On the east central coast of the island is a small hidden bay called Chwaka. There are velvet-smooth white sand beaches here and long lines of palm trees, under which the sailors used to lie while waiting for the coffles to be rushed down from the town to their ships. Apparently the British officers did not know of this bay until sometime in the 1850s—at least they never mentioned it in their reports—and by then it had become a favored haunt of slavers.

After Chwaka was discovered by the British, the slavers employed a device worthy of a Rider Haggard romance. Fifteen miles north of Zanzibar city, on the west coast of the island, is a small village called Mangapwani. About a quarter of a mile inland from the village there is a cave which goes down into the ground for some fifty feet. At the bottom is a pool of clear water, and steps have been cut in the stone sides of the cave so that women from the nearby villages can descend to fill their water jars. From the bottom of this cave an underground passage, cut through the rock during the centuries by the overflow of the pool, runs out to the coast. It emerges in the side of low cliffs some thirty feet above the beach, and here the Arabs carved out of the rock a subterranean chamber with carefully concealed stone steps leading down from it to the beach.

A slaver could sail into Zanzibar harbor and anchor under the watching eyes of the British frigates. Ostensibly she was looking for a cargo of spices, ivory, or some of the Persian carpets brought down by the dhows from Arabia. In the maze of tangled streets the ship's captain would meet his Arab contact and the two men would retire to a coffeehouse or to a private residence fronted by one of the great carved Zanzibar doors and guarded by eunuchs with scimitars. (The manufacture of eunuchs was a considerable industry in Zanzibar, almost the only place where little slave boys could be purchased for no more than a dollar or two. Cost was an important consideration, as the Arabs removed all the genital organs and only one child in twenty is said to have survived the operation.)

The slaver would contract for, say, one thousand slaves. Such a number would make a coffle over half a mile long or require a huge coastal barracoon—either of which would be sure to attract the attention of the watching British. The slaver, however, would return to his ship, make what purchases were necessary to justify his presence in Zanzibar, then weigh anchor and sail north along the coast. Meanwhile the slaves were being brought to the mouth of the cave in small gangs drawn from various parts of the island. The mouth of the cave was well hidden by brush, and its presence was not suspected by the British. The slaves were hurried along the underground passage, and as many as possible were kept ready in the subterranean chamber until the slaver hove in sight. Fast fishing vessels known as *mapatas*, with sails made of woven rushes and planks tied together by ropes, were borrowed from Mangapwani to rush the slaves out to the waiting vessel. She could be loaded in three hours and then, with the northeast monsoon filling her sails, race south for the Mozambique Channel and the cape.

Few ships were overhauled by the clumsy, old-fashioned frigates which the British were using to suppress the trade, and no American slavers were ever captured off Zanzibar, but the following extracts from Lieutenant Barnard's record of a three years' cruise off Mozambique show how slave ships could be taken in coastal waters. Barnard's frigate was anchored in Quelimane harbor when two American brigs came in. Their names, he says,

> were the *Anna* and *Kentucky;* they were loaded with mud for ballast and they were anxious that I should look at them; however, I learnt quite sufficient to feel certain that had not the coast been well guarded, they would have delivered one of them over for slaves. In fact, the master of the *Anna* told me that proposition had been made to him. I slept on board the *Anna* that night and little thought that I should ever command her as a prize. . . .
>
> On the 20th of October 1844, we anchored again off Quillimane and Parker and myself took boats up the river. I boarded the American brigantine *Porpoise* and the boat's crew recognized two of the men who had belonged to our prize the *Defensivo* [a slaver captured some weeks before]. She also had as passengers the captain of the *Defensivo* and Tavaces, a slave-agent. I learnt that the captain had been very active in shipping slaves, having gotten off 600 in the *Kentucky* and 400 in the *Anna.*
>
> On November 30th, 1844, we started for the Cape of Good Hope and in the afternoon two sails were reported ahead at anchor, a brig and a schooner, off the northern Zambezi. As we approached we observed them interchanging signals and two large boats leave them and run in for land. I first boarded the brig and found her quite deserted with a slave-deck laid and loaded with slave provisions. She was well found, rigging new and in capital order and royal yards across. In the cabin numerous broken bottles and glasses shewed that they had strengthened the inward man before deserting. Her papers and colours had disappeared but I recognized her as my old friend the *Anna.*
>
> On July 5th, 1846, we were again in Quillimane where they said the *Cleopatra* [another British cruiser] had "played the devil" at Angonha, burning a brig called the *Kentucky* which was the same vessel that I had seen in company with the *Anna.*

Sometimes the Arab and the Yankee slavers worked together as a team. In 1857 HMS *Hermes* saw signal fires leaping from headland to headland as a warning to the slave ships taking on cargo in the bays. Off Inhambane she came upon a vessel apparently trying to escape. It was a long chase, but the wind dropped, and, as the *Hermes* was a paddle-wheel frigate, she managed to overtake the stranger. She was Portuguese, with an Arab captain, and there was nothing suspicious on board. Later the *Hermes* discovered that the vessel had been sent out as a decoy, to distract attention from an American slaver loading up a river. On this occasion the slaver escaped.

What to do with the slaves after a vessel had been captured was, if possible, an even greater problem on the east coast than on the west. Lieutenant Barnard describes a slave brig under Portuguese colors driven ashore near Mozambique and deserted by her crew. On board were 420 slaves battened under hatches and left to drown or suffocate. As the local judge was "a coloured man, formerly a gentleman's servant and one of the greatest slave-dealers in the place," the lieutenant in command of the boats' crew knew there was no use appealing to him, so he turned the slaves loose to swim to shore and fend for themselves. One hundred and ten were immediately retaken by the local inhabitants for resale. The rest fled into the interior but, as most of them had probably come from villages hundreds of miles from the coast, it was doubtful whether any reached home.

As a partial solution—there was no real one—the British established two new colonies for freedmen, one on the Seychelles Islands a thousand miles northeast of Zanzibar and another at the Cape of Good Hope, these being the nearest points at which the Negroes were safe from being re-enslaved. The problem that remained was how to transport the rescued slaves to one of the two colonies. There were no accommodations on the frigates for such numbers of people, and either voyage would take a warship out of patrol service for a number of weeks. At first the answer was simply to put the captured slaver in charge of a prize crew; but a disaster that occurred in 1843 put a virtual end to this practice.

The *Cleopatra* captured a slaver called the *Progresso*, flying no flag and claiming no nationality, off Mozambique with 447 slaves on board. The slaves when freed from the hold immediately ran wild, breaking open the casks of liquor and bolting the ship's supply of food. They fought among one another, trampling the weaker ones in their struggle to reach the rum and water casks. Finding some chickens in crates, they devoured the still living birds. The English seamen forced the half-mad Negroes back into the hold. The next morning 54 were dead. The prize crew made all sail for the Cape of Good Hope, but they ran into a storm and the voyage took 50 days. When the captured slaver reached the Cape—according to Lieutenant Barnard, who was serving on board the *Cleopatra*—177 more slaves were dead, and another 63 died after being landed.

The Reverend Pascoe G. Hill, chaplain of the *Cleopatra*, had chosen to sail to the Cape with the prize crew. When he returned to England he published an account of the voyage, calling it *Fifty Days on Board a Slave-Vessel*. "One of the Spaniards," he says, referring to a member of the *Progresso*'s original crew, "gave warning that the consequences" of battening down the slaves under hatches instead of keeping them in irons and bringing them up for air during the day "would be 'many deaths.' The next day the prediction of the Spaniard was fearfully verified. Fifty-four crushed and mangled corpses lifted up from the slave deck were thrown overboard. Antonio tells me some were found strangled, their hands still grasping each other's throats. The bowels of one were crushed out. They had been trampled to death for the most part in the madness and torment of suffocation. It was a horrid sight as they passed one by one—the stiff, distorted limbs smeared with blood and filth—to be thrown into the sea. Some, still quivering, were left on deck to die. Antonio reminded me of his last night's warning. He actively employed himself with his comrade, Sebastian, in distributing their allowance of water, rather more than half a pint each, which they grasped with inconceivable eagerness."

In Hill's account the Spaniards of the slaver's original crew are presented as the heroes of the voyage—and indeed they probably were, having had more experience in handling cargoes of terrified Negroes than had the English seamen. Questions were asked in Parliament as a result of the chaplain's story. Church and anti-slavery groups held protest meetings, and the Admiralty ordered an investigation. From that time rescued slaves had to be transported on the frigates themselves, to prevent a repetition of the *Progresso* disaster. The frigates spent weeks away from their cruising stations, their decks crowded with often resentful semi-captives, while their officers tried to solve unfamiliar problems of discipline and sanitation. They cursed what they called the "sentimentalists" at home, who had never known the practical difficulties of handling hundreds of confused and panic-stricken persons on a small vessel. They cursed the slaves too, though their resentment against them does not seem to have been chiefly a matter of racial prejudice, since all the officers speak highly of West African Krumen, often comparing them with English seamen to the disadvantage of the latter. Most of all the officers of the squadron cursed the Yankee skippers in the trade and the Arabs carrying slaves in their elusive dhows.

Although many and indeed for a long time most of the east-coast slaves were carried to Brazil or Cuba, the great majority of those from Zanzibar were shipped northward to the Persian Gulf. This Arabian branch of the slave trade was the one that proved hardest to suppress. Except for its connection with the East Coast Slaving Squadron, it lies outside the scope of the present narrative, but it continued long after 1873, the year when Zanzibar ceased to be an export market for slaves. There is, in fact, a considerable body of proof to show that slaves are still being exported to Arabia and that the great powers are too much concerned with oil diplomacy to investigate the situation. The worst cruelties, the widest ravages, the greatest loss of human life in the slave trade occurred during the 1870s and 1880s, after the Atlantic trade had been effectively abolished. Those were the years when the famous Tippu Tib, with his Arab companions and black mercenaries, had literally depopulated most of the Upper Congo forest, penetrating the country, as Henry M. Stanley said in 1887, "with only one dominating passion, which was to kill as many of the men and capture as many of the women and children as craft and cruelty would enable them." It was Tippu Tib and his Arab raiders who furnished the excuse for King Leopold's equally disastrous exploitation of the Congo—but all that is part of another story.

The slave trade from Zanzibar to Arabia was formally abolished, but not suppressed, by the Hamerton Treaty of 1847. By terms of the treaty, it was still permissible to ship slaves from the mainland to Zanzibar, and the cruisers of the Slaving Squadron were forced to watch helplessly while dhow after dhow loaded with slaves sailed into Zanzibar harbor to the beat of drums and the blowing of conch-shell horns. Hamerton, the first British representative to the sultan of Zanzibar, estimated that forty thousand slaves a year were being landed on the island. Supposedly they were "for domestic use only," but this was a ridiculous pretense, considering that the whole population of the island, Arab, East Indian, and Negro, was only sixty thousand. It was obvious that slaves were being reshipped from the island in great numbers, but the cruisers could do nothing until the slave-laden dhows were outside the sultan's territorial waters and headed north for the Persian Gulf.

The sense of frustration of the British officers is reflected in Captain Sulivan's account of watching a dhow enter Zanzibar harbor.

> I went on deck just in time to see a huge dhow pass under our stern; her upper bamboo deck so covered with slaves squatting there, that not a square foot of it was visible. As she passed, every face on board of her was turned towards us and the Arabs from the raised deck or poop abaft, gave a most derisive cheer, followed by laughter, and one of them seeing Jumah [the cruiser's interpreter] hailed him which produced more cheers and laughter.
>
> "What does he say, Jumah?" I asked.
>
> "He say, Ah! ah! why you not come and take us, are you afraid?"
>
> Jumah replied, "We catch you another time."

"I got lots of slaves on board, tell the captain to come and see."

This was followed again by laughter as she passed inside, lowered her sail, and anchored within pistol shot of us. In an hour from that time, every slave was doubtless in the market and another dhow ready to take them north.

The Arab slavers were ruthless men and determined fighters. They were not natives of Zanzibar, but came from Oman, where they lived a semi-piratical existence. Devereux of the *Gorgon* saw them cut the throats of 240 slaves and throw the corpses overboard when a dhow was chased by his paddle-wheel frigate. The slavers were trying to lighten the vessel so they could escape. In 1861 a group of these buccaneer slavers temporarily seized the town of Zanzibar, parading through the streets waving their swords and muskets while the sultan hid in the upper floor of his palace. If there were no slaves to their liking in the market or if prices were too high, they sometimes kidnaped Zanzibarian citizens and carried them off bound hand and foot. Their dhows, which were of ten to a hundred tons with one or two masts, were armed with ancient three-pound cannon, while the crews carried flintlock muskets, spears, daggers, and two-handed swords.

Generally, however, the dhows did not put up much resistance to the squadron; they relied on speed rather than force. If speed failed them, their crews would try to run them aground and escape, leaving the slaves in the hold to drown or live as might be. It was the task of the pursuing cruiser to capture the dhow before she could be beached.

Until the squadron began to use steamers in the 1840s, overtaking a dhow running before the wind was almost impossible for the clumsy frigates. With the coming of steam, the cruiser had the advantage. Coal, however, was almost prohibitively expensive —it cost £8 a ton on the Zanzibar station as against a few shillings a ton in England—and a steamer could carry only seventy-six tons of the precious fuel, enough for three days of steady cruising. As a result, the frigates proceeded under sail; they got up steam in the boilers only when a suspected dhow was in sight.

If the dhow had no slaves on board, the frigate's commander was answerable to the Admiralty for the coal he had wasted. One officer lamented during a chase that, if the dhow was not a slaver, the pursuit was costing him twenty-five shillings an hour.

Often a dhow reached shore before it was overhauled, and then boats had to be sent through the surf to rescue the slaves. The fact that English crews and captains received "head money" for every slave rescued may have inspired them to take risks that they would not have taken for purely humanitarian motives, but those motives were also present. One confusing circumstance was that a surprising number of slaves—generally young girls destined as concubines for some wealthy Arab's harem—did not want to be rescued and would claim to be mere passengers on the dhows. The Arabs, incidentally, counted on making a high profit from the sale of such girls; it was one of their reasons for making their wholesale slave raids.

The Slaving Squadron had troubles other than those with the dhows and their cargoes. When the seamen landed to replenish their supplies of food and water, they were often attacked by local tribes that depended on the slave trade for a living. Coastal chiefs were always threatening to put their realms under French or German protection if the English interfered with their share of the trade, and the threat was often effective, since the British did not wish to see their commercial and military rivals firmly established in an area from which they could menace the sea route to India. There was also the problem of public sentiment in Europe. When Great Britain sent cruisers to close off the Zanzibar slave trade, she was denounced in Europe as an international bully meddling in the affairs of a small but proudly independent nation. When, rather than send troops against the sultan, Britain agreed to permit the coastal trade, she was again denounced as betraying the noble principles of Clarkson, Wilberforce, and Buxton. Some said that Zanzibar would starve if deprived of the slave trade. But when the British tried to set up industries on the island, they were denounced, once again, for using the suppression of the trade as an excuse to further their own commercial interests. If the officers of the Slaving Squadron tried to coerce the mainland chiefs, they were brutal imperialists. If they did not coerce them, they were callous monsters indifferent to the plight of the miserable thousands in the coffles and barracoons.

Meanwhile the East Coast Slaving Squadron had become, for its officers, a semi-independent realm and a complete way of life, with its own joys and sorrows, its own lingo, and its own traditions. We read of the officers' worry about shore leave, which had to be granted, but which almost always led to an outbreak of malaria and dysentery; we read of a steady diet of "quinine and grog"; of irresponsible crews who refused to use mosquito nets because they cut down the circulation of air, and who looted the captured dhows like pirates; of sea shells used as drinking cups after all the crockery had been broken in an engagement with an armed slaver; of the shore fights with natives; of the problem of conserving coal and, when fires were out, the torture of a two-hour delay in getting up steam; then we read about the terror of smallpox, the occasional floggings of sullen seamen, the long cruises in open boats to catch slavers up shallow rivers, with the men plagued by insects and keeling over with sunstroke, and finally we read of the frustration and bitterness—against the reformers at home, against the American skippers, against the Arabs, against the slaves themselves, and against the Admiralty that sent them out with no knowledge of the situation.

It is to the credit of the officers that, in spite of their frustrations, they did not suggest abandoning the fight against the slave trade. They had seen too much not to know that it was an unmitigated evil. Captain Moresby of the *Menai* reported of one dhow that it shipped three hundred slaves and that only twelve of them were alive ten days later. The dhow had been becalmed in the run from the mainland to Zanzibar, usually a two-day trip. "Those in the lower portion that died," Moresby says, "could not be removed; they remained until the upper part died and were thrown overboard. When the *Lyra* took a dhow carrying 112 girls," and these were valuable slaves intended for concubines, "each man as he went into the hold fainted." The beach in the harbor of Zanzibar was covered with dying slaves who had collapsed during the passage from the mainland and had been abandoned there. Hamerton in 1842 counted the bodies of fifty being eaten by dogs. Yet the slaves who died on the beach were not the only unfortunates. The sultan charged an import tax of one dollar per slave landed, and so the dhow captains flung sick slaves into the harbor to save the dollar. Visitors to Zanzibar were always impressed by the "lovely white shells" covering the bottom of the bay and clearly visible through the gin-clear water. The shells were the bones of slaves.

# 12

# The Dream of a Slave Empire

*I have lost two out of three [of my slave ships]. I have been in it for the grandeur and been fighting for principle. Now I am in it for the dollars.*

—C. A. L. Lamar

By THE YEAR 1850 THE OFFICERS OF THE SLAVING SQUADRON BEGAN to feel that they were making progress in their long fight to suppress the trade. There were then 24 British warships on the African coast, including some of the new steam frigates, and they carried 154 guns. They had obtained the right to board and search any merchant vessel in African waters, unless it flew the French or the American flag. About the French flag there was not much difficulty. France maintained an effective African squadron of her own, and it had put an end to French slaving, except in the disguised form of recruiting indentured laborers. That was a new problem for humanitarians, but not for the British officers, who were concerned only with the traditional forms of slaving. Their great and increasing difficulty was with the American flag, which now sheltered most of the slavers on the coast.

In 1850, however, the difficulty seemed less acute than it would shortly become. The United States was then maintaining a squadron of five warships on the African station. Two of these—the sloop-of-war *Yorktown* and the brig *Perry*, which was commanded by Lieutenant Andrew Hull Foote—had been sent to patrol the coast of Angola, where no American warships had previously appeared, although it was a famous haunt of American slavers. Foote made a few captures, most notably the ship *Martha*, already mentioned, and temporarily disrupted the Angola and Congo trade. He also pleased the British by giving them somewhat more cooperation than other American commanders had offered in the past, or would offer again before the Civil War. The British officers told him that their squadron, since 1839, had captured about seven hundred slaving vessels, a number that equaled the entire merchant marine of some middle-sized European countries. They said that the trade had diminished from an average of 105,000 slaves exported each year in the early 1840s to only 37,000 in 1849, and they were expecting a further reduction in 1850, since the slavers were becoming afraid to approach the coast. The coastal barracoons, they reported, were crowded with unsold slaves. Foote went home to make his own report in a book, *Africa and the American Flag*, which proved to be prematurely optimistic. What he failed to take into account was the power of the slave interest in Washington.

Yet the British Slaving Squadron seemed to have sound reasons for optimism in 1850. With the help of the Foreign Office and various colonization societies, English and American, it had closed nearly half of the West African coastline to the slave trade. The effectively closed areas included Senegambia, Sierra Leone, Liberia, the Gold Coast (where the British had taken over the old Danish forts), and more recently the Portuguese settlements in Angola.

Most of the slaves exported during the 1850s were to come from areas still controlled by native rulers. Notably they would come from the region between the Gambia and Sierra Leone (later divided between Portuguese Guinea and French Guinea); or they would come from the Slave Coast (now Togo, Dahomey, and Western Nigeria), or from the region north and south of the Congo River, or else from the east coast rivers that flowed into the Mozambique Channel. These were areas rich in slaves, and the British were trying to close them all.

Perhaps their most strenuous efforts during the 1850s were directed toward the Slave Coast, with its famous ports of Lagos, Porto Novo, Whydah, and Badagry. Slaves poured into all of them as a result of the annual wars between the Dahomans and the Yoruba. The English moved first against Lagos, which was controlled by the Yoruba. In 1851 a squadron of six warships under Commander Bruce attacked Lagos but was repulsed. Bruce enlisted the help of Akitoye, a pretender to the local throne, and Akitoye's men were told to wear white neckties, supplied by the British, so that they could be distinguished from the other army. With this native help, the second attack succeeded. Akitoye was installed as king of Lagos, but he later went into slave trading on his own account, as did his successor, and a British governor took over the area in 1861.

Step by step Great Britain was becoming established as a colonial power in Africa, but the evidence seems to show that the early steps were anything but deliberate. Often they were taken, as at Lagos, simply as a means of suppressing the slave trade. A naval officer on the scene sometimes moved faster than his government wished him to move. Thus, on the east coast, Captain Owens seized Mombasa in 1823 to keep slavers out of the port. The sultan of Zanzibar protested, and Owens' act was promptly disavowed by the government. When Captain Colomb suggested that part of the east-coast slaving area might be acquired by purchase, the Foreign Secretary pointed out to him that the sultan of Zanzibar was an independent monarch who could not even consider selling part of his country. "You might as well talk of purchasing Germany," the secretary added.

The same scruples were displayed on the west coast, where diplomacy instead of force was used in persuading King Gezo of Dahomey to abolish the trade. After stoutly refusing to do so many times, he finally signed a treaty in 1852, but slaves from Dahomey continued to reach the coast. The British then instituted a close blockade of Whydah, his principal port. As late as 1862, Palmerston was writing Lord John Russell, the Foreign Secretary, "As to conquering Dahomey, nobody would think of that nor would it be at all necessary. It would be quite enough if we could stop the bung holes through which the Dahomey slave trade issues and these are but few: Whydah, Porto Novo, Badagry."

On the other side of the Atlantic, the market for slaves was contracting. The French in 1848, the revolutionary year, had abolished slavery in their colonial possessions, thus closing a minor market, and the Dutch were talking of abolition. Brazil, which had been the largest consumer of slaves, had taken steps of its own to suppress the trade after Admiral Reynolds blockaded the coast in 1849. Cuba seemed to be the only market that remained, and during the 1850s it was importing from thirty to forty thousand slaves a year. Slowly, however, a new development began to make itself evident. American capital went into the slaving business on a rather large scale, for the time, and American-owned vessels began landing their cargoes not only in Cuba but also directly in Georgia and the Gulf states.

This new development was one that the Slaving Squadron found it hard to combat. The new American slavers, instead of being brigs or topsail schooners, were among the largest and fastest sailing ships of their time; several of them were clippers built for the China trade. Instead of carrying two or three hundred slaves, they took on a human cargo as large as that of an ocean liner: for example, the *Martha* had intended to buy 1800 Negroes. They specialized in buying boys and girls, who made less trouble and took less space than adults. British warships could not search them, and American warships were becoming less active on the African coast; time after time a larger appropriation for the African Squadron was voted down or filibustered to death in Congress. Moreover, the capture of a slaver did not put its owners out of business. The owners, in many cases, were a syndicate controlling several vessels and able to reckon that the profits on two or three successful voyages more than counterbalanced the losses on four or five.

There is a famous letter that reveals how the American spirit of business enterprise was applied to slave smuggling. The letter was written in 1858 by Charles A. L. Lamar, oldest son of Gazaway Bugg Lamar, who, in spite of his fantastic name, was the leading financier of Georgia. Its purpose was to obtain another stockholder for the boldest of all slaving ventures. The italics in the text are words underlined by the younger Lamar:

> I have in contemplation, if I can raise the necessary amount of money, the fitting out of an expedition to go to the coast of Africa for a cargo of African apprentices *to be bound for the term of their natural lives,* and would like your co-operation. No subscription will be received for a less amount than $5000. The amount to be raised is $300,000. I will take $20,000 of the stock and go myself. I propose to purchase the "Vigo," an iron screw steamer of 1750 tons, now in Liverpool for sale at £30,000 cash. She cost £75,000. G. B. Lamar [his father, that is] can give you a description of her. . . . She is as good as new, save her boilers, and they can be used for several months. If I can buy her I will put six Paixhan guns on deck and man her with as good men as can be found in the South. The fighting men will all be stockholders and gentlemen some of whom are known to you, if not personally, by reputation. My estimate runs thus:
>
> | | |
> |---|---:|
> | Steamer $150,000; repairs, guns, small arms, coal, etc., $50,000 | $200,000 |
> | Supplies, $25,000; money for purchase of cargo, $75,000 | 100,000 |
> | | $300,000 |

I have, as you know, a vessel now afloat, but it is, in my mind, extremely doubtful whether she gets in safely, as she had to wait

on the Coast until her cargo could be collected. If she ever gets
clear of the Coast, they can't catch her. She ought to be due in
from ten to thirty days. I have another now ready to sail which
has orders to take a cargo of 1000 or 1200 to be in readiness the
1st of September, but to be kept, if necessary, until the 1st of
October—which I intend for the steamer—so that no delay may
occur. With her I can make the voyage there and back, including
all detentions, bad weather, if I encounter it, etc., in ninety days,
certain and sure; and the negroes can be sold as fast as landed at
$650 per head. I can contract for them "to arrive" at that figure,
*cash*. The "Vigo" can bring 2000 with ease and comfort, and I
apprehend no difficulty or risk, save shipwreck, and that you can
insure against. I can get one of the first lieutenants in the navy
to go out in command, and we can whip anything if attacked,
that is on that station, either English or American. But I would
not propose to fight; for the "Vigo" can steam eleven knots, which
would put us out of the way of any of the cruisers.

In another letter Lamar computed the returns from a single
voyage: "1200 negroes at $650, $780,000, which leaves net profit
and steamer on hand, $480,000." In spite of his glowing prospectus,
Lamar did not raise money enough to buy the *Vigo*. That same
year, however, he embarked on another slaving venture that made
its share of history. We shall come back to Lamar, who represented, with some other bold spirits, what threatened to become
a new age in American slaving.

The new age resulted from the long conflict between the South
and the North over the slavery question. At first the Southerners
were content to defend their peculiar institution as one that was
necessary for the time being; they held that if the North did not
interfere with slavery, it would gradually wither away. Nobody advanced that argument after 1830. Abolitionists in the North were
attacking slavery as an absolute evil, and the Southerners' answer
was foreordained: slavery, they said, was the necessary feature of
an ideal society. The Negroes were ideally designed to serve, and
the whites were ideally designed to rule in leisure and cultivate
the arts of life and government. Slavery, in short, was an absolute

good, and it was their patriotic and human duty to give it the widest possible extension.

Some of the Southern extremists argued, tongue in cheek, that the North should enslave the Irish and German immigrants. It would be an act of kindness, they said, since the immigrants would then be better fed and housed than they were on the daily wages that Northern capitalists were paying them. Other extremists proposed, more seriously, that the South should establish its own cotton mills operated by slave labor. Said M. Tarver, Esq., of Mississippi, writing in *De Bow's Review,* "It would no doubt be true, that grown negroes taken from the field would be found awkward and clumsy in the labour of the cotton mill, but slaves put into factories when young, and raised up to that employment, would make the most efficient and reliable operatives to be found in any country. . . . They would be more reliable, because they would have no right to prescribe the hours for working; there would be no striking for higher wages; and they would have no right to leave the employment at pleasure, as is the case with free laborers. These would be eminent advantages in favour of those who employed this species of labour."

Still other extremists argued that the price of slaves should be reduced, so that every white man in the South, without exception, could own a Negro. That, said Edward A. Pollard of Virginia, would be the salvation of the poor white. "He would no longer be a miserable, nondescript cumberer of the soil, scratching the land here and there for a subsistence, living from hand to mouth, or trespassing along the borders of the possessions of the large proprietors," Pollard continued in his book of Southern apologetics, *Black Diamonds.* "He would be a proprietor himself; and in the great work of developing the riches of the South, from which he had been heretofore excluded, vistas of enterprise and wealth would open to him that would enliven his heart and transform him into another man. He would no longer be the scorn and sport of 'gentlemen of color,' who parade their superiority, rub their well-stuffed black skins, and thank God that they are not as he."

In the same book Pollard offers another prospect that seems to have engrossed many of the bolder spirits in the South. It was the dream of extending the benefits of slavery to the Latin countries beyond the Gulf of Mexico. "Looking into the possibilities of the future," Pollard says, "regarding the magnificent country of tropical America, which lies in the path of our destiny on this continent, we may see an empire as powerful and gorgeous as ever was pictured in our dreams of history. What is that empire? It is an empire founded on military ideas; representing the noble peculiarities of Southern civilization; including within its limits the isthmuses of America and the regenerated West Indies; having control of the two dominant staples of the world's commerce—cotton and sugar; possessing the highways of the world's commerce; surpassing all empires of the age in the strength of its geographical position; and, in short, combining elements of strength, prosperity, and glory, such as never before in the modern ages have been placed within the reach of a single government.

"What a splendid vision of empire!" Pollard continued. "How sublime in its associations! How noble and inspiriting the idea, that upon the strange theatre of tropical America, once, if we may believe the dimmer facts of history, crowned with magnificent empires and flashing cities and great temples, now covered with mute ruins, and trampled over by half-savages, the destiny of Southern civilization is to be consummated in a glory brighter even than that of old, the glory of an empire, controlling the commerce of the world, impregnable in its position, and representing in its internal structure the most harmonious of all the systems of modern civilization."

It was a dream as grandiose and almost as fatally persuasive as Hitler's dream of the Third Reich. There are indications, moreover, that it was shared by many or most of the Southern Fire-Eaters, as the extremists were called, and even by supposedly responsible statesmen. Seizing Cuba was regarded as a first step toward realizing the dream. Three filibustering expeditions set out for Cuba in the years from 1849 to 1851, and in 1854 the

American ministers to England, France, and Spain issued the Ostend Manifesto, in which they declared that if Spain would not sell Cuba for a fair price, the United States was justified in taking the island by force. William Walker's expedition to Nicaragua was, according to Pollard, an act of Southern patriotism. One of Walker's announced aims, when he became president of Nicaragua for a brief period, was to introduce slavery and the slave trade. Agitation in favor of Caribbean conquests was carried on all through the 1850s. "About the middle of the year 1859," says the *Annuaire des Deux Mondes* in its 1860 issue, "in the cotton-growing states, and especially in Louisiana and Mississippi, there was formed a mysterious association whose statutes were veiled in impenetrable secrecy and whose members were called the Knights of the Golden Circle." Of course that Golden Circle— a phrase often used at the time—was the circle of new slave states to be formed around the Caribbean and the Gulf of Mexico. Later, during the Civil War, the Knights became a secret order of Southern sympathizers in the Northern states.

The dream of a Golden Circle was among the minor causes of secession and war. The dreamers were playing for high stakes, and they were eager to cut loose from the North, with its cautious merchants and troublesome abolitionists. But it was useless to conquer new slave states in Latin America unless they could buy slaves to people them. Cuba had a fairly plentiful supply, and that helps to explain why seizing the island was regarded as a necessary first step in Southern expansion. But the only inexhaustible source of slaves was Africa, and the dreamers of empire faced the issue squarely. At first in private meetings, then loudly in public, they began to argue for the repeal of all laws that prohibited or merely penalized the African slave trade.

It was in South Carolina that the issue came into the open. In 1854 the South Carolina Committee on Coloured Population recommended that the trade should be reopened, for the reason among others that "it would confer a blessing on the African race." The statement attracted little attention, but two years later

Governor James H. Adams, in his annual message to the South Carolina legislature, argued at length for reopening the trade. "Shall Africa be left to her barbarism and all to ruin Europe and America?" he asked. "The Northern policy . . . is to settle our territories as hireling States and to bring them, as such, into the Union more rapidly than the South can introduce slave States. . . . They receive annually from four to five hundred thousand European emigrants to swell their numbers while we have not received for fifty years a single negro!"

At the time his words struck Southern ears as "a thunder clap on a calm day," and the thunder had a long reverberation. In 1857 Henry St. Paul, also of South Carolina, asked the legislature for permission to import 2500 "free black laborers from the Coast of Africa to be indentured as apprentices to labor for a term of years which the parties may agree upon." The *New Orleans Daily Crescent* reported that his suggestion produced "a burst of applause from hundreds of auditors in the lobby." Governor Wickliffe of Louisiana declared in 1858, "It is just and right that the Federal Government and the Northern States bow to the immutable decrees of natural law and not resist the South in the spread of her institution to regions so palpably pointed to by the finger of destiny for her occupation." The agitation spread to Congress, where Representative Crawford of Georgia, with the approbation of many other Southerners in the House, argued vigorously for the reopening of the trade. Senator Alexander Stephens, later Vice-President of the Confederacy, said in his farewell address to his constituents, "Slave states cannot be made without Africans. . . . [My object is] to bring clearly to your mind the great truth that without an increase of African slaves from abroad you may not expect or look for many more slave states."

It must be emphasized that a great many Southerners resisted these efforts to reopen the trade. The resistance was strongest in the border states, which had a surplus of slave labor and which feared that fresh imports from Africa would reduce the value of their property. Even in the Deep South, however, there were many cotton planters who opposed the trade for humanitarian reasons. The Fire-Eaters were a minority, and a small one at first, but they were active in gaining converts. All through the 1850s they carried on their propaganda by means of newspaper editorials, pamphlets, speeches at agricultural-society meetings, and face-to-face arguments. The Southern Commercial Convention, representing a fairly broad sector of Southern opinion, held its annual meeting at Vicksburg in 1859. It was urged to raise a fund "to be dispensed in premiums for the best sermons in favor of reopening the African Slave Trade." It also discussed a resolution that, "in the opinion of this Convention, all laws, State or Federal, prohibiting the African slave trade, ought to be repealed." The debate became so heated, with threats of personal violence, that a dozen moderate members withdrew from the convention. The resolution was then passed by a majority of forty to nineteen. Tennessee voted against it, and the border states of Virginia, Maryland, Kentucky, and North Carolina did not vote; perhaps their representatives were among those who had withdrawn.

That helps to explain why the slave trade, after all this agitation, was outlawed by the Confederate constitution. Even the Fire-Eaters recognized that if they did not prohibit the trade, they would lose the allegiance of the border states and would probably not be recognized by Great Britain. They seem to have believed, however, that the prohibition could be overridden by the laws of the separate states, which retained their sovereignty. Accordingly they went off to war, still fighting for their dream.

There is one more thing to be said about the effort to reopen the slave trade that continued almost until the firing on Fort Sumter. Although it had little effect on legislation, Federal or Confederate, it did have a number of practical effects. It prevented Congress from sending more ships to the African station or from voting more than the smallest appropriations for the ships already there; in some years no money was voted at all. It encouraged American naval officers—many of whom were Southerners—to be tolerant of slavers and lackadaisical in pursuing them.

It created a climate of opinion that made slavers hard to convict in United States courts. It prevented secretaries of state from making the slightest concession in their long dispute with Great Britain about the misuse of the American flag. In regard to the capture of one vessel, the *Rufus Soule*, which had been flying the American flag and was clearly a slaver, Secretary Lewis Cass wrote to London, "Whether this vessel was then engaged in the slave trade is one thing, but whether she was entitled to the protection of the flag of the United States is another and quite different thing and depends not upon the nature of her employment, legal or illegal, but upon her national character." In other words, the British could not search a truly American slaver, and American naval vessels were almost never there to search her, with the result that most of the slave ships, in the 1850s, not only flew the American flag but were owned by American citizens. Many of the owners were Northern merchants from New York or Boston, and these preferred the Cuban trade as being a safer investment. Others, however, were Southern Fire-Eaters themselves, like C. A. L. Lamar, and these preferred to forget the risks and land their cargoes on Southern soil. They had gone into the business not only for profit but also as a practical and patriotic step toward realizing their dream of a slave empire, a Golden Circle.

"To have boldly ventured into New Orleans," said an article in the *New York Herald* for August 5, 1860, "with negroes freshly imported from Africa, would not only have brought down upon the head of the importer the vengeance of our very philanthropic Uncle Sam, but also the anathemas of the whole sect of philanthropists and negrophilists everywhere. To import them for years, however, into quiet places, evading with impunity the penalty of the law, and the ranting of the thin-skinned sympathizers with Africa, was gradually to popularize the traffic by creating a demand for laborers, and thus to pave the way for the *gradual revival of the slave trade*. To this end, a few men, bold and energetic, determined, ten or twelve years ago, to commence the business of importing negroes, slowly at first, but surely; and for this purpose they selected a few secluded places on the coast of Florida, Georgia and Texas, for the purpose of concealing their stock until it could be sold out."

That picture of a conspiracy headed by a few bold and energetic men is a tempting one for those who accept the devil theory of history. It may even be close to the truth, but it is impossible to confirm. What we do know, from contemporary evidence, is that after 1850 more and more Guinea Negroes began to appear in the cotton states. They were seen in the great slave markets at New Orleans and Memphis. They were advertised for sale in weekly newspapers. The *Mobile Mercury* reported, "Some negroes who never learned to talk English, went up on the railroad the other day." An agricultural society offered a "premium of twenty-five dollars for the best specimen of a live African imported within the last twelve months." Congressman Crawford of Georgia told the Democratic convention at Charleston, in 1860, "If any of you northern democrats will go home with me to my plantation, I will show you some darkies that I bought in Virginia, some in Delaware, some in Florida, and I will also show you the pure African, the noblest Roman of them all. I represent the African slave trade interest in my section."

As testimony from the other side, we have a speech by the Little Giant, Stephen A. Douglas, which is summarized in the *27th Report of the American Anti-Slavery Society*. Douglas said (1859) "that there was not the shadow of doubt that the Slave-trade had been carried on quite extensively for a long time back, and that there had been more Slaves imported into the southern States, during the last year, than had ever been imported before in any one year, even when the Slave-trade was legal. It was his confident belief, that over fifteen thousand Slaves had been brought into this country during the past year. He had seen, with his own eyes, three hundred of those recently-imported, miserable beings, in a Slave-pen in Vicksburg, Miss., and also large numbers at Memphis, Tenn." There are no figures to confirm or disprove Douglas's estimate, but we do know that the import trade was growing. An "interested person" boasted to a senator, about 1860, that between sixty and seventy slave cargoes had been successfully landed in the Southern states within the past eighteen months. The *New York Tribune* doubted the statement, but a Virginian insisted that it was correct. "I have had," he said in a letter to the paper, "ample evidences of the fact, that reopening the African Slave-trade is a thing already accomplished, and the traffic is brisk, and rapidly increasing. . . . The arrival of cargoes of negroes, fresh from Africa, in our southern ports, is an event of frequent occurrence."

There was still, in 1961, a living witness to, or piece of evidence confirming, the importation of slaves during the 1850s. The oldest person on the Social Security rolls was Charlie Smith, of Polk City, Florida, who was 118 years old and a former slave. According to records at the Department of Health, Education and Welfare, Mr. Smith had been kidnaped off the coast of Liberia at the age of twelve and had been sold in the New Orleans slave market in 1855, probably with others from the same cargo.

Our best record of how the cargoes were landed is a series of letters written by Charles A. L. Lamar, discovered long after his death and printed in the *North American Review* of November 1886. Lamar, to judge from the letters, was a typical young Fire-Eater, quick-tempered, bold, and flamboyant. He is described as a heavy man with a big red mustache, about five feet, nine inches tall, and "coarse-spoken," according to the cook of his vessel the *Wanderer*. That was, incidentally, his third vessel, coming after the *E. A. Rawlins* and the *Richard Cobden*, both of which had already been dispatched to the coast of Africa. The *Rawlins* had first been detained for eight days by the collector of the port of Boston, who suspected her of being a slaver. After she was released, Lamar sent a bill for damages of $1320 to his kinsman Howell Cobb of Georgia, who was Buchanan's Secretary of the Treasury. "I did not, in my other communication," Lamar wrote him, "disclaim any intention of embarking in the Slave-trade, nor did I say anything to warrant you in supposing I was not engaged in it. I simply declared that there was nothing on board except what was on the manifest, and that I insist there was nothing suspicious on it."

Lamar always had his nerve with him, as well as a conviction of his utter rightness. He seems to have entered the slaving business in 1857, "fighting for a principle," as he later said, but "now I am in for the dollars." He thought in big terms. While still negotiating for the iron-screw steamer *Vigo*, in the spring of 1858, he formed another syndicate and bought the flagship of the New York Yacht Club for use as a slaver. This was the famous *Wanderer*, built the preceding year for a wealthy member of the club who wanted the fastest vessel afloat. She was a two-masted schooner of 260 tons, with an over-all length of 104 feet, not counting 23 feet of bowsprit. Her mainmast was 84 feet tall, and its topmast was 35. Her builder liked to say that she could fly instead of sailing.

The *Wanderer* was sold to Captain W. C. Corrie, who was secretly acting for the syndicate, and Corrie, a jovial type, was promptly elected to the Yacht Club. He then sailed for Charleston, where the *Wanderer* had water tanks capable of holding twelve thousand gallons installed below her berth deck. She also took on a sailing master, Captain Semmes, who was said to be a brother of Raphael Semmes, later rear-admiral in the Confederate Navy. The *Wanderer* was flying the pennant of the New York Yacht Club, and Corrie announced that he was taking her on a pleasure cruise in the West Indies. Instead he made a quick passage to the west coast of Africa.

Having arrived at the mouth of the Congo, Corrie found the British cruiser *Medusa* on patrol. The *Medusa* had the reputation of being one of the fastest vessels in the Slaving Squadron, and Corrie, in his role of an elegant yachtsman, challenged her to a race, which the *Wanderer* won handily. Afterward there was an elaborate dinner, with plenty of wine. At one point Corrie suggested to the British officers that his floating palace would make an excellent slaver; then he begged them to examine the yacht for extra water tanks, a slave deck, and shackles. The officers burst out laughing and went back to drinking their port.

Confident now that his yacht could outrun the cruiser, Corrie—or rather his sailing master—went up the Congo and took on a cargo of 750 young Negroes between the ages of thirteen and eighteen. He made another fast crossing and, by prior arrangement, met Lamar on Jekyll Island, at the mouth of the Little Satilla River near Brunswick, Georgia. Lamar had paid $15,000 to the owners of the island for permission to land the cargo. The Negroes were distributed to different areas; some were sent up the Little Satilla, and the *Wanderer* took 150 of them up the coast to the Savannah River. In a postwar interview, A. C. McGhee, a member of the syndicate that financed the venture, tells how they were smuggled past the fort at the mouth of the river. "Captain Semmes," he says, "crept into the mouth of the Great Ogeechee by night and ascended the river to the big swamp, and there lay concealed while he communicated with Lamar in Savannah.

"Lamar thereupon announced that he was going to give a grand ball in honor of the officers and garrison of the fort, and insisted that the soldiers, as well as their superiors, should partake of the good cheer. When the gayety was at its height the *Wanderer* stole into the river and passed the guns of the fort unchallenged in the darkness and made her way to Lamar's plantations, some distance up the river. The human cargo was soon disembarked and placed under the charge of old rice-field negroes, who were nearly as savage as the new importations."

The adventure was reported in the newspapers, the *Savannah Republican* giving a detailed account on December 11, 1858. Such an outcry was raised by Northern abolitionists that, as Lamar expressed it in a letter to a friend, "I tell you, things are in a hell of a fix." United States District Attorney Ganahl made a personal issue of the case. Lamar wrote: "The yacht has been seized. . . . They have all the pilots and men who took the yacht to Brunswick here to testify. *She will be lost certain and sure,* if not the negroes. Dr. Hazlehurst testified that he attended the negroes and swore they were Africans, and of recent importation. . . . All these men must be *bribed.* I must be paid for my time, trouble and advances.

. . . Six of those who were left at Mont's, who were sick, died yesterday. I think the whole of them now sick will die. They are too enfeebled to administer medicine to. I am paying fifty cents a day each for all those I took up the country. It was the best I could do."

Lamar had taken a number of the slaves to an isolated plantation to hide them from the district attorney's agents. But he was betrayed by the plantation owner and could not repossess his property. He wrote to another friend: "I am astonished at what Governor Phiniz has written me. . . . The idea of a man's taking negroes to keep at fifty cents a head per day, and then refusing to give them up when demanded simply because the law does not recognize them as property, is worse than stealing."

The yacht was confiscated by the government and offered for public sale at Savannah. Lamar turned up at the auction and announced that as the vessel was his property, wrongly taken from him by the Northern abolitionists, he would punch the head of anyone daring to bid against him. But the warden of the local jail did bid, and it cost Lamar $4000 to regain her. Having got his ship back, Lamar kept his promise by knocking the warden down.

In spite of all these difficulties, the voyage was a success. McGhee stated that "slaves that had been purchased for a few beads and bandanna handkerchiefs were sold in the market for from $600 to $700 apiece. The owners of the vessel paid Captain Semmes $3500 for his services and cleared upwards of $10,000 apiece on the venture for themselves." But Captain Corrie was not to escape scot-free. The New York Yacht Club expelled him, and he was refused permission to continue flying their pennant.

Lamar himself, now "in for the dollars," next formed the design of sending the *Wanderer* to China for a shipload of coolies. "They are worth from $340 to $350 each in Cuba," he wrote to a friend in New Orleans, "and cost but $12 and their passage." It was a time when coolie labor had become so popular in Cuba that it had lessened the demand for Negro slaves. But for some reason—we do not know why—Lamar abandoned the design, and the *Wan-*

*derer* sailed back to the Congo. A. C. McGhee tells us that Captain
Semmes traded with the same local monarch, King Dahominey,
from whom he had bought his first shipload of slaves.

> On the second occasion [McGhee says] he had to go further up
> the river to secure the cargo, but he succeeded in delivering six
> hundred captives at the mouth of the river. They were more in-
> telligent than the first cargo, lighter in color, and better in many
> respects than those captured nearer the coast. A number of them
> died during the voyage, and the *Wanderer* was put to her best
> speed on several occasions to get away from undesirable acquaint-
> ances, but she was never overhauled. . . . In attempting to
> enter Jekyl Creek, between Jekyl and Cumberland Islands, she ran
> aground one stormy night, and a number of the captives escaped
> from the hold and jumped into the sea and were drowned. . . .
> The negroes were sent to New Orleans and sold, except a few that
> were scattered about among the Georgia planters. The profits
> were quite as large as from the first expedition, and but for the
> breaking out of the war and the blockading of the port at Savan-
> nah, the *Wanderer* might have made another voyage in 1860.

As a matter of fact, she did make another voyage, and perhaps
two, but under different captains. Lamar had quarreled with
Semmes, and he wrote a letter explaining the reason. "He claimed
he was to have received $30 a head for every one [of the slaves]
who *had life in him,* that was landed, independent of his condition,
even though he might die before he could be housed. Such was
not the contract." Semmes, who thought it *was* the contract, went
off in a rage.

Lamar then hired as captain a man who was variously known as
Potter, Dresser, Walker, and Martin; we shall call him Martin. In
October 1859 Lamar asked the collector of the Port of Savannah to
seize the *Wanderer* because, although he had sold Martin a considerable interest in the vessel, Martin had never paid him, and
"I have just about made up my mind that I have to deal with a
damned rascal." Martin heard about the complaint and acted
promptly. He got some sailors to bring stores on board, then
shanghaied them and put to sea. When the men protested, Martin
produced a horse pistol, a cutlass, and a revolver. Going from man

to man, he stuck the pistol in their ears and asked in turn, "Do you really want to go ashore?" All the men changed their minds. Martin then brought out a case of champagne for the crew.

"He has undoubtedly gone to the coast of Africa for a cargo of slaves," Lamar wrote. "And if he is as smart there as he has been here, he will get one." Lamar was right in his suspicions. Martin was "after a cargo of niggers," as he told the shipping master before dropping him when the *Wanderer* set sail. But in his hurry to get away he had neglected to take along either charts or chronometer, and he was forced to chase every vessel he met so the captain could tell him where he was. He was drunk from morning to night and drove the ship along under such a press of sail—she logged 340 miles in one day—that the mate afterward said, "It was a wonder he didn't run her under." On reaching the Azores, Martin kidnaped two girls, whom he intended to exchange for a number of Negro slaves, having heard that Negro kings liked to have white women in their harems. The ship was bound for the Slave Coast, but, lost as usual, Martin hailed a French vessel off the Canaries and went on board her. The mate took advantage of his absence to seize the ship, with the cordial cooperation of the sailors, who had begun to dislike Captain Martin. The mate took the *Wanderer* to Boston and surrendered her to the federal authorities.

Lamar heard the news, hastened to Boston, and, in December 1859, claimed the vessel on the ground that she had been stolen from him. The court ruled in his favor. He then took the *Wanderer* to Savannah, found her another captain, and she is said to have made still another voyage to Africa. If she did make that fourth voyage, she came somewhat closer to deserving the name by which she is generally known, "the last slaver."

The *Wanderer* had some further adventures. She was seized by the Union Navy, commissioned as a cruiser, then later used as a hospital ship till the end of the war, and she ended her days in the Central American copra trade. Caught in a gale, she was driven ashore and wrecked. As for Lamar, he had lost interest in the slave trade with the approach of hostilities. He raised a Georgia regiment, became its lieutenant colonel, and survived four years of fighting. On the night of April 16, 1865—a week after Appomattox—he was killed by a stray shot in the streets of Columbus, Georgia. Union General James H. Wilson, whose forces had just taken the town, said later that Lamar "was the last conspicuous man, of whom I have any knowledge, killed during the rebellion."

There were other ships that claimed the title of "last slaver." George Howe, a medical student from Mississippi, sailed on one of them, partly against his will, and later he wrote an account of his round trip to Africa. Actually the *Rebecca*, as the ship was called, fell short of winning the title by a year or two, since she landed her cargo during November 1859, but still she had an exciting voyage. The *Rebecca* was a Baltimore clipper with a record, Howe says, "of 14 knots to windward, sailing inside of four points from the wind. We could easily make 320 to 340 miles daily." Speed proved to be the *Rebecca*'s salvation. When she was loading slaves from native sloops at the mouth of the Congo, the lookout at the masthead shouted, "Sail ho! Away to the southward." It proved to be the *Vixen*, a British steam frigate, but the *Rebecca* continued taking on slaves until the frigate was within gunshot. Then, Howe says,

> The Spanish captain cried out: "Let go!" The pin holding the staple in the anchor chain was cut, and the chain parted. Sail was hoisted rapidly, the Negroes in the sloops climbed over the ship's side, and as the sloops were emptied they were cast adrift with their single occupant, a Krooman. They scattered like frightened birds.
>
> We seemed a long time getting headway, and everybody was looking very anxious, as other sails were set; studding-sails were added, stay-sails hoisted, and a large square sail on the mizzenmast from the deck to topsail—such a cloud of canvas that I felt sure the masts would go overboard. The *Vixen* was now within one mile and she seemed to have wonderful speed; again she changed her course and there followed a puff of smoke. That was

too close for comfort, I thought, as the splashing sea showed
where the ball ricocheted, and so very near. We seemed to have
gained some distance during this maneuver, and the wind grew
stronger the farther we got from land. A cloud of black smoke
showed that a grand effort was being made by our pursuer to recover the distance lost while changing her course to fire at us. We
were now easily going ahead and the distance was greater between
us, the wind so strong that we were compelled to take in the lofty
studding-sails. Another hour, and it was getting near night, with
the cruiser at least five miles astern, still holding on, hoping something would happen to disable us yet. Night fell, but we continued our course without change until midnight, when we sailed
south-southwest until daylight, so that if anything should happen
to our masts, we should be far from the route of our pursuer if he
still followed us.

"But the pursuer was lost," Howe says, and the *Rebecca* made a
successful run to Cuba, where she landed her slaves. Afterward the
ship was burned to escape being detected by her smell, and Howe,
paid off as her surgeon, took passage back to New Orleans, his
pockets full of gold.

About six months later a romantic young man named Edward
Manning joined the crew of the Baltimore-built clipper *Thomas
Watson*, of 348 tons, sailing out of New London, Connecticut. He
must have been reading *Moby Dick*, for he thought he was going
on a three years' whaling cruise, and he signed the ship's articles
under the fictitious name of Edward Melville. Soon he discovered
that the whaling voyage was fictitious too. After the ship reached
the Azores, the crew was set to work breaking out the stores in the
hold, and these—Manning says in his book *Six Months on a Slaver*
—were found to include a supply "of rice, hard-tack, salt beef,
pork, etc., in quantities large enough to feed a regiment for a long
time." Next the sailors were ordered to lay a slave deck. Most of
them "seemed to be well pleased at the new phase the voyage had
taken," Manning says, "and were anxious for the time to come
when the ship would be well filled with 'blackfish oil,' as they
termed the negroes, and her bow pointed toward the States." Man-

ning gained the ill will of the captain by being the only one to
protest.

The *Thomas Watson* shipped her black cargo near the mouth of
the Congo, got away from the coast without being sighted by a
cruiser, and landed more than eight hundred Negroes on the south
coast of Cuba in December 1860. She was then taken into the Bay
of Campeche and fumigated to remove the sickly sweet smell that
persisted. Manning reached New Orleans in January and found
the city in a state of "most intense excitement"; he thought it wise
to take the first train leaving for the North. Later he served as a
volunteer officer in the United States Navy, while the *Thomas
Watson* became a Confederate blockade runner. Pursued by Union
cruisers, she was driven on a reef outside Charleston harbor and
was burned to the water's edge.

There were still other "last American slavers." In April 1860,
while Ensign (later Commodore) George Hamilton Perkins was
master of the USS *Sumter,* he wrote home to his New England
family. "The clipper ship *Nightingale* of Salem," he said, "shipped
a cargo of 2000 negroes and has gone clear with them. . . . She is
a powerful clipper and is the property of the captain, Bowen, who
is called the 'Prince of Slavers.' " The *Nightingale* was a lovely
ship of a thousand tons, built long, low, and fast for the China
tea trade. In January 1861 she reappeared on the African coast and
began a game of hide-and-seek with the cruisers. Finally on April
21, nine days after the firing on Fort Sumter, she was captured by
the United States sloop-of-war *Saratoga* while she was taking on
slaves at Cabinda. Of the 961 Negroes she had already shipped,
160 died before they could be put ashore at Monrovia. Her captain, Francis Bowen, besides being the prince of slavers, was the
kinsman of some prominent abolitionists. Another Francis Bowen
was the professor of moral philosophy at Harvard College, thus
illustrating the curious relationship that existed in New England
between sometimes unscrupulous merchants and high-minded
reformers. The slaving Bowen was permitted to escape at São
Thomé by a naval lieutenant with Southern sympathies. The

*Nightingale* herself was condemned at New York and did service through the war as a supply ship for the blockading squadron.

The blockade was effective, but there was still a demand for slaves in the cotton states during the first year of the war, and it would appear that a few cargoes escaped the Union cruisers. The *Pensacola Observer* reported in the spring of 1861, "A cargo of 600 Africans has been landed on the Florida coast near Smyrna." The vessel, name unknown, was burned by her crew. As late as December 16, the *Augusta* (Georgia) *Chronicle* said that 270 slaves, "guaranteed real Congo negroes," had been landed by another unnamed slaver and had arrived at a plantation on the Savannah River. But a named vessel with more than a chronological claim to being the last American slaver was the *Erie*, Captain Nathaniel Gordon. It was the *Erie* case that put an end, practically speaking, to slaving by American captains.

She was a ship of 476 tons, built in Warren, Rhode Island, and her captain, who was said to have made three earlier slaving voyages, hailed from Portland, Maine. In August 1860 Gordon shipped a fourth cargo—this time of 890 slaves, including 106 women and 612 children—from a beach near the mouth of the Congo. The indictment says that he "thrust them, densely crowded, between the decks, and immediately set sail for Cuba." Fifty miles off the African coast he was intercepted by the steam sloop-of-war *Mohican*. The slaves were landed in Liberia. The *Erie* and Gordon were taken to New York for trial.

At first the case attracted little attention. It seemed to be like all the other cases that had ended with the captain's jumping bail or had dragged through the courts for years and then been nol-prossed. It did not matter that slaving was still defined as piracy under the law of 1820. President Buchanan and his Secretary of the Navy, Isaac Toucey of Connecticut, had been making an effort to suppress the trade, unlike most of their predecessors, and the results of it are shown in the record of slavers captured after 1858. Still, not one of the slaving captains had ever been sentenced as a pirate. When Gordon's first trial produced a hung jury, everything seemed to be following a familiar pattern. One thing had changed, however, since Gordon's capture: the United States was now at war with the slaveholders, and the new district attorney regarded himself as the agent of a government fighting for its life. He felt that Gordon had to die as an example to others. There was a second trial in November 1861, lasting two days before a half-empty courtroom, and the jury almost immediately brought in its verdict of guilty.

Gordon, who regarded himself as a victim, was in truth not much worse or better than a hundred other slaving captains. He was not a prince of slavers or even a baronet. He was, however, more faithful than some to a thieves' code of honor, and he did not betray his owners even after he had been sentenced to death. The owners, who also faced death if convicted, were probably respected merchants. There are indications that persons of influence were trying hard to save Gordon, and the governor of New York appealed to President Lincoln for clemency. The appeal was not answered. It was rumored that a mob would storm the jail, so a company of Marines marched over from the Navy Yard and stood guard with fixed bayonets. Somebody smuggled in a dose of strychnine for Gordon. He swallowed it at three o'clock in the morning of the day when he was to be hanged at noon; then, as the poison began to take effect, he rolled on the floor, shouting at his guards, "I've cheated you!" The prison doctor saved him for the gallows.

Gordon was the only American slaver who was executed, and his death on February 21, 1862, was almost the last episode in the American slave trade. Congress at its previous session had appropriated $1,800,000 to suppress the trade. It was the first serious appropriation for the purpose, and, with the cotton-state congressmen all in Confederate service, it passed with little opposition. In June 1862 the United States and Great Britain proclaimed a treaty granting the warships of both nations the right of search and establishing mixed courts for the trial of captured slavers. By that time a British squadron was maintaining a close blockade of the

Cuban coast, although slavers occasionally slipped through with their cargoes. It was reported to the Senate that the *Ocilla* of Mystic, Connecticut, had landed slaves in Cuba in 1862, and that the *Huntress* of New York had landed others in 1864. Nothing more is known about the *Huntress*, which seems to have been truly the last of the last American slavers.

No more captures were being made, and in 1867 the British withdrew their Atlantic Slaving Squadron as being no longer needed. The mixed courts for slaving trials were abolished in 1868 and 1869; no cases had come before them in several years. There is the possibility that a few cargoes were landed in Cuba or Brazil or both as late as the 1880s, but for practical purposes the Atlantic slave trade was ended. It had lasted the better part of four centuries, during which it had involved, by a conservative estimate, the forced migration of fifteen million Negroes, besides causing the death of perhaps thirty or forty million others in slave raids, coffles, and barracoons. What it had produced in Africa was nothing but misery, stagnation, and social chaos. In England and France—also at a considerable cost in lives—it had created greater accumulations of wealth than had been known in previous centuries, and thus it had played its part in the Industrial Revolution. In the Western Hemisphere, besides introducing a vigorous new strain of immigrants, it had created the plantation system, it had opened vast areas to the cultivation of the four great slave crops—sugar, rice, tobacco, and cotton—and it had also encouraged the fatal and persistent myth of Negro inferiority. The trade itself was almost impossible to suppress as long as chattel slavery flourished in a powerful country; in fact it was being revived in the 1850s. It helped to bring about the Civil War, and nothing less than a war could end it. One might say that the doom of the slave trade was sounded by the guns at Fort Sumter and was sealed at Antietam and Gettysburg.

# Bibliography

THE AUTHOR AND HIS COLLABORATOR HAVE NOT ATTEMPTED TO
compile a complete bibliography. This is simply a list of the more
useful works consulted in preparing the various chapters of *Black
Cargoes*. The most useful work of all was Elizabeth Donnan's
four-volume collection, *Documents Illustrative of the History of
the Slave Trade to America* (Washington, 1930–1935), which unfortunately stops short with the end of the legal trade to South
Carolina on December 31, 1807. For the period of legal slaving,
Miss Donnan includes extracts from all the important source material except the one best source, *Minutes of the Evidence delivered before a Select Committee of the whole House . . . to
whom it was referred to consider of the Slave-Trade*. These minutes, printed in four folio volumes, give a detailed picture of all
aspects of the trade as it was carried on from England in 1790.
For the period of illegal slaving, 1807–1865, there is no single work
that presents the whole story, though W. E. B. Du Bois, *The Suppression of the Slave Trade* (1896) has not been superseded as
an account of the political struggles over the trade.

Longer bibliographies, including the titles of many books on
the African background, can be found in the paperback edition of
Melville J. Herskovits, *The Myth of the Negro Past* (Boston,
1958) and in Basil Davidson, *The Lost Cities of Africa* (Boston,
1959).

## Chapter 1/The Beginnings

An early account of the Indian uprising in Hispaniola is to be found in a book by Antonio Herrera de Tordesillas, with the resounding title *Historia general de los hechos de los Castellanos en las islas y tierra firma del Mar Oceano* (1601). It was translated by J. Stegens (London, 1725) and excerpted in Vol. V of Awnsham Churchill's *Collection of Voyages and Travels* (London, 1732).

For Las Casas see Lewis Hanke, *Bartolomé de Las Casas* (The Hague, 1951). There is a good account of the beginnings of the Asiento in Vol. I, Part I of Elizabeth Donnan's *Documents*.

For a general picture of the African background of the slave trade, see Basil Davidson, *Black Mother* (Boston, 1961). Davidson also recounts the deeds and misdeeds of the Portuguese in the ancient kingdom of Kongo. A recent work on African ethnology is George P. Murdock, *Africa, Its Peoples and Their Culture* (New York, 1959). The best account of the tribal origins of the Negroes brought to America is in Herskovits's *The Myth of the Negro Past* and in his article "On the Provenience of New World Negroes" (*Social Forces*, Vol. 12, 1933).

For Ghana and Timbuktu see E. W. Bovill, *The Golden Trade of the Moors* (London, 1958), also Carter G. Woodson, *The African Background Outlined* (Washington, 1936). For Benin see H. L. Roth, *Great Benin* (London, 1903). For a greater culture than that of Benin, see F. Willett, "Ife and its Archaeology" (*Journal of African History*, Vol. 2, 1960).

The African voyages of Sir John Hawkins are recounted in the last volume of Hakluyt's *Voyages* (3 vols., London, 1598–1600; also in Everyman's Library, 7 vols.). The strange adventures of Andrew Battel can be found in John Pinkerton, *A General Collection of the most interesting Voyages and Travels* (London, 1814).

## Chapter 2/Slaving in the Seventeenth Century

Elizabeth Donnan's *Documents*, previously mentioned, is rich in material concerning the seventeenth-century chartered companies in the slave trade. See also George F. Zook, *The Company of Royal Adventurers Trading into Africa* (*Journal of Negro History*, Vol. 4, No. 2, 1919).

There are several first-hand accounts of voyages to Africa at the end of the century. Perhaps the best is William Bosman's *A New Accurate Description of the Coast of Guinea* (London, 1705), but there are several good ones in Churchill's *Voyages*, as note particularly:

Father Jerom Merolla da Sorrento, *A Voyage to the Congo 1682*, Vol. I.

John Barbot, *A Description of the Coasts of North and South Guinea*, Vol. V.

James Barbot, *An Abstract of a Voyage . . . in the* Albion-Frigate, Vol. V.

James Barbot, Jr., *An Abstract of a Voyage to the Congo River . . . in the Year 1700*, Vol. V.

Thomas Phillips, A *Journal of a Voyage made in the* Hannibal *of London 1693–1694*, Vol. VI.

A version of Sieur André Brue's *Voyages and Travels along the Western Coast of Africa* is printed in Thomas Astley, A *New General Collection of Voyages and Travels*, Vol. II (London, 1745).

## Chapter 3/The Early American Trade

For slavery in the West Indies, the best source is still Bryan Edwards, *The History, Civil and Commercial, of the British Colonies in the West Indies*, 3 vols., London, 1801. Other good contemporary sources are Edward Long, *The History of Jamaica*, 3 vols., London, 1774; Sir Hans Sloane, A *Voyage to the Islands of Madera, Barbadoes . . . and Jamaica* (London, 1707–1725); and the *Minutes of the Evidence*, previously mentioned.

For the first Negroes on the mainland, see R. R. Wright, "Negro Companions of the Spanish Explorers" (*American Anthropologist*, Vol. IV, 1902) and *The Journal of Alvar Nuñez Cabeza de Vaca*, translated by Fanny Bandelier (New York, 1922).

U. B. Phillips, *American Negro Slavery* (New York, 1918) contains a well informed account of slavery in the colonies, north and south. For the status of the first Negroes in Virginia, who were treated as indentured servants, see John H. Russell, *The Free Negro in Virginia* (Baltimore, 1913), and John Hope Franklin, *From Slavery to Freedom* (New York, 1956).

Eric Williams, *Capitalism and Slavery* (Chapel Hill, North Carolina, 1944) has a good deal to say about white indentured servants. The enslavement of Indians is discussed in many histories of colonial times.

For early Massachusetts slavers, see George H. Moore, *Notes on the History of Slavery in Massachusetts* (New York, 1866). The voyage of the *St. John* (or *St. Jan*) of New Amsterdam is documented in Donnan I.

## Chapter 4/Flush Times on the Guinea Coast

Most of the statements about the extent and profits of the Liverpool trade are taken from A *General and Descriptive History of the Ancient and Present State of the Town of Liverpool* (1798), sections of which, with additional material, are reprinted in Donnan II, 625–32. See also Gomer Williams, *History of the Liverpool Privateers and Letters of Marque with an Account of the Liverpool Slave Trade* (London, 1897), a colorful and dependable book. For the economic results of the trade, see Eric Williams, *Capitalism and Slavery*. For the parallel growth of Nantes, see Gaston-Martin, *Nantes au XVIII⁰ siècle: l'ère des Négriers, 1714–1744* (Paris, 1931).

For traders on the African coast, see Nicholas Owen, *Journal of a Slave-dealer* (Boston, 1930); Francis Moore, *Travels into the Inland Parts of Africa* (London, 1734), the best account of English trading on the Gambia; Lt. John Matthews, RN, A *Voyage on the River Sierra-Leone on the Coast of Africa* (London, 1788); John Atkins, A *Voyage to Guinea, Brazil and the West Indies . . .* (London, 1737); and William Smith, A *New Voyage to*

*Guinea* (London, reprinted 1774), which is in some respects a sequel to Atkins' story.

For pirates on the coast see, besides Atkins, Capt. William Snelgrave, *A New Account of Some Parts of Guinea, and the Slave-Trade* (London, 1734). Snelgrave makes it clear that piracy in the early eighteenth century was a blind sort of proletarian revolt.

For narratives of enslaved Africans, see Thomas Bluett, *Some Memoirs of the Life of Job, the Son of Solomon* . . . (London, 1734), a story continued in Francis Moore's *Travels.* Job seems to have been the most engaging of many African "princes" freed, fêted, and sent home by the directors of the Royal African Company. See also *The Life of Olaudah Equiano or Gustavus Vassa written by Himself* (London, 1790) and *A Narrative of . . . the life of James Albert Ukawsaw Gronniosaw, an African prince, as related by himself* (Bath, 1780).

For the agitation that led to Parliamentary hearings on the trade, see Wylie Sypher, *Guinea's Captive Kings* (Chapel Hill, 1942); John Newton, *Thoughts upon the African Slave Trade* (London, 1788); Alexander Falconbridge, *An Account of the Slave Trade on the Coast of Africa* (London, 1788); and Thomas Clarkson, *The Impolicy of the Slave Trade* (London, 1788).

The best single source for English eighteenth-century slaving is *Minutes of the Evidence*, already mentioned. The minutes were printed in four volumes: No. I (1789), No. II (1790), No. III (also 1790), and No. IV (1791). These are difficult to find in the United States, but microprint copies can be obtained from London, where they are filed under *British Sessional Papers 1731–1800. House of Commons. Accounts and Papers. Vol. 28* (1789) to *Vol. 31* (1791). Thomas Clarkson, with the help of others, prepared an *Abridgement of the Minutes of the Evidence*, in 600 pages, which became the basis of many other abridgements and abstracts. The most effective of these was Clarkson's own *Abstract of the Evidence* (1791).

There are several accounts of the Old Calabar massacre; the fullest is in Gomer Williams, *The Liverpool Privateers.* The ironic sequel to the massacre comes from a letter printed in Donnan II, 533.

For travels with a slave coffle, see Mungo Park, *Travels in the Interior Districts of Africa* . . . (2nd ed., London, 1799).

## Chapter 5/The Middle Passage

Most of the sources of this chapter are books already mentioned. They include Bosman, Thomas Phillips, and James Barbot, Sr. and Jr., from Chapter 2; Edward Long and Bryan Edwards from Chapter 3; and William Snelgrave, John Newton, Alexander Falconbridge, and Gomer Williams from Chapter 4, as well as the invaluable *Minutes of the Evidence*, supplemented with material from Vol. II of Elizabeth Donnan's *Documents.*

For the Zong case the standard source is Prince Hoar, *Memoirs of Granville Sharp* (London, 1820), excerpted in Donnan II, 555–57.

Other new sources are William Richardson, *A Mariner of England* (London, 1908); Capt. J. G. Stedman, *Narrative of a Five Years' Expedition against the Revolted Negroes of Suriname* (London, 1796); Père Dieudonné Rinchon, *Le Trafic Négrier* . . . (Brussels, 1938), which contains statistics of losses in the French trade; and George Howe, "The Last Slave-ship" (*Scribner's Magazine*, July 1890).

## Chapter 6/Captains and Crews

For the story of Captain Billy Boates and the letter from Captain Joseph Harrison, see Gomer Williams, *The Liverpool Privateers.*

For John Newton see *An Authentic Narrative of Some Remarkable and Interesting Particulars in the Life of ****** committed in a Series of Letters to the Rev. Mr. Haweis* (London, 1786). The letters were from Newton, who wished to remain anonymous. See also Richard Cecil, *The Works of the Rev. John Newton and Memoirs of His Life* (New York, 1851).

For the full story of the last legal English slaver, see *Memoirs of the late Captain H. Crow of Liverpool . . . with descriptive sketches of the Western Coast of Africa* (London, 1830).

The life of sailors in the Guinea trade is best revealed in *Minutes of the Evidence,* but the statistics of mortality are from Thomas Clarkson, *An Abstract of the Evidence.* Independent narratives are William Richardson, *A Mariner of England,* and James F. Stanfield, *The Guinea Voyage* (Edinburgh, 1807), which latter has to be approached with caution.

## Chapter 7/The Yankee Slavers

Vols. III and IV of Elizabeth Donnan's *Documents* are rich in custom-house records, in slaving items from colonial newspapers, and in letters from Yankee skippers. They are the principal source of this chapter, but also note the following.

The story of Capt. James deWolf is told at length in George Howe, *Mount Hope: A New England Chronicle* (New York, 1958), and the story of the *Charlestown* comes from the last chapter of Mungo Park, *Travels in the Interior Districts of Africa.*

For Peter Faneuil's slaving venture, see W. B. Weeden, *Economic and Social History of New England* (Boston, 1890). Capt. Samuel Moore's two voyages up the Gambia are retold from Francis Moore's *Travels,* but there are additional details of the second voyage in a letter reprinted in Donnan III, 41.

For records of Rhode Island families engaged in the trade, consult the index to Donnan III. Do not consult the *Dictionary of American Biography,* which regards slaving as an unmentionable subject. For the slaving activities of Simeon Potter and the deWolf brothers, see *Mount Hope,* Chaps. IV and VII.

The tables of African origin are modified slightly from those in Melville J. Herskovits, *The Myth of the Negro Past.* Herskovits had compiled them from two longer lists of imported slaves in Donnan IV, and these might also be consulted for their fascinating footnotes.

## Chapter 8/The Fight to Abolish the Trade

For Benezet see George S. Brookes, *Friend Anthony Benezet* (Philadelphia, 1937).

For the New England attitude toward slaving, see "Slave-Holding New England and Its Awakening" (*Journal of Negro History*, Vol. 13); also Elizabeth Donnan, "The New England Slave Trade after the Revolution" (*New England Quarterly*, Vol. 3); also John Hope Franklin, *From Slavery to Freedom.*

In addition to Clarkson's *History of . . . the Abolition of the Slave-Trade*, there are interesting accounts of the battles in Parliament in R. Coupland, *The British Anti-Slavery Movement* (Oxford, 1933), and in W. L. Mathieson, *British Slavery and Abolition* (London, 1926). The literature of the Abolition Society is treated at length in Wylie Sypher, *Guinea's Captive Kings.*

For Clarkson see E. L. Griggs, *Thomas Clarkson—Friend of Slaves* (London, 1936). For Wilberforce see R. J. Wilberforce and S. W. Wilberforce, *Life of William Wilberforce* (Philadelphia, 1839), and R. Coupland, *Wilberforce* (Oxford, 1923).

For the invention and effects of the cotton gin, see *The World of Eli Whitney*, by Jeanette Mirsky and Allan Nevins (New York, 1952).

The book by blind Joseph Hawkins is *A History of a Voyage to the Coast of Africa* (Philadelphia, 1797). The letter to James deWolf is reprinted in George Howe, *Mount Hope*, 122–23. There is rich material on the Charleston trade, 1804–1807, including the bookseller's lament, in Donnan IV, 502–549.

## Chapter 9/Contraband

Useful books dealing with Great Britain's effort to suppress the trade include Thomas Fowell Buxton, *The African Slave Trade and Its Remedy* (London, 1840); W. L. Mathieson, *British Slavery and Abolition* (London, 1926), and *Great Britain and the Slave Trade* (London, 1929); A. Mackenzie-Grieve, *Last Years of the African Slave Trade* (London, 1941); and Christopher Lloyd, *The Navy and the Slave Trade* (London, 1949), which is rich in anecdotes, but is not to be followed uncritically.

For a different point of view, see Louis Lacroix, *Les Derniers Négriers* (Paris, 1952). Lacroix was a retired sea captain willing to believe the worst of the British Navy.

For statistics and interpretative material on the Brazilian trade, see Gilberto Freyre, *The Masters and the Slaves* (New York, 1946).

For a longer discussion of why the West African coastal states were unwilling or unable to abandon the trade, see Basil Davidson, *Black Mother*, Part 6. Slaves were the only African product—except palm oil in the Bight of Biafra—that they could exchange for European weapons.

The table of expenditures and receipts for an illegal slaving voyage is from

*Captain Canot, or Twenty Years of an African Slaver*, written out and edited by Brantz Mayer (New York, 1854).

For the changing designs of sailing vessels, see Carl C. Cutler, *Greyhounds of the Sea* (New York, 1930); H. I. Chapelle, *The Baltimore Clipper* (Salem, 1930); and Howe and Matthews, *American Clipper Ships* (Salem, 1926).

For the long controversy with Great Britain over the right of search, see W. E. B. Du Bois, *The Suppression of the Slave Trade*, and Hugh G. Soulsby, *The Right of Search and the Slave Trade* (Baltimore, 1933).

Edgar S. Maclay, *Reminiscences of the Old Navy* (New York, 1898) tells the story of the *Cyane*. The disappearance of the *Redwing* is related in Vol. II of Sir Henry Huntley, *Seven Years' Service on the Slave Coast of Western Africa* (London, 1850).

## Chapter 10/The Roaring Eighteen-Forties

For the *Amistad* see William A. Owens, *Slave Mutiny* (New York, 1953). For the *Creole* see Peter Freuchen, *Book of the Seven Seas* (New York, 1957). There are accounts of both cases in John R. Spears, *The American Slave-Trade* (New York, 1900).

There are two American books about joint cruising by officers assigned to the African service: *Journal of an African Cruiser by an Officer of the United States Navy* (Horatio Bridge), edited by Nathaniel Hawthorne (New York, 1845), and Andrew Hull Foote, *Africa and the American Flag* (New York, 1854). See also *Adventures and Observations on the West Coast of Africa* (New York, 1860), by the Rev. Charles W. Thomas, who was chaplain of the American squadron, 1855–1857. For the diplomatic aspects, see Soulsby, *The Right of Search and the Slave Trade*, and Mathieson, *Great Britain and the Slave Trade*. Christopher Lloyd is the best source for sea fights between British cruisers and slave ships.

For the adventures of Richard (or Philip) Drake, see *Revelations of a Slave Smuggler; being the Autobiography of Capt. Richard Drake, an African Trader for Fifty Years—from 1807 to 1857* (New York, 1860). As much of Drake's story as anyone needs to know is excerpted in George Francis Dow, *Slave Ships and Slaving* (Salem, 1927), together with many other slaving narratives.

Most of the material on the West Coast mongos comes from *Captain Canot*. Researches by his great-grandnephew, J. B. Conneau, have proved, first, that the book was chiefly by Canot (or Conneau) and not by Brantz Mayer; second, that Conneau's narrative is much more accurate and trustworthy than it was formerly held to be.

## Chapter 11/Slave Catching in the Indian Ocean

For historical and general information about Zanzibar see F. D. Ommanney, *Isle of Cloves* (Philadelphia, 1956); Richard F. Burton, *Zanzibar* (London, 1872); and *A Guide to Zanzibar* (Zanzibar, 1952).

For American traders see C. T. Brady, Jr., *Commerce and Conquest in*

East Africa (Salem, 1950), which pays special attention to the Salem trade with Zanzibar.

For the history of the East Coast see Basil Davidson, *The Lost Cities of Africa*, which deals with the early history; R. Coupland, *East Africa and Its Invaders* (Oxford, 1938); Mrs. C. E. B. Russell, *General Rigby, Zanzibar and the Slave Trade* (London, 1935); Mabel V. Jackson, *European Powers and South-East Africa* (London, 1942); and Edward Hutchinson, *The Slave Trade of East Africa* (London, 1874).

For the picturesque history of the East Coast Slaving Squadron, see Lt. Barnard, RN, *A Three Years' Cruise in the Mozambique Channel for the Suppression of the Slave Trade* (London, 1848); Capt. G. L. Sulivan, *Dhow Chasing in Zanzibar Waters* (London, 1873); Capt. Colomb, *Slave-Catching in the Indian Ocean* (London, 1873); and W. Cope Devereux, *A Cruise of the Gorgon* (London, 1869).

## Chapter 12/The Dream of a Slave Empire

Edward A. Pollard's arguments for reopening the slave trade are taken from *Black Diamonds Gathered in Darkey Homes of the South* (1859). Pollard's book is less ambitious, but also less crotchety and more to the point, than George Fitzhugh's more famous *Sociology for the South* (Richmond, 1854), another book which presented the dream of a slave empire.

Political efforts to reopen the slave trade are discussed in W. E. B. Du Bois, *The Suppression of the Slave Trade*, and in Chap. VI of William E. Dodd, *The Cotton Kingdom* (New Haven, 1921). See also W. J. Carnathan, "The Attempt to Reopen the African Slave Trade, 1857–1858" (Southwest Political and Social Science Ass'n., Sixth Annual Convention, 1925); Stella Herron, "African Apprentice Bill" (Mississippi Valley Historical Ass'n., Proceedings Vol. 8, 1914–15); and almost every issue during the 1850s of *De Bow's Review*.

The letter about buying the *Vigo* was first printed in a series of extracts from the letter-book of Charles A. L. Lamar (*North American Review*, November 1886). There are conflicting stories about the three (or four) voyages of the *Wanderer*. Besides Lamar's letter-book, some of the best sources are the October 1920 issue of *Yachting*, the May 22, 1926, issue of the *Marine Journal*, and Chap. XIX of Spears' *The American Slave Trade*.

For George Howe's account of his voyage, see *Scribner's Magazine*, July 1890. For Edward Manning see his book *Six Months on a Slaver* (New York, 1879), also excerpted in Dow's *Slave Ships and Slaving*. For cargoes landed in the Southern states as late as 1861, see pp. 153–54 of Eric Rosenthal, *The Stars and Stripes in Africa* (London, 1938).

The trials and the execution of Nathaniel Gordon were reported in contemporary New York newspapers. See also Chap. XX of Spears' *The American Slave Trade*.

# Index

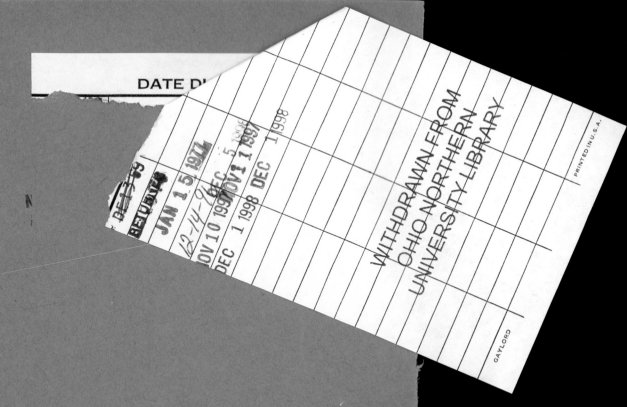